T5-CRQ-662

LIFE

LIFE
An Enigma, a Precious Jewel

Daisaku Ikeda

Trans. by Charles S. Terry

KODANSHA INTERNATIONAL
Tokyo, New York & San Francisco

Distributed in the United States by Kodansha International/USA, Ltd., through Harper & Row, Publishers, Inc., 10 East 53rd Street, New York, New York 10022.

Published by Kodansha International Ltd., 12–21 Otowa 2-chome, Bunkyo-ku, Tokyo 112 and Kodansha International/USA, Ltd., 10 East 53rd Street, New York, New York 10022 and 44 Montgomery Street, San Francisco, California 94104. Printed in Japan.
First edition, 1982

Library of Congress Cataloging in Publication Data
Ikeda, Daisaku.
Life, an enigma, a precious jewel.
Translation of: Seimei o kataru.
Includes index.
1. Buddhism—Philosophy. 2. Man (Buddhism)
I. Terry, Charles S. II. Title.
BQ4040.I3813 294.3′42 81-20942
ISBN 0-87011-433-6 AACR2
ISBN 4-7700-0994-1 (in Japan)

CONTENTS

PREFACE

For any human being, the most difficult question in life is what his own life means. Man's scientific eye has probed into matter and discovered the world of atoms and electrons; in its search for the infinite, it continues to push the limits of the cosmos farther and farther away. Yet life itself—the nearest thing of all, the thing that should be the easiest to grasp—remains a mystery, despite the rapid advance in the past few decades of what we call the life sciences.

Why is this? Is it not because life is constantly changing, because it has countless complex levels and an understanding of it requires perfect serenity and the light of perfect wisdom? As many philosophers have recognized, an understanding of life is man's greatest basic problem, but the questions posed are so intricate that most philosophical speculation has led merely to the magnification of the riddle. This, I am sure, is because the refining of life and the deepening of wisdom have not kept pace with scholarship.

In the Orient, a man who faced the mystery of life squarely and found the perfect solution was the founder of Buddhism, Shakyamuni—the Sacred One of the Shakya Tribe, Gautama Siddartha, called the Buddha, the Enlightened One. Life is not an abstract concept. It involves living and being in the world of the here and now, achieving enlightenment in the midst of reality, coping with the laughter and sorrow, pleasure and grief, of this present world. Shakyamuni himself spent most of his life, not attempting to explain an abstract understanding of the riddle of life, but trying to teach men how to overcome the suffering of this world and find a path to happiness.

In order to find the enlightenment that came to Shakyamuni, it is necessary to refine and purify one's life and to develop the highest and most trenchant form of wisdom. This is the practice of Buddhism. In the forty years of his ministry after the enlightenment, Shakyamuni strove valiantly to teach his disciples how to practice Buddhism, so that they might transmit the principles of his understanding to later generations. The enlightenment itself he preached in the Lotus Sutra.

The purpose of this book is to show the relationship between the Buddhist answers to the mystery of life and the empiric solutions modern science has offered to the same or similar questions. We are not attempting to adduce scientific proof of the truth of Buddhism, which transcends science, but merely to indicate ways in which Buddhist truth may be illustrated in modern scientific terms.

While we can by no means pretend to have arrived at the state of enlightenment achieved by Shakyamuni, we are able to take advantage of the traditional Buddhist theories as developed by such geniuses as Nagarjuna, Vasubandhu, and Chih-i. Furthermore, we are familiar with the Buddhism of Nichiren Daishonin, who explained the riddles of life even more clearly than Shakyamuni and who established a way whereby enlightenment with respect to the cosmic life-force can be achieved simultaneously with solutions to the problems we face in this world.

Today scientists throughout the world are throwing more light on the phenomena that bring life into being. Important clues as to the various special qualities of life are continually being discovered. As a general tendency, we can say that the discoveries of modern science offer confirmation of the teachings that have come down to us from Buddhist thinkers of the past. In fact, in the latter part of the twentieth century, scientific theory appears to be coming ever closer to Buddhism.

Buddhism is a great treasure house. It is a treasure house of infinite capacity, supplying mankind with the answer to life's eternal questions and providing mankind with goals worth living for. But because of Buddhism's tremendous profundity and its enormous breadth, and because it has all too rarely been explained in terms easily applicable to everyday reality, it has been, even in the Orient, a hidden treasure house, sadly in danger of falling into oblivion.

The person who showed me the wonderful treasures Buddhism abounds in was my mentor, Josei Toda, the second president of Soka Gakkai. After President Toda's death, it became my mission and my responsibility to protect the principles of Soka Gakkai, to watch over its religious activities, and to spread the faith for the sake of world peace and universal happiness. My goal was to tell as many people as possible about the great treasure house of the Buddha's Law and to convince them of its infinite splendors. I studied, I meditated, and I attempted whenever possible to talk to people, particularly students and other young people. This book may be regarded as one fruit of this effort.

The central theme, of course, is the Buddhist view of life. In the first part, The Cosmos and Life, I have discussed spatial and temporal aspects of life and its spread throughout the universe. The approach from this angle is relatively easy for modern man, since it can often be illustrated by scientific information. Many current scientific theories tend to agree with traditional Buddhist concepts.

In the second part, The Buddhist View of Life, I have dealt with the self-realization of individual lives, with varying degrees of freedom, and with the corresponding differences in happiness and unhappiness. Stressed in this central portion of the book is the fact that each life is constantly changing and is consequently susceptible to an inner revolution, by means of which the individual may achieve happiness and fulfillment.

The third part, Life and Death, is concerned with the question of what happens to our selves after we die. Do we return to nothingness? Do we continue to exist in some state imperceptible in ordinary life? Or are we born again in one form or another? The questions discussed here are of a sort that human beings, whether Oriental or Occidental, cannot keep from asking themselves. For this very reason, they have often been answered in facile and superficial ways. As it happens, however, science—particularly medical science—has in very recent years become vitally concerned with questions of life and death. While touching on a number of recent theories, I have tried to explain the Buddhist interpretation of death and what follows it.

The first part, then, is devoted to an examination of such concepts as life-time, life-space, and life-force, while the third section deals mainly with questions of temporal continuity, or, more specifically, the absence of discontinuity between life and death. The second part is concerned with varied aspects of our inner lives and life activity. I have used the word Buddhist in the title of the second part only, but the first and third parts are also based on Buddhist ways of thought.

The Japanese version of this book, entitled *Seimei o Kataru* (*Dialogue on Life*) was first published in 1973. In the intervening decade scientists have published many new discoveries, a number of which would have been suitable for incorporation in the present volume. To attempt to keep the book scientifically up to date, however, would have imposed a heavy burden on the translator and the editors, and would have even further delayed publication of the English version. In view of the fact that no new finding disagrees with my basic discussion—indeed, the more scientific knowledge we obtain, the more modern science appears to be in harmony with Buddhist theory—I feel it best to publish the original in its present form.

I am grateful to the translator, Charles S. Terry, for his diligent and sensitive treatment of the many difficult Buddhist terms used in the original, as well as for his efforts to render into fluent English a text that is complicated even in Japanese. I am also grateful to the publishers, Kodansha International, who have previously published English editions of several of my other books.

DAISAKU IKEDA

January, 1982

I

THE COSMOS AND LIFE

THE BODY AND THE SPIRIT

THE STRANGE PHENOMENON OF LIFE

A book called *The Physics and Chemistry of Life*, published in 1956, begins with this statement: "There are three riddles—three fundamental riddles in the world. First, what is the universe? Second, what is matter? And third, what is life?" The book, compiled by the editors of *Scientific American*, attacks the third riddle, "What is life?" with all the wizardry of contemporary science, and at one point the authors confidently state: "Scientists of the second half of the twentieth century declare that the 'mysteriousness' of life and the myths concerning it are a matter of ancient history." But this is quickly followed by the admission that "still, even now the mystery of life, clothed in new forms, remains deep and remote."

I do not wish to belittle the accomplishments of modern scientists, but it does seem to me that as more and more of the elements of life are revealed, the number of mysteries discovered increases. It is almost as though the purpose of scientific progress was not to solve the mysteries, but to search out new ones. It is still a truism that the more we know, the more we find we do not know. I doubt that science will ever completely remove the veil in which life is shrouded.

We know now of forms of life that would have been considered impossible only a few decades ago. For example, microbiologists at the University of Tokyo have recovered from oil wells organisms that feed on petroleum. They exist 2 thousand meters underground, where there is no free oxygen, and are constituted in such a way as to be able to obtain oxygen by breaking down molecules of nitric acid, which is, of course, highly corrosive and a deadly poison to what we normally think of as living beings. Recently, the Soviet geophysicist Chudinov succeeded in reviving a type of microorganism imbedded in potassic rock formed around 250 million years ago. After being dormant for eons, this tiny speck of life began to move and multiply again when it was placed in the proper culture medium.

Dr. Kenzo Tonomura has discovered a bacterium called K62 which thrives on mercury, and still other organisms feed on iron or manganese. When it comes to viruses, microbes smaller than bacteria, even more curious phenomena are encountered, for some of them seem to shuttle back and forth between organic and inorganic states. One such is the tobacco mosaic virus, which causes one of the more serious diseases of the tobacco leaf. It was first isolated by W. M. Stanley, who thought he was working with a crystalline substance like salt or ice, but he found to his astonishment that under certain circumstances the "crystals" started to move. He was forced to conclude that the virus could alternate between living and non-living forms.

Truly, the forms in which life manifests itself are infinite, and I am sure that as science progresses, ever more complex manifestations will be discovered, some explainable by known laws of physics and biology, others not. Most likely, we will also find new functionings of a spiritual nature that as yet are relegated to the realm of the supernatural.

It is clear today that many aspects of life go beyond the limits of what we once considered common sense, and it follows that common sense is not a very reliable source of information about the true principle of life.

If we stop and think, we soon realize how varied and intricate life is. Life is photosynthesis—that marvelous process whereby plants absorb the energy of the sun and use it to transform water and carbon dioxide into oxygen and organic compounds. Life is the nitrogen cycle—microscopic parasites drawing their energy from the roots of plants, fixing atmospheric nitrogen, and converting it into nourishing compounds. Life is the blossoming of flowers in the spring, the ripening of fruit in the fall, the rhythm of the earth and of nature. Life is the cry of cicadas signalling the end of summer, migratory birds winging south in a transparent autumn sky, fishe frolicking in a stream. Life is the joy beautiful music instills in us, the thrilling sight of a mountain peak reddened by the rising sun, the myriad combinations and permutations of visible and invisible phenomena. Life is all things.

People used to think the stars had a fixed place in the heavens, shining with their own light throughout eternity. Now we know even stars share the fate of men and other living creatures—birth and death—and astronomers tell us our sun itself will grow dark and die in another 5 billion years. At this very moment, somewhere in the universe, a new star is coming into being; somewhere else an old one is disintegrating in a blinding flash of light. And the universe—this corpus of life encompassing everything from the giant stars to the tiniest microorganisms—is constantly expanding at a tremendous rate, as each element within it pursues its own destiny. The cosmos in its entirety is acting out a never-ceasing drama of life and death.

In a spatial sense, the universe extends from electrons and protons through atoms and microbes to stars, galaxies, and the great unknown beyond. In a temporal sense, the cosmos contains the infinitesimal lifespan of the subatomic particles as well as the multi-billion-year life cycle of the great galaxies. What we call life includes the infinity of movement in this vast expanse of space and time.

The riddles of the universe, matter, and life are infinitely broad and infinitely deep. No wonder the thinkers of past and present have felt lost before their vastness. No wonder scientists have sighed in dismay and frustration. Faced with the unlimited variations in which life manifests itself, some scientists have tried to fit things into the laws of physics, while others have sought solutions in physiology or psychology. We stand in awe before their achievements, and rightly so, for it is important to examine the workings of life objectively using the advanced scholarly techniques that we have developed. In the search for the secret of life, however, we must go beyond the findings of science, for science cannot teach us the basic underlying principle that gives being to the myriad of phenomena that exist.

What produces life? What fundamental reality causes life to manifest itself as life? When we have answered these questions—or rather *this* question, because it is really only one—I think we will be able to solve the riddles of the universe, matter, and life. Ultimately the three riddles are not separate one from the other, but thoroughly interrelated.

It is the purpose of religion and philosophy to search out the principle that underlies all existence and to cause this principle to be reflected in all human life, bringing to men both happiness and the potentiality for creativity. While we must take cognizance of the many great intellectual achievements of the past, we must also try to go further and examine the true and fundamental source of life and the universe.

THE HUMAN BODY

Where does human life reside? The question, seemingly simple and direct, is difficult to answer. Any child can tell you where his heart or his brain is, but if you ask him where life is, he has to stop and think, as indeed do those of us who are not children. And yet this is one of the most basic conundrums of life, and the one most closely related to our personal sense of reality.

Alexis Carrel (1873–1944), who received the Nobel Prize for Physiology or Medicine in 1912, remarked in his *Man, the Unknown*, "In fact, our ignorance is profound. Most of the questions put to themselves by those who study human beings remain without answer. Immense regions of our inner world are still unknown." Carrel added, "If Galileo, Newton, or Lavoisier had applied their intellectual powers to the study of body and consciousness, our world probably would be different today."

On the whole, we fall into the illusion that we know ourselves, but Carrel is right in suggesting that we know ourselves least of all. Few of us understand the delicate equilibrium maintained by our bodies, let alone the source of our feelings and desires. And yet, without knowing these things, we cannot give a sensible answer to our question, "Where does human life reside?" And it is folly even to try to consider such imponderables as life after death.

Such being the case, it is questionable whether we are in a position to lead full lives or to open up a path of human happiness in the sense Carrel intended. In my opinion, to understand where the essence of one's life resides is the point of departure for a philosophy of life. It may also be the ultimate goal of that philosophy. At the very minimum, understanding one's own life is a necessary condition for leading a full and happy life.

If we attempt to analyze human life in the most down-to-earth terms, we may start with the fact that the human body, which carries out the actions of life, is composed of matter. Chemical analyses show that the body is made up of cells, which are in turn made up of such components as DNA molecules and proteins. These too can be broken down into carbon, nitrogen, and other elements found everywhere in the universe. There are no chemical elements in the human body that do not exist elsewhere. Still, even though the elements into which the body can be broken down do not differ from elements found in inorganic matter or machinery, the functions performed by the human body set it entirely apart from even the most complicated computers or precision machines.

There was a time, during the late eighteenth and early nineteenth centuries, when the view that the human body was in a class with machinery was dominant in Europe, but this was before the full complexity of its operations was understood. Over two hundred years ago Julien de La Mettrie (1709–51), who was in a general way a follower of Descartes, asserted that the human body was indeed a moving machine. The heart is a pump, the teeth are scissors, the lungs are a bellows—that sort of thing. Descartes himself had recognized the special nature of the human spirit and had confined himself to saying that animals were machines, but La Mettrie decided the spirit was an emanation of the flesh and concluded even humans were machines.

Shortly after he published his views in *L'Homme-machine* (1747) in Holland, an entirely opposite view was being published in London under the title *L'Homme-plante* (1750), and it turned out that La Mettrie had written this book also. Presumably after giving a logical analysis of the human body as a machine, he remained sufficiently unconvinced himself to write a refutation of his own theory.

What *is* the difference between a human body and a machine? Is it not this difference that constitutes life?

I am inclined to think so. Today's machines are a great deal more intricate than they were in Descartes's time. Some of our computers and robots function in an almost lifelike fashion, and this will probably be even truer as time goes on. Even so, no matter how complex machinery becomes, it differs in certain basic respects from living beings.

First of all, a machine must be designed by a human being, and in order for it to work, it must be provided with an outside source of energy, for it cannot of itself create all the energy it requires. There is, after all, no such thing as a perpetual motion device. A living being, on the other hand, can gather energy with its own strength and create its own movements. The necessary strength and intelligence are inherent in what we call life. Life, then, is at once the creator and the created.

The second fundamental point is that a machine does not function until it has been put together. Only in science fiction does a half-finished watch give the correct time or an automobile run without an engine.

The human body is different; each of its tiny cells is a living entity, and the cells and organs work together in a complicated kind of rhythm to produce a larger unified whole. And in the harmony of the individual parts and the entire body, we find the fundamental rhythm of life. Unlike machinery, a human body is in a sense in an incomplete state, always growing and changing. Nevertheless, at any given instant it is a complete functioning whole.

The human body is composed of about 60 trillion cells, performing a multitude of functions that staggers the imagination. Normally, we are unconscious of all but a tiny fraction of the processes going on within us. In the liver alone, some two hundred types of detoxification and metabolic activities are carried out, and if the liver cells do not perform these functions smoothly, not only the body but the mind as well can become disturbed. Defective metabolism of copper or amino acid, for one example, can cause sleepwalking or hallucinations. A certain Japanese scientist has calculated that a factory manufacturing all the chemicals made by the human liver would have to be several times as large as the entire Tokyo-Yokohama industrial area.

The liver is nothing compared to the brain, where there are something like 20 billion cells more or less constantly in action, enabling us to calculate, to remember, to think, to reach decisions. In the average adult, all this activity goes on inside a gray mass of convoluted nerve tissue weighing about 1,500 grams. If a computer duplicating all the brain's functions were to be constructed with the techniques now available, it would cover the surface of the earth. Whether it would actually work or not is another matter.

The human body contains an astounding array of statistical wonders. The total length of the blood vessels in an adult, for example, is about 96 thousand kilometers, more than twice the circumference of the earth; in order to breathe, we use 300 million lung cells. The most marvelous aspect of all is the harmony with which all these cells and organs work together to produce a living being with a creative mind of his own. No doubt it is this mysterious unifying power that has caused most thinkers to reject the idea of the body as a machine and cling instead to the theory of some mysterious vital force.

The ancient Greeks called this *pneuma*: something whose presence within the body gives life, and whose absence means death. It was because people were not really satisfied with the popular concept of man as some sort of complicated machine that pneumatism was revived, this time in the form of modern science. An important modern exponent was the German embryologist Hans A. E. Driesch (1867–1941), whose experiments with the blastula of the sea urchin led him to a belief in a vital principle in life which does not exist in non-living objects. Driesch called this entelechy, but whether one speaks of pneuma or of entelechy, one is postulating an outside element, theoretically existing apart from matter and space. I think this is wrong.

I believe that the principle or law that unites the cells and organs into a living being exists *within* life and *within* the body, and there is no need to set up a deity or a pneuma outside of man's own existence. If man were made to live by some outside force, his body would indeed be no more than a machine, and he himself a mere puppet. The pneumatists have opposed the mechanists, but by postulating a supramaterialist life-force, they have committed essentially the same mistake as the mechanists.

To avoid this vicious circle, we must look to the body as the manifestation of life, for the life-force is inherent in the body. It is this force which, among other things, harmonizes the body's parts and enables man to absorb from without that which is necessary to maintain life. This active, positive life-force within the body is the fundamental essence of life, and it is one with the life-force of the universe.

Two physiological phenomena offer striking support for this idea. One is the ability of the human body to renew itself and under certain circumstances to heal itself. The other is the process of immunization.

The self-regenerative capacity of the body is by no means confined to man. On the contrary, it appears more dramatically in the lower forms of life. If you cut off an ordinary lizard's tail, it will grow back, and the same thing can be observed in many other animals. Humans, of course, do not grow new limbs to replace severed ones, but if no more than about a third of a human liver is excised, it will grow back. More important, if you cut yourself, new groups of cells called granules form to heal the wound. The whole practice of surgery is dependent on this phenomenon.

With respect to immunization, I am speaking particularly of natural, rather than artificial, immunization. We have in our bloodstream polymorphonuclear leucocytes (white corpuscles) that are able to attack and ingest germs and other poisonous substances entering our bodies. In the case of a single harmful germ, the white corpuscles can search it out and devour it in about a minute. We also have in our systems cells capable of producing large numbers of antibodies. These are substances, mostly protein in composition, which attack and deactivate specific harmful bacteria. They were postulated by Paul Ehrlich (1854–1915), who explained them by an oft-repeated analogy to a lock and key. The antibody is the lock, so constructed that it fits around a particular germ, which is the key, and thus puts it out of commission.

The really interesting feature of immunization is the ability on the part of the body to distinguish what belongs inside the body from what does not. When germs enter the body, antibodies form to attack them, but the antibodies do not attack the cells of the body itself, even though these, like the germs, are proteinaceous matter. This is crucial, of course, because if there developed antibodies that attacked red corpuscles, life in the body would be destroyed. There is, then, a sort of intelligence in the body's cellular mechanism, since only antibodies hostile to intruding cells are created.

The life-force expresses itself in living beings. It embodies the innate intelligence of the human body. But in order for this life-force, which is the essence of life, to operate, it must gather physical matter from the cosmos and manifest itself in a living body. The body is, then, the place where the life-force expresses itself in its earthly phenomenal form.

In his *Orally Transferred Teachings* (*Ongi Kuden*), Nichiren Daishonin explained the word *kimyō*, which we use to mean devoting oneself to the Buddha and the Law. He said, " 'Devotion of one's life' means both the physical law of life and the spiritual law of life. The ultimate principle reveals that these two laws are an inseparable aspect of every single life." This means, in the final analysis, that devotion to the Buddha and the Law resolves itself into faith in one's own life, which is a perfect unity of the physical and spiritual laws of life. I shall return to Nichiren Daishonin's statement later, but at this point I am interested in the term *physical law of life*, which in Japanese is *shikihō*. Both the *physical law of life* and its complement the *spiritual law of life*, or *shimpō*, are technical terms in Buddhist philosophy, and we must form a fairly exact concept of their meaning.

Our world is made up of matter. Our bodies are no exception, but I do not think Nichiren Daishonin intended "physical law of life" to refer to physical matter. As we have seen, the human body is not simply a concatenation of physical elements, but a well-ordered and rhythmical life-complex that creates and re-creates itself. Indeed, each tiny cell in the body is a particle of life, each has its own individuality, and each functions in rhythmic harmony with the other cells.

The fundamental life-force, moving with the miraculous rhythm of the cosmos, manifests itself in an infinity of mysterious forms. It exists in non-sentient objects as well as in the lives of the birds and butterflies. The human body is simply the most delicate and marvelous manifestation of this life-force, but what we speak of as the "physical law of life" includes not only the human body and its workings, but the entirety of this dynamic here-and-now world in which the life-force manifests itself in perceptible form.

By searching into the world of perceptible phenomena, one can discern not only the life-force, but the inherent law that governs its functioning, and this is an essential part of the physical law of life. Chemists experiment with inorganic matter and discover chemical laws, while physiologists study living beings and discover organic laws. It is important to remember that these laws are only specific manifestations of the physical law of life. The physical element itself is the whole perceptible world, in which the life-force is manifest as both law and generative power.

One must conceive of the physical element not as passive, static matter, but as the totality of matter and the dynamism that keeps it constantly in flux. In an explanation of the Ten Factors (see page 48), Nichiren Daishonin wrote that the first factor, appearance, is the color and form of our bodies. This is intended, I think, in a very broad way to mean the physical workings of our bodies, but also our bodies as the place where spiritual activities occur.

In other words, the physical law of life at its most obvious in man is the body, but we must remember that this body is the location of spiritual activity, such as the working of intelligence, the exercise of conscience, and the choice between good and evil. By observing the physical element, we can see manifestations of the spiritual element. It does not follow, however, that one can get at the roots of the spiritual law of life simply by analyzing the workings of the brain.

Without the brain cells, there would be no spiritual phenomena, but the brain cells are themselves not life. They are the manifestation of the life-force which conducts spiritual activity. To understand the true nature of the spiritual law of life, which is an integral part of life, we must look more deeply into the essence of the life-force.

PROBING THE DEPTHS OF THE MIND

A brilliant intellect can often find surprising and important truths in the most common everyday occurrences. Such was the case with Sigmund Freud, who invented psychoanalysis. Being a good nineteenth-century man who wanted answers to all questions, Freud began wondering if the little things people do ostensibly by chance were really a matter of pure accident. Was there actually no cause, he asked, for such lapses as forgetting promises, writing down a word wrong, or leaving one's umbrella somewhere? Freud thought not. After all, the study of natural science had demonstrated the universality of cause and effect in nature: there were logical physical reasons why the earth revolves around the sun, and why a rock thrown into the air falls down again. Why should it be different with actions performed by people?

Freud concluded that it was not different, and that behind the seemingly accidental quirks in human behavior there were invariably psychological causes. A person breaking a promise might not be conscious of wanting to break it, but somewhere in the recesses of his mind the desire to break it is present in sufficient strength to becloud his memory. If one writes a word wrong, somewhere inside one has an urge to write it wrong. Although some people considered Freud's way of thinking perverse, his findings did give new depth to the study of human behavior.

His principal conclusions have been borne out over the years, even though other scholars have disagreed on some points. In particular, his discovery of a subconscious mind lurking beneath consciousness, which I regard as his greatest achievement, became a cornerstone for all later research into the human mind. In Freud's analogy, the mind is like an iceberg floating in an ocean. The ocean represents life itself, and just as most of the iceberg is submerged and invisible, so most of the mind's activity is unconscious.

The analogy, simple though it is, appeals to me. If we carry it a little farther, we may surmise that in the deep sea of life surrounding our mental activity, there are any number of wondrous sights still awaiting discovery. Even in the physical world, the deeper we delve into the ocean, the stranger the inhabitants we find. Doubtless there remain today innumerable forests of coral occupied solely by sea creatures we have never seen.

In the sea of life lie many hidden forces, moving us to conscious or unconscious action and in other ways sustaining the workings of the body. Some, like hunger and the sex urge, are instincts and we share them with lesser animals; others, such as fear, uncertainty, and joy, can be classed as emotions. On a more complex level are intelligence, conscience, lust for power, and lust for money. There may also be grotesque impulses creating emotional storms of which we are totally unaware. Whether we are conscious of them or not, there is a galaxy of forces forming an entity, which is the substance of our inner life. This is what is called in Buddhist philosophy the spiritual law of life (*shimpō*), and it is this inner element that is constantly manifesting itself in the movements of the physical law of life (*shikihō*), creating life as it does so.

In *The Ten Factors* (*Jūnyoze-ji*), Nichiren Daishonin said, "The [second] factor, nature, is the nature of our spirits." This is generally understood to mean our individual personality or character, but I think we can go beyond this and say that nature is the unity created by the fusion of all mental and spiritual activity.

Each human being forms his own world of the spirit. Some appear to be born with strong instinctive urges; others suffer constantly from emotional disturbances. Still others are filled with love and compassion, which are forms of spiritual desire.

A medical man once related to me a remarkable example of how a mental stimulus can affect not only a human being's actions, but his physiological state as well.

In a certain hospital, two women were taking care of a sick child. One was the child's mother, the other a hired nurse. After giving a series of blood tests to both women, the doctor came to the conclusion that when the child was doing well, both of them had a normal pH level. When the child's illness approached a critical state, however, the mother's blood contained a much higher acid content. Her anxiety, in other words, affected even the content of her blood. This did not happen in the case of the nurse, though there was no reason to believe she was unfeeling, or that she was not doing her best to help the child to recover. It is, of course, only natural for the mother to be the one most deeply affected by the child's illness, but it is of extreme interest that her mental state caused such a remarkable change in her physical condition. Here, certainly, is an illustration of how the working of the spirit can become manifest in the world of the physical.

Another interesting example was reported in connection with child training by Medard Boss, a physician specializing in psychosomatics.

It seems there was a healthy, mischievous boy of seven who was crazy about chocolates. To keep him from eating too many, his mother put the chocolates on a high shelf. But while she was not looking, the child placed a stool on a chair and climbed up high enough to reach the chocolates. His mother discovered this and, to punish him, tied his hands and put him on a high table where he could see, but not reach, the chocolates.

After this punishment had been repeated a few times, the boy began to show signs of emotional instability, and an eczema resembling measles broke out all over his body. His insensitive mother could not figure out what was wrong with him, but a doctor pointed out to her that the instinctive urge to eat the chocolates, coupled with anger, fear, frustration, and uncertainty, was exerting a strong adverse effect on both his mind and his body. The punishment was discontinued, and the boy soon returned to normal.

The story is depressing. It reminds one of how often we unwittingly cause mental injury to the very young. Surely the mother could have devised a more humane way of teaching the boy to control his appetite. But before we condemn her, we must ask ourselves whether we really have an adequate understanding of the unconscious working of the mind. If we do not really understand life, we cannot effectively impart to the young the self-control they need to become healthy, well-rounded adults.

The world of the spirit is not confined to such matters as intelligence, judgement, and desire. There is also mental activity at a lower level, in the subconscious and the unconscious. If there were not, the action of intelligence, conscience, judgement, and emotion would indeed be accidental, and the fundamental source that gives birth to these would remain obscure.

Opinions are divided on the nature of these lower levels of mental activity. Freud thought that instinctive desire was at the root of everything. Nietzsche and Adler thought it was the will to power or to perfection. Herbert Marcuse held that it was a life wish or a death wish. All these men, however, believed that whatever it was, it was present in human beings from the time of birth. There is no doubt today but that impulses, instincts, and the desire for power can exert a strong influence over intelligence or judgement. I believe that there is, still deeper in man's unconscious, a more basic source from which these instinctive urges emanate.

Jung, who along with Freud is regarded as one of the giants of depth psychology, thought that, basically, all men's lives shared a common foundation. He called this the *collective unconscious* and believed it contained a heritage going back to the very beginnings of mankind. Jung is credited with being the scholar who built a bridge between psychology and religion, and there is indeed something closely related to religion in the idea that all the 3.7 billion people in the world share a common memory of sorts.

The more progress science makes, the closer it comes to Buddhist ideas, but I think we must go even deeper to find the common source of all human mental activity. Living beings receive their life-force from the fundamental cosmic existence, which supplies the energy for the rhythmic movements of life throughout the cosmos. The wisdom of Buddhism long ago recognized the existence of this life-force.

In the innermost depths of all beings, there is the primal life-force and it causes living beings to live. The same force supports inorganic matter and works it into the harmonies and rhythms of the great cosmic existence. In Buddhism, this all-sustaining force is called by a number of names, but the best is *Myōhō*, the "Mystic Law." This is the active force necessary for all life, the force that creates and re-creates all existence, spiritual and physical.

When this force manifests itself in the physical world, it appears as the laws governing the inorganic world, which make possible chemical compounds and control the physical pulsations of the universe. In other words, the laws of physics, chemistry, and astronomy are simply particular phenomenal manifestations of the Mystic Law of the cosmos. Similarly, the life-force constructs the world of the spirit, creates intelligence, gives birth to conscience, gives force to urges and instincts, and thus creates all variations of mental and spiritual activity. It is what is called God in other religions, but it is different from God in that it is perfectly immanent in the cosmos and in human life. It is not a force outside the cosmos. It is the cosmos itself. The true nature of the cosmos and of life is the fusion into entity of the physical law of life and the spiritual law of life. This fusion is the process whereby life is created and made to spread out into the infinite.

Nichiren Daishonin said in his *Orally Transferred Teachings* (*Ongi Kuden*), "Earth is comparable to the physical law of life (*shikihō*); cosmic space is comparable to the spiritual law of life (*shimpō*). The two are inseparable."

Cosmic space, the Buddhist concept called in Sanskrit *śunyata* and in Japanese *kū*, has been translated as "nothingness" or "the Void," but is actually the spiritual law of cosmic life as a whole. Perhaps the best way to understand this interpretation is to consider that nothing exists except in relation to everything else, which is to say, the totality of the cosmos. The spiritual law of life, then, is one and the same as the spiritual law of the cosmos.

Nichiren Daishonin's meaning was that the universe is performing the rhythmical movements in which the physical world and the cosmic spirit are one.

The universe may appear to be a purely material existence, but there is within it the world of the life-force inherent in all the physical wonders of the cosmos. If we see the Mystic Law as the fundamental source of all universal phenomena, I think we can understand the fusion of the physical and spiritual laws of life.

The life of a human being is a form of cosmic life action and is connected with the innermost source of cosmic being. In the lives of men, as in the life of the cosmos, life consists of the inseparable entity of physical and spiritual elements. Nichiren Daishonin was referring to this, I think, when in explaining the word *kimyō*, meaning "devoting oneself to the Buddha and the Law," he wrote, "*Ki* refers to the physical law of life; *myō* refers to the spiritual law of life."

This statement goes directly to the fundamental relationship between the cosmos and human beings. The physical element forming the body of life is composed of everything in the universe, but everything ultimately reverts to the cosmic life. The process is a continuous, cosmic metabolism. The *ki* in *kimyō* is the process whereby the physical element within us returns to the cosmic body.

In contrast, while the spiritual element resides in the constantly changing physical element, it remains the continuing unified harmony of life, within which burns forever the vital fire that creates life. The force that causes the constant shifting and transformation of matter is in the innermost reaches of the spiritual law of life and is the fundamental life-force of the cosmos. Hence, *myō* in *kimyō* is the inherent life of the universe.

The spiritual law of all living beings is founded on cosmic life itself. The life of the universe and the life of a human being have at their nucleus the fundamental life-force, and they both partake in the fusion and rhythmical movements of this life-force. In both there is continuous and constant change.

On the human level, it has been proven that the material elements of the human body are constantly being renewed. If the radioactive isotope of sodium, Na^{24}, is injected into human beings, it spreads within 5 seconds to the heart, the lungs, and throughout the circulatory system, but after only 75 seconds, it begins to emerge in sweat. After a month even that portion of the chemical that had entered the bones and the teeth is ejected.

About half of the protein in the liver is renewed every two weeks; that in muscle tissue is completely exchanged in four months.

Matter, then, is always flowing and moving. And it is the same with spiritual or mental activity. We all know how a thought or feeling will float into our conscious minds for a moment and then disappear somewhere into our unconscious minds. Within our bodies, matter and mind become two aspects of the same entity, functioning together inseparably, expressing our own form of fusion and interaction between the physical law of life and the spiritual law. If we can understand how this fusion and interaction take place within our own bodies, it is easier to conceive of the life of the universe in similar terms.

After stating that *kimyō* means "devoting oneself to the Buddha and the Law," Nichiren Daishonin said the two laws "are an inseparable aspect of every single life." If we consider this from the practical viewpoint, it becomes evident that as human beings we are special manifestations of the fundamental life-force of the cosmos. We are differentiated one from the other, but we should all strive to draw more and more energy into ourselves from the all-sustaining cosmic life-force.

What Nichiren Daishonin meant by "ultimate principle" was the life essence of the cosmos, in other words, the embodiment of the Mystic Law. To base our lives on the Mystic Law is the fundamental way toward achieving strength and happiness as human beings, and this is the only proper line of action for human beings to follow. There are too many people in the world today who do not receive an adequate flow of cosmic energy from the fundamental source, and who consequently suffer from distress and unhappiness. I want to say that the fundamental meaning of the practice of Buddhism is to bring a human revolution to these people.

2
MAN AND NATURE

ONLY ONE COSMOS

There is a poem by Walt Whitman called "Miracles," which expresses in exquisitely simple terms the beauty and mystery of nature:

> Why, who makes much of a miracle?
> As to me I know of nothing else but miracles,
> Whether I walk the streets of Manhattan,
> Or dart my sight over the roofs of houses toward the sky,
> Or wade with naked feet along the beach just in the edge of
>   the water,
> Or stand under trees in the woods,
> Or talk by day with any one I love, or sleep in the bed at night
>   with any one I love,
> Or sit at table at dinner with the rest,
> Or look at strangers opposite me riding in the car,
> Or watch honey-bees busy around the hive of a summer
>   forenoon,
> Or animals feeding in the fields,
> Or birds, or the wonderfulness of insects in the air,
> Or the wonderfulness of the sundown, or of stars shining so
>   quiet and bright,
> Or the exquisite delicate thin curve of the new moon in spring;
> These with the rest, one and all, are to me miracles,
> The whole referring, yet each distinct and in its place.

Whitman was not the only American writer to deal with the splendors of the awakening American continent. In the works of Emerson, Mark Twain, Thoreau, Melville, and others, the miracle of the great dynamic harmony of nature is alluded to again and again. It seems to me, however, that Whitman best expresses the idea of a life-force pulsating not only in himself, but in all that he saw. I think he deeply felt the power of the unifying force through which all life is brought together in one great totality. There echoed in him the rhythm of the universal order, and he keenly sensed the mysterious link that made him one with his fellow men, with the birds and the insects, and with the sun and the moon and the stars.

No form of life can exist in complete isolation. Even when the connection between living things and their natural surroundings is not obvious, careful examination invariably reveals a connection of some sort, for a delicate thread of life joins all objects and beings in the universe. To form a viable modern concept of this thread, one needs a certain foundation in scientific theory. The theoretical understanding provided by science fits in remarkably well with the Buddhist concept of the universe.

Most of us know little about the bacteria living in the soil or the plankton in the sea, but these tiny organisms play an important role in the maintenance of human life. It is an accepted scientific principle among ecologists that all living beings are connected with all other living beings, and we may see here scientific support for what I have called the thread of life.

In the forests and woods around us are countless living creatures: little birds chirping in the trees, insects buzzing amid the grasses and flowers, and untold numbers of worms and parasites and bacteria in the soil. Some insects harm crops; others perform functions useful to men. According to the calculations of a Japanese biologist, if we take one step in a forest, we are likely to have something like forty thousand microorganisms under our foot, all of them joined by the thread of life and involved in a complicated pattern of communal existence. Insects feed on plants, birds and animals on insects, and when birds and animals die, microbes convert their decomposing bodies into food for plants. In the complex scheme of nature, plants, animals, and insects all carry out their life cycles and their functions, and in a broad sense, all living beings, humans included, participate in the maintenance of life.

The food cycle in the ocean is another illustration. There, everything becomes food for something else. As a form of coexistence it is curious in a way, for all the organisms are constantly struggling against others. If they gave up the struggle, they would all die. Plantlike plankton absorb sunlight and become food for animal plankton, which are eaten by small fish, which are eaten by large fish, which die, decompose, and become food for the plantlike plankton. But spread a large quantity of petroleum on the ocean surface, as so often happens by accident today, and the chain is broken.

Other substances, more insidious than oil, do not attack the marine food cycle directly, but ride it, so to speak, until they end up in food which can be fatal or harmful to human beings. Among these are such toxic compounds as PCB, BHC, and the methyl mercury that causes the dread Minamata disease. We have in the course of industrial development discarded these chemicals in rivers or in the ocean in what was until recently considered safe quantities, but now it turns out that even very small quantities are not safe. Indeed, as far as humans are concerned, small quantities can be more dangerous than larger ones, because they can all the more easily enter the marine food cycle and gradually become concentrated in pathogenic quantities. In the water, the poisonous particles are first ingested by vegetable plankton, and as they rise higher in the food cycle, the amount of poison in a large fish may be from ten thousand to a hundred thousand times the original concentration in the water.

The whole of nature is alive: it is a complex of flowing, interrelated movements as wonderful as the biological system of a living human being. Nature is one vast organic movement directed by a single life-force and operated by means of a single gigantic nervous system, a majestic and harmonious order in which countless living organisms coexist and cooperate, but also devour each other to keep the system alive.

In an article on the origin of life in the universe, the molecular biologist Itaru Watanabe says, "It is possible now to consider the entire earth as one vast organism—or at least I think the day will soon come when we shall have to consider it in that fashion." My only disagreement is that Dr. Watanabe is too conservative. It seems to me quite evident, even without additional scientific data, that the planet earth is a single organism with a life of its own.

And what a fantastic organism it is, turning for eons on its axis, revolving around the sun, building its continents, nestling its oceans of life-giving water, providing air for the creatures inhabiting its surface. Consider too its times of trouble, when typhoons and hurricanes attack forests and living beings, when the ground trembles and breaks, when flaming lava spews forth from volcanoes.

The earth has been through much and has been subject to awesome cataclysmic changes. One wonders sometimes how it has survived. In the glacial period, from about a million years ago until the end of the Diluvian period only 10 thousand years ago, oceans, rivers, and earth alike were frozen. In the past 320 thousand years, the earth's magnetic field has been reversed at least five times, the north magnetic pole suddenly becoming the south magnetic pole, and vice versa. And yet the earth has moved on in its journey through infinite space, its core burning at temperatures up to 4,000°C., but its surface cool enough to support some sort of organic life over a period of at least 3 billion years.

In June, 1972, a Conference on Human Environment was held in Stockholm for the purpose of discussing ways to protect the world from pollution. Attended by ecologists and medical researchers from all over the world, this U.N. conference ended by adopting a formal resolution with several articles, but the theme and the prevailing feeling at the meeting were amply summed up in its slogan: "Only One Earth." Whether the words are strictly accurate or not is a matter of opinion, for there may well be in the cosmos other planets like earth on which there is organic life. Still, as far as we, and probably our children and our children's children, are concerned, our planet is the only earth we have.

We should not allow the idea of Only One Earth to cause us to forget that the earth is a part of a larger entity. Certainly we must consider, for example, the sun to be a part of our organic existence, because it gives light and energy to everything on earth. If the temperature of the sun were to undergo only a slight change, the whole order of life on earth would be affected. With any appreciable rise in the sun's heat, the surface of the earth would heat up and the ice caps would melt, changing the whole world into one vast ocean. Or if the sun cooled, the earth might be covered with ice. In effect, human life and human activity are so intimately connected with the sun that even a relatively small change in solar conditions could put an end to life as we know it.

Though it is less obvious, the earth is also connected to the stars, which like the sun contribute to the formation of the universe. The English astrophysicist Dennis Sciama emphasized the closeness of the relationship as follows: "If you throw a ball high into the air, you feel the resistance of the ball in your hand. The reason is that all the stars in the sky are trying to prevent you from throwing it. They are exerting the force of gravity."

In the Milky Way alone are more than 100 billion star systems, joined by an invisible cosmic thread which we call Newton's Law of Universal Gravity. The whole great universe, which has given being to the earth, is bound together by ecological links. Stars are linked with stars, and solar systems with solar systems, by complicated, intricate physical laws. To a modern physicist the entire cosmos is a magnificent complex of harmonies, similar to the Buddhist concept of the cosmos.

Think of the universe as an orderly progression from the individual human being to groups of people to earth to sun to solar system to galaxy. Then consider the size of a single human being with regard to the galaxy as a whole. Our bodies contain about 60 trillion cells, which make up our organs and our musculature, as well as our nerves and lymph glands. If you think of each person or animal in the world as a cell, then groups of people may be considered cell groups and the earth and solar system compare with the heart, the liver, the kidneys, the nose, the eyes, the ears, or the teeth of the cosmos. And the physical laws making up the cosmic thread of life can be likened to the nervous system and the blood vessels that maintain harmony and order in the human body.

Just as the body can be paralyzed if a blood vessel breaks or if the nervous system ceases to function properly, if the cosmic thread of life were to break, the effects would immediately spread throughout the universe. No matter how small or distant the damage, not one of the living cells we have called human beings would remain unaffected.

Because of this universality, my own feeling is that the Conference on Human Environment might have done well to adopt the slogan: "Only One Cosmos." This does not deny the principles behind Only One Earth, but instead gives them broader meaning. Only One Cosmos fits in with my theory of life and it has the ring of truth, for if the peace and happiness of mankind are not founded on harmony with the rhythm of the universe, they will be castles built on sand. In order to maintain respect for the lives not only of human beings, but of all living things, we must not interfere with the workings of terrestrial and cosmic order. Not in the smallest way. All existence in the universe forms one great unified life system.

In likening the universe to the body of a man, we should not overlook the cancers and cancerous actions which can destroy the universe just as they eat away a man's body. A cancer is a treacherous cell. It works for itself alone, pushing aside or killing other cells and growing with abnormal speed. It tries to monopolize our nourishment, it puts forth poisons, and it eats at our vital organs. But after the cancer has killed us, it has nothing to do but to die itself. This feature has caused the cancer cell to be described as a "demented cell." If we are to save the universe and its subtle intricacy, we must not, as human beings, become cancerous growths in the body of the universe. There are people today who are as selfish as cancers and we must be on guard lest we join them. What we must remember is that the universe with its systematic and rhythmic movements is the only universe we have. We must make every possible effort to ensure that human beings themselves do not become demented cells.

ENVIRONMENT AND ADAPTABILITY

In his *Geography of Human Life*, Tsunesaburo Makiguchi, the first president of Soka Gakkai, provides a penetrating insight into the influence of the environment on the human spirit. Makiguchi deals extensively with the whole of nature and society, but I am particularly fond of a passage on mountains: "Mountains are natural teachers who comfort the human spirit and illumine the human heart. The people, who are loved and protected by the mountains, respect the mountains as a child respects its parents. Could there be anyone who does not love mountains? The love is such that the human being, confronting the mountain, accepts it as a member of his own society, even though it is so different from him. He forms a personal relationship with it and transforms it into a sentient being."

Concerning plants, Makiguchi wrote, "Plants awaken the aesthetic feeling within us, soften our murderous tendencies, inspire us to poetry, and thus nurture our hearts and minds."

Intrigued with the working of the social mind, Makiguchi said, "Men fear the sanctions of society and rejoice in its approval, which means that men recognize a mind at work in society. . . . Society, like individual human beings, should be recognized as having mental activities: wisdom, emotion, thought." He goes on to point out the basis for all social thought, which is the individual spirit: "Each person's brain is a cell forming part of one large organic brain that is society's, and the individual cells must stimulate each other and communicate with each other until all members working together can give birth to a social spirit."

Pres. Makiguchi's comments on the interrelation between the spirit of human beings and their natural, social, and cultural environment emphasize the point that the thread of life does not consist merely of physical phenomena, but contains spiritual and emotional elements as well. If we do not carefully observe the spiritual influences of our environment, then even if we are spared bodily harm, we are likely to suffer spiritual pollution culminating in social confusion or upheaval.

In considering the relationship between man and his environment, we should do so in the light of a famous passage from Nichiren Daishonin's *On Good Omens* (*Zuisō-gosho*), which says, "The world is objective environment; the sentient beings are subjective existence. For example, if the objective is a shadow, the subjective is the body. If there is no body, there is no shadow. If there is no subjective existence, there is no objective environment. But subjective existence expresses itself in the objective environment."

Here "the world" means our environment or the whole of space. *Objective environment* (*ehō*) is a Buddhist term and may be taken to mean elements of the visible environment. *Subjective existence* (*shōhō*) is the totality of living entities, called in Buddhism *sentient beings* (*shujō*). If we interpret subjective existence to be human beings, then the objective environment is human environment.

Nichiren Daishonin illustrated his meaning with an analogy to the body and its shadow. The body moves and transforms the shadow, but at the same time, the body is in a sense created by the shadow, for the body would not be a body if it did not cast a shadow. In other words, the body is given being and identity by the environment, and vice versa. In my opinion, it is only by synthesizing this dialectic that we can arrive at full understanding of the interrelation of our lives and our environment.

The living entity we call a human being is produced and nourished by harmony and unity among such diverse forces as the total pull of gravity in the universe, the flow of energy from the sun, and the somatological thread that encompasses all nature like a net.

In my opinion, the implication of the passage is this: although human life is created by the material world, and spiritual activity by the totality of elements in the universe, it is necessary for the human being to reach out for the sustenance and support of his environment. If the human being could not convert the support and sustenance of the physical world into his own flesh and blood, if he were able to make no active effort to accept it, he could not continue living.

To give a simple illustration, one can eat the most nourishing of feasts, but if one cannot digest what he eats, it will not contribute to the growth or well-being of one's body. One can read the world's most valuable books, but if one lacks the mental capacity to understand them, they are only paper and ink.

In the case of food, ingestion is not enough. There must also be digestion. The digestive tract is thought of by laymen as an interior organ of the body, but from the medical viewpoint, it is contiguous with the great outdoors. If food is not digested and absorbed, it is simply pushed through a long narrow strip of environment, as it were.

The relationship of the active forces in our bodies to the environment is measured by doctors in terms of what is called *adaptability*. Besides being able to digest and absorb nourishment from the alimentary tract, we must be able to breathe in air, extract oxygen from it, and breathe out the carbon dioxide; we must have a variety of defensive mechanisms against infection; we must adjust ourselves to the changing seasons. A healthy body does all this, of course. In the summer, the sweat glands go to work to adjust the temperature of the skin; in the winter, the capillaries near the surface of the skin contract to preserve heat. A properly functioning body also absorbs through the eyes and ears the information needed to respond intelligently to phenomena occurring around us.

If we analyze the life-force deep within us, we find that it manifests itself in innumerable forms, making possible the actual operation of the mind and body necessary for a creative life. The life-force is the source of all activity, because it responds to environmental stimuli and causes us to adapt to them. The person who leads an active life can face any environment and select from it that which is to be learned or digested. Depending on his activity, there are subtle changes in the meaning of the environment. The life-force in the human body not only makes possible the manifestation of life, but changes and re-creates the objective environment.

Kant, whose philosophical system I regard as one of the high points of Occidental thought, made some very trenchant observations about man's power of cognizance. It was his belief that man has an innate ability to understand the world about him; that we are born with the ability to see, for example, that there is a desk nearby, or that someone else is present, or that the stars are shining, or that an airplane is flying overhead, or that an object is moving. This is not to say we are born with an innate knowledge of what these various phenomena are, only that we have the ability to learn what they are, in terms of what Kant called categories.

Unless I am mistaken, Kant was the first Occidental thinker of modern times to recognize this ability as being inherent in life. This discovery, it seems to me, brought Western thought a step closer to Buddhism.

In general, Western philosophy of the modern period can be divided into two streams, rationalism and empiricism. With regard to the outside world, the rationalists, among whom we find Descartes, Spinoza, and Leibnitz, believed our understanding was based on certain innate ideas, which is to say on inborn intelligence. The empiricists, including Hobbes, Locke, Berkeley, and Hume, held that this understanding was accumulated from without. Locke, for instance, likened the human mind to a piece of blank paper on which ideas were imprinted through sensation. Kant rose above the dichotomy by postulating a living mechanism within human beings that permits them to comprehend the empiric world about them. If my interpretation is correct, he believed our comprehension of experience is an intuitive process based on a sensitivity to certain categories, among them time and space.

As a simple example, there is a cup in front of me right now. Its form is spatially apparent to me. From the temporal viewpoint, I am aware it was there some time ago. If no one had ever told me this was a cup, I would nevertheless know instinctively that it has been occupying the space there for a certain length of time.

Or let us suppose it is snowing outside. I can apprehend as a spatial concept the shapes and sizes of the snowflakes. With respect to time, I know the snowflakes I am looking directly out the window at were not there just a moment ago, and in another moment they will be on the ground. Such basic understandings, which Kant called Pure Reason, develop into more complicated ideas and thoughts. Kant conceived of the process whereby we intuitively recognize things outside ourselves as a function of the *transcendental analytic.*

From the epistemological viewpoint, if we take Kant's transcendental analytic, which is the innate ability to understand, as the subjective existence, then the thing understood is the objective environment. Depending on the nature of the subjective existence, the objective environment can take on an infinity of forms.

Living beings recognize objects by means of sense organs, but what is seen differs tremendously with the nature of the eye or the ear perceiving it. Amoebas and earthworms can sense only the presence of light and receive only a vague light and dark impression of what is around them. The compound eyes of insects cannot put together a coherent image as the human eye does, but they are very sensitive to movement. A wasp, I am told, cannot distinguish between a motionless fly on the wall and the head of a nail, but a dragonfly can immediately recognize a mite, a potential meal, passing before its eyes.

If a motion is very rapid, human eyes are apt not to resolve it into an image, but an insect's eyes often will. Cats and other animals can see better than people in the dark, because their pupils become relatively much larger in the dark than in the light. In short, the nature of what is seen depends upon the see-er.

People in general all have from birth the same sense organs and roughly the same capability to comprehend. They consequently see the physical world about them in pretty much the same way, at least so far as eyesight is concerned. What they make of what they see depends upon the manner in which their life-force functions.

Given that people share to a large degree a common set of biological features, their bodies have much the same degree of adaptability to various stimuli and they have similar capacities for building the environment—what we call society and culture. This ability to create society and culture is a unique feature of human beings, as opposed to animals or other living things. In the passages quoted above from *Geography of Human Life*, Tsunesaburo Makiguchi pointed out that the organism we call the social spirit is composed of individual spirits. In other words, the spirit of society, which is part of the environment in which individuals live, is formed by the active life-force of its many individual members. Conversely, if men did not have the ability to form societies, there would be no such thing as a collective social spirit.

At the core of the human spirit, there is a potential love for other human beings and for nature. There is also an irresistible urge to challenge the riddles of life and the universe, an impulse to search for aesthetic beauty and scientific truth. Love, the longing for beauty, the thirst for religion, the yearning for truth: these are all eminently human energies, and through the expression and manifestation of these energies great changes are brought about in human environment.

In the passage from *Geography of Human Life* about mountains, Makiguchi pointed out that to the minds of human beings, mountains could become living things. He meant quite simply that the force of human love can transform a cold inanimate mountain into a warm, pulsating, compassionate spirit. The soul that can appreciate the beauty of a plant can rest in a world brimming with richness and lyricism, and the world men who love nature live in can have the same life-force and feeling as themselves.

The human being who loves the earth and is at rest in the workings of the planet partakes of the immense reflection of the earth-become-spirit. The mind of the philosopher nestled in the womb of the universe can spread to encompass the universe. The spirit that loves nature, loves mankind, and pursues the infinite beauties of the earth and the cosmos to their fundamental source is inspired by poetic feelings, enlightened by the wisdom of science, moved by the wisdom of philosophy, and overpowered by the urge toward religious faith.

Dr. Akira Miyawaki, one of our leading ecologists, has likened the features of nature to the eyes and cheeks of a human face. The eyes, he notes, are easily damaged, but the cheeks are relatively impregnable to such outside forces as wind, cold, and rain. The natural features corresponding to the eyes are river basins, soggy plains, steep slopes, and mountain ridges. To try to build concrete highways in places like this is equivalent to putting a lighted match to a human eye. The place for roads is on the earth's cheeks, which have much greater power of resistance.

Dr. Miyawaki sees the earth as a living body and diagnoses its ailments as he would those of a human being. For him, the earth is not an inanimate object. It is a living organism with warm, flowing lifeblood.

It is profoundly true that the objective environment responds to and is transformed by the life-force of men. All living beings, man included, possess the life-force, which creates their environment, and, of course, reflects themselves.

This is why Nichiren Daishonin said, "If there is no body, there is no shadow. If there is no subjective existence, there is no objective environment." If the life-force within a living being leaves the body, its reflection also dissipates. Animals have animal shadows; men have human shadows. The environment of each living being differs with the state of existence within which it lives.

Unfortunately, there are humans who cast shadows very like those of beasts. Though physically they look like human beings, we must conclude that the true condition of their lives is akin to that of beasts. Let us hope for the day when men will lead lives that cast truly human shadows.

ACTION AND REACTION IN LIFE

Just after the passage from *On Good Omens* (*Zuisō-gosho*) cited above, there is this statement: "Consequently, if the five sense organs of the sentient beings are about to be destroyed, everything in the surroundings cries out with vexation. If the country is about to be ruined, there are ominous signs: the mountains crumble, the plants and trees wither, and the rivers run dry. When the eyes and ears and other sense organs are bewildered, there are natural disasters, and when men's spirits are not firm, the earth trembles."

The "sentient beings" include animals as well as people, but the reference is primarily to people. The five sense organs are the human body, and the environment around the body is its reflection. The over-all meaning, I think, is that destruction of the living body evokes destruction or violent change in the environment.

The passage also says that the destruction of the natural surroundings (*i.e.*, the "country") is preceded by forewarnings. When the crumbling of mountains, the withering of plants and trees, the drying up of rivers throw people into consternation, neither heaven nor earth can fail to be affected. This is my interpretation of the passage, and it seems to me it is intensely applicable to the world in which we now live—a world in which the evils of society and civilization threaten to destroy mankind itself. One does not have to look far today to find crumbling mountains, withering plants, or depleted rivers!

When changes in the environment seem to be a threat to human existence, it should not be overlooked that the cause of the evil is often within human beings themselves. Those who have allowed themselves to become slaves of greed, ignorance, and egoism, and who have thereby lost their essential humanity, are tearing away at the soil of the earth, provoking untimely seasons, disturbing the normal movements of the seas, and thus gradually destroying the basis for life on our planet. This, I think, is what Nichiren Daishonin meant when he said, "if the five sense organs of the sentient beings are about to be destroyed, everything in the surroundings cries out with vexation."

What about, "When the eyes and ears and other sense organs are bewildered, there are natural disasters, and when men's spirits are not firm, the earth trembles"? We know already of the close connection in the physical world between the activities of human beings and the natural environment. Can we take this latter statement to mean that in the depths of the human being there is a similar interaction between the physical and the spiritual? And if so, what is its nature?

These are difficult questions. It is comparatively easy to see how man's attitude toward nature affects the physical environment, because the attitude expresses itself in concrete, conscious actions. Spiritual phenomena are not so easy to grasp, though the life-force that manifests itself in our attitude toward nature and society is the same life-force that motivates our inner spiritual activity. For this reason, it is impossible to arrive at a complete explanation of human life in connection with its environment without taking into account the relationship between subjective existence and objective environment within the world of the spirit.

An interesting modern view of nature is expressed in Martin Heidegger's theory of existence, to which it may be profitable to refer at this point. Heidegger's theory itself is difficult, partly because he invented a terminology of his own, but his general idea of nature is fairly easy to explain.

We are always expressing wonder at the harmony of nature, but most of us do not look beneath the surface of things. Heidegger became convinced that the entire cosmos must be one living entity, because otherwise the movements of the universe would not be orderly. He conceived of a fundamental and rudimentary existence that gives birth to the harmonious interaction of all things, and he called this the *Urnatur*.

Heidegger being an existentialist, it must have been something of a struggle for him to develop this concept. I consider the *Urnatur* an exceptionally profound idea, but if it is not an eternal existence encompassing all of our individual lives, I do not think it can be regarded as the ultimate essence of the universe.

Heidegger seems to consider that when men die, they revert to nothingness. Consequently, though his *Urnatur* is the basis for the existence of nature and man, he does not believe the lives of men and other beings are eternal in nature.

From the Buddhist viewpoint, *Urnatur* is somewhere between nature and the ultimate reality, which is the Mystic Law. The Mystic Law itself is the eternally indestructible cosmic life that must underlie the *Urnatur*. To the average person, the idea of the entire cosmos being a single living body may seem strange at first, but if we regard the Mystic Law as being immanent in every phase of life, it is not hard to think that all things in the cosmos are manifestations of it.

The reason why I suggest that we think in terms of Only One Cosmos instead of Only One Earth is that Only One Cosmos strikes at the absolute truth: the universe is the embodiment of the Mystic Law, which pervades all existence.

In *The True Entity of Life* (*Shōhō Jissō-shō*), a letter Nichiren Daishonin wrote to a disciple, he said, "All beings and their environments in any of the Ten Worlds, from Hell at the lowest to Buddhahood at the highest, are, without exception, the manifestation of *Myōhō-renge-kyō*. Where there is an environment, there is life within it. Miao-lo states, 'Both life (*shōhō*) and its environment (*ehō*) always manifest *Myōhō-renge-kyō*.' "

I shall have occasion later to take up the unique Buddhist concept of the Ten Worlds, or Ten States of Being, of which Hell is the lowest and Buddhahood is the highest, but for the time being, it is sufficient to note that "all beings and their environments in any of the Ten Worlds" means all living beings in the cosmos, and the overall meaning of the passage is that everything having life is a manifestation of the Mystic Law.

To be more precise, one can comprehend from this passage the actual relation between human life and its environment in both the physical and the spiritual world. As suggested earlier, the statement that "where there is an environment there is life within it" should not be taken to mean that the two phenomena simply coexist. The explanation in the commentary, which says that both "always manifest *Myōhō-renge-kyō*," indicates tersely how the dynamic rhythm of human life and its environment is related to the cosmic life we call the Mystic Law.

The Mystic Law is the force and wisdom inherent in the entire cosmos, which is itself the source of all physical and spiritual phenomena. From the innermost depths of the cosmos, the Law gradually becomes manifest in definite form, and as this happens, human lives take on individuality. Simultaneously, the individual environment takes form as objective environment, or shadow. The subjective existence and the objective environment make up a single existence, which takes form as the life-force residing in cosmic life becomes manifest. That this existence can be divided into two is unthinkable. The formation of a human life as a subjective existence is identical with the formation of that life's environment. They can no more be separated than can the growth and development of animals and plants be separated from the world in which they live.

Each human life, together with its environment, partakes of the fundamental life-force of the entire cosmos. It follows that any change in the life condition of a single human being can, in the inner reaches of life itself, exert an influence on other human lives. And since nature and the cosmos are living entities, the waves emanating from one human life can not only shake the foundations of other living beings, but can affect things usually thought to be lifeless.

Experiments in extrasensory perception offer definite indications of how human beings can influence each other in the purely spiritual realm. These are empiric, scientific experiments, and they are consequently carried out entirely in the physical world, but many scientists employing a variety of methods have obtained results that seem to have a bearing on spiritual matters. At least the findings cannot be explained by known physical laws.

In one experiment, of a type often carried out by students of ESP, two rooms separated by a distance of 200 meters are employed. The rooms are connected only by an electric buzzer. A teacher sits in one room, and a student in the other. When the buzzer is sounded, the teacher picks up a card from a pack on the desk before him and attempts by concentration to communicate the image or number on the card to the student in the other room. The student then concentrates on picking a card corresponding to the one selected by the teacher. There are no conventional signals; the teacher simply focuses his mind on the card in his hand and tries mentally to convey what he sees to the student. Sometimes the student picks up the right card. Sometimes he does not. The procedure is repeated many times to reduce the element of pure chance.

If agreement between the teacher's card and the student's card were indeed a matter of chance, over a large number of trials, the number of times the cards match should follow the laws of statistical probability, but in fact this is not the case. In an extended experiment in which several students participated, there was a distinctly higher rate of matching among students who respected and trusted the teacher than among students who did not. By sheer probability, this difference in response itself should appear only one time in about a million, which is as good as saying that the results could not be a matter of sheer chance.

According to parapsychologists, the only possible explanation for the results in this case is telepathy between teacher and students. There was a time not many years ago when serious talk of telepathy was apt to be greeted with jeers. Today it is widely believed that information can under certain conditions be transferred from one mind to another without the use of conventional methods of communication.

Parapsychological experiments also suggest the possibility of clairvoyance, kineticism, and foreknowledge, though evidence is still to a large degree inconclusive, and much study remains to be done. It can at least be said that we have arrived at a stage where it is no longer considered scientific to dismiss out of hand a number of phenomena formerly scoffed at as spiritualistic.

Perhaps the card experiment means only that the brain waves of the teacher affect those of the students. It may also be, however, that the inner life-force of the teacher has influenced the life-force of the students. We tend to associate premonitions with unfortunate events such as death or accidents, but I think it is possible that genuine premonitions occur as the result of the spiritual activity of the life-force, for there are pleasant premonitions as well. Certainly everyone has had the experience of deciding, for no particular reason, to visit a friend and then being greeted with the words, "I had a feeling you would come today." It is a common occurrence, and often there is a perfectly ordinary explanation, but I think it quite possible that between two friends there is a form of mental or spiritual communication that does not require the use of either the five senses or overt communication. Within the inner lives of two individuals there is an interaction of the forces of love or trust, moving them to seek each other out, just as there may be an interaction of the forces of revulsion or suspicion, keeping them apart. Expressed in terms of fundamental and reflected phenomena, this means that the human life and its environment are in the deeper meaning fused into one and are continually exerting influence on each other. The interaction between the life-force in one human being and that in others takes place not only in the physical realm of objective environment, but in the spiritual realm as well. It is certain, I think, that the pulsating force that moves one life can also sway the inner being of other lives in a truly occult fashion.

We must no doubt take into consideration many variable factors, such as the strength and purity of the life-force in the individual human being and any special circumstances which may surround the lives of the people with whom he is associated. We must also keep in mind the oneness and indivisibility of the physical and spiritual realms and the continuously interacting influences between the individual and others in both realms. The consequences of the interaction are therefore not always easy to predict by scientific methods. It seems to me significant, however, that the inner influences of our life-forces on other lives, so long postulated by Buddhism, is now being examined and demonstrated by non-Buddhist parapsychologists.

One parapsychologist, Whately Carington, has come very close to the Buddhist viewpoint. Like Jung, he believes in a collective unconscious shared by all men, but he goes on to hypothesize that it functions as a single entity.

In the ancient Greek view, which served as the basis of Heidegger's philosophy, man and nature were of homogeneous character, and man could become an integral part of nature. The Greeks referred to nature as the *physis* or the cosmos, and considered it to be a living entity, just as men and animals are living entities. When conflict arose between man and nature, it was to be regarded as a necessary step in the creation of a new harmony. In effect, nature, men, and animals were all living entities whose minds and hearts were capable of mutual interactions. On the whole, the Greeks did not spend much time contemplating the spiritual interaction of the human mind and nature, and this aspect of existence remained largely unexplored by later Occidental philosophers and scientists.

In contrast, in the Buddhist view, the profound unity of subjective existence and objective environment leads naturally to the idea that the life-force of one human being can affect other living beings and even the fundamental being of mankind as a whole. Furthermore, the minds of mankind fuse into one and exert a continuous influence, both physical and spiritual, on other living beings and on the whole of nature. As time goes on, I think scientists and philosophers will throw greater light on the collective unconscious and its relationship with non-human life and nature in the broadest sense.

Since the influence of one human life-force is far-reaching and extends to the inner spirit of mankind as a whole, the future of mankind rests ultimately on the acceptance of human life as the fundamental phenomenon in our world. The future depends on the life pattern of each individual and on the manner in which he expresses the life-force of the cosmos. If human beings open their eyes to the harmonious rhythm of the universe and coexist peacefully with all forms of life, they will enhance the function of the thread of life and move toward the creation of a new universe in which mankind will be full of love, trust, and compassion, and the workings of the human mind will cause that living being which is nature to continue its creative work. The harmonious operation of the cosmic body, supported by beings who cherish Only One Cosmos, will in turn work to support each human life as fully as though there were Only One Life. This is the way human life and behavior should be within the unity of subjective existence and objective environment.

But if human beings remain slaves of greed, ignorance, and egoism, if they hate and kill each other, if the mind of mankind becomes a black cancerous growth, then mankind will destroy other living beings and even nature itself, cutting as it does so the vital thread of life that links the cosmos. Our planet will become bleak and moribund, and mankind will be cut off at its very roots.

We are free to choose the path we follow, and the ability to follow the right one is innate within man. The question is how to develop the potential wisdom inherent in our life-force so that it works for life and creativity in the universe. Even if a human being possesses the ability to love and trust, if the motivating force within him is weak, he is not apt to influence other human beings, let alone human life as a whole. On the other hand, if a person has a strong motivating force, but is beset by doubt, suspicion, and antagonism toward others, he is apt to destroy himself, and perhaps mankind as a whole. When we have discovered how to employ our life-force for the creation and furtherance of life on both the human and the cosmic levels, and when we have found out how to live in true harmony with the universe, the philosophy of the unity between subjective existence and objective environment will have become the great saving practical philosophy of mankind.

EYES THAT CAN SEE LIFE

WHAT ARE DREAMS?

Some time ago there was a literary controversy over whether *Ten Nights of Dreams*, a collection of stories by the Japanese novelist Natsume Sōseki, was purely fictional or based on Sōseki's actual dreams. The cerebral physiologists involved came to the general conclusion that the dreams were in large part real. Prof. Junji Matsumoto of Tokushima University, for example, citing such phrases as "pure white cheeks," "huge red sun," and "red letters in the black dark," argued that the frequency and distribution of sensory images in the stories were very much the same as in genuine dreams.

The application of scientific analysis to a literary work may seem insensitive, but it can at times yield fascinating new insights into the subconscious mind of the author. With that in mind, I reread *Ten Nights of Dreams* and came away pondering once again the curious nature of dreams. They develop along unrealistic lines, jump from incident to incident, and rarely come to a definite conclusion, and yet in sleep the mind somehow accepts them. Sōseki's *Dreams* are fictionalized to some extent and have a certain continuity. Real dreams are usually almost completely lacking in coherence. Still, they penetrate deep into our subconscious thought and reveal hidden secrets—often secrets our conscious mind would just as soon have remain secret. When we awake, the dream we have had usually seems to have no connection with reality, but psychoanalysts would disagree.

Even asleep we apparently react in our dreams to outside stimuli. Freud noted that when a sleeping patient's nose was tickled with a feather, he dreamed he was being tortured, and that tapping on scissors with pincers caused another patient to dream of a bell ringing. The reaction in the dream, however, is quite different from the stimulus.

Examination of brain waves tends to prove that everybody dreams. People who think they do not are simply quick to forget their dreams upon awakening. As a general rule, dreams are thoroughly unpredictable, and in the past they have been regarded as the opposite of reality. Indeed, to be "living in a dream world" means to deny reality. Freud and his followers, however, showed that dreams have an important connection with fundamental reality in that they furnish a means of examining our innermost thoughts. We have then a paradox: dreams are intimately related to our personal reality, but they appear to have no direct relationship to the here-and-now reality in which we live.

Ambiguity is by no means limited to dreams. Many other phenomena in human life defy common-sense explanations. But common sense, as we have already observed, helps us little in explaining even such basic things as consciousness and the human mind. It seems certain that consciousness is within the human body, but where in the body? Traditionally, such expressions as "in my heart" or "deep inside me" have been employed, but consciousness is certainly not located in the heart or the bowels. In the brain cells? Again no. Though much of the activity involved in consciousness takes place in the brain, consciousness is not necessarily confined to the brain. It is impossible to pick out a place in the body and say, "This is where consciousness resides." At the same time, human consciousness does not exist outside the body. In some respects, the workings of consciousness, mind, and spirit are as mysterious in real life as in dreams.

When we are asleep and motionless, are we our real selves? When we are dreaming, our eyeballs move constantly, but aside from that, is the still, motionless body the true self, or is the true self the self-image we see floating about in the dream? One can assert that a dream is a purely mental phenomenon occurring during sleep, even that the images in the dream are hallucinations of a sort, but this is not the whole story. The dream is related to our real self, for in a dream we experience happiness, sadness, and the whole gamut of human emotions.

I think dreams offer a clue to the nature of the Buddhist concept of *kū*. As we have seen, *kū* has been called "nothingness" or "the Void," but *kū* is a concept transcending the dualism of existence and non-existence. Like dreams, *kū* both is and is not.

Dreams cannot be fitted into customary concepts of reality because they are independent of the two most important measuring rods of ordinary reality, time and space. If they do have their own temporal and spatial framework, it is different from the ordinary one. I think we could say dreams represent a pretemporal, prespatial chaos.

How does Buddhism explain such a condition? Having started with dreams, we have reached a point where we should ask how Buddhism deals with the various phenomena of life which cannot be measured in terms of time and space.

A CONSTANTLY CHANGING WORLD

A cardinal principle of Buddhist philosophy is that all things are composed of elements that are constantly changing and combining with each other in different ways. An important analysis of human life is the theory of the Ten Factors, which was summarized by Nichiren Daishonin in the following passage:

> That we are the true and indestructible essence of the Three Bodies of the Buddha in One is explained in the Lotus Sutra [listing the Ten Factors of life, which are] appearance, nature, entity, power, influence, inherent cause, external cause, latent effect, manifest effect, and consistency from beginning to end. The first of these, appearance, means the appearance of our bodies in color and form. This is also called the Manifest Buddha (*ōjin nyorai*), which is Provisional Perception (*ketai*). Next, [the second factor] nature refers to our spirit, which is also called the Buddha of Reward (*hōjin nyorai*). This is Perception of the Latent (*kūtai*). The third, entity, is the entirety of our body. This is also called the Buddha of the Law (*hosshin nyorai*), or Perception of the Middle Way (*chūtai*).

Of the many technical philosophical terms here, which I must eventually explain, at the moment I am particularly concerned with three: Provisional Perception (*ketai*), Perception of the Latent (*kūtai*), and Perception of the Middle Way (*chūtai*). These three basic concepts necessary to an understanding of Buddhist epistemology are usually spoken of collectively as the Three Perceptions (*santai*).

Perception (*tai*) means something that is clear and apparent. If one examines things with respect to these Three Perceptions, one can understand the essential character of life and of all things in the universe. This idea is based on the teachings of the great Chinese Buddhist thinker Chih-i (538–97; also called T'ien-t'ai Ta-shih, or, in Japanese, Tendai Daishi).

It is important to note that in Buddhist philosophy in general it is not considered possible to reach an understanding of such complex and intangible phenomena as life by examining them from a single fixed viewpoint. Instead, one must be flexible and adopt a number of viewpoints.

This approach is part and parcel of modern science, where it is constantly being found that one theory will not fit all the facts. A simple example can be drawn from the field of mathematics.

For centuries it was accepted as absolute truth that given a straight line and a point outside it, one and only one line parallel to the first could be drawn through the point. This fifth postulate of Euclid was and is valid if one is dealing with Euclidean space. Modern scientists, however, have come to realize that Euclidean geometry is only one among many possible concepts of space, and not an entirely satisfactory one at that.

Suppose you reject Euclid's postulate and start from the assumption that the number of parallel lines is infinite. Reasoning backward, you can arrive at a different geometry and a different concept of space. The same would be true if you started from the assumption that there is not even one parallel. This would by no means be idle speculation, because owing to the inevitable imperfection of our equipment and our powers of observation, it is impossible to demonstrate empirically that two lines are parallel, whereas it can always be shown that they may not be.

If one postulates that the surface of a sphere is flat—which means, in effect, that the arc formed by the sphere and a half circle running through the middle of the sphere is considered to be a straight line—then there is no parallel line running through any point outside the straight line on the surface of the sphere. Conversely, on a hyperbolic-paraboloid surface like a saddle an infinite number of parallel lines is possible.

Non-Euclidean geometry was developed from such considerations as these, and non-Euclidean geometry, which was used to establish Einstein's theory of relativity, is now a basic tool of mathematics and physics. Today the actual space of the cosmos is generally considered to be non-Euclidean in character, and Einstein himself postulated a four-dimensional space, finite but not bounded, as the actual space of the universe. According to this concept, if one were to go straight up without limit one would go to the edge of the universe and return to the point of departure without changing directions. The simplest way of conceiving of a finite, unbounded space is to imagine an ever-expanding balloon. The balloon grows larger and larger, but a point moving "straight" along its surface eventually arrives back at the place from which it started.

Modern mathematics was developed by discarding the traditional viewpoint and adopting a multiple approach, and this is an important point. In looking at such fundamental matters as life and the universe, a fixed viewpoint is not enough. One must always keep in mind that what one seems to see is not necessarily the whole truth.

A child born with built-in green sunglasses would presumably go through life thinking everything is green. He might form for himself a beautiful theory of what the world is like, but the theory, no matter how beautiful, would have no validity for anyone else. Similarly, if one regards life and the cosmos from a single fixed viewpoint, one might construct an ingenious philosophy, but whether it would explain the whole of life and the universe is very doubtful.

The flexibility of the Buddhist viewpoint has in the past caused many to dismiss Buddhist philosophy as vague or unrealistic. This failure to appreciate the true nature of Buddhist thought is probably due in part to the mystic, poetic, abstract, and metaphysical language found in the Buddhist sutras. In contrast, the rigid yes-or-no method of argument employed in most Western philosophy and science of the past has exercised a strong appeal because of its straightforwardness and seeming certainty. Despite the difference in language, I consider it almost inevitable that people will begin to reassess the flexible, multipolar, and intuitive Buddhist way of looking at things. We live in an age when science has explored many delicate and complicated aspects of life and the universe, things neither known nor imagined only a few decades ago, and I believe our present state of knowledge calls out for a reexamination of the traditional wisdom of the Orient, and particularly the relativistic ideas of Buddhism.

In the passage quoted above from one of Nichiren Daishonin's writings, appearance was defined as the appearance of our bodies in color and form. The passage can be interpreted on several different planes of physical existence, but its fundamental meaning is that appearance, which is equated with Provisional Perception, means all things we can detect with our senses. The body, in other words, is the physical aspect of existence, and I include in this minute particles and the like, which we can see only with electron microscopes, as well as invisible phenomena such as sound waves. In short, anything that can be measured quantitatively. In Buddhist thinking, all these things are temporary or transitory, and they are constantly undergoing change, being brought together or dispersed by causes and conditions. In a sense, nothing can be said to exist, because a moment before it was different from what it is now, and a moment later it will be again different.

While we say all aspects of reality as we see it are transitory or temporary, the suggestion is that there must exist a deeper permanent truth. The question arises as to how we are to conceive of this.

In the view of modern science everything in the universe is indeed constantly moving and changing. Science deals primarily with physical being, but Buddhism emphasizes the continuous change going on in human life, pointing out that our perceptible lives on earth are constantly undergoing birth, maturation, destruction, and latency. It follows that in Buddhism, to cling to life as a permanent and unchanging entity is to violate the truth and has the consequence of bringing on human suffering.

If, as Buddhism teaches, "all is in flux, and there is no permanence," how do we cope with the world around us? Do we flee from it? Do we challenge it? Fleeing does not accord with Buddhism, for it implies that the truth of impermanence is somehow repugnant. Many people seem to think that if all life is transitory, there is nothing to do but resign oneself to the fleeting nature of life. In the Japanese language, for example, the character used for writing "perception" in the Three Perceptions has also come to be used for a word meaning to *resign oneself* or to *give up*. From this narrow etymological viewpoint, when a person sees how things really are, he abandons unrealistic wants or ambitions.

Actually, the realization of the constantly changing nature of all things is the key to true happiness, for it means that no matter how bad a situation is, it will change. No misfortune is permanent; no evil insuperable.

In Buddhism, all things in the universe are transitory, but they come together harmoniously as the result of causes and conditions. In the case of the sentient beings, which includes human beings, each individual is thought to be a fusion of the Five Aggregates. These are form, perception, conception, volition, and consciousness. They are constantly changing, constantly re-fusing in response to certain causes and conditions. I shall have occasion to go into this subject more fully in a later chapter, but at this point I would like to emphasize that the idea of these Five Aggregates accounts for the presence of countless individual lives, all put together from the same essential elements, but all different and all constantly changing.

Earlier I referred to the use of radioactive tracers to show how the cells of the human body are constantly undergoing metabolism. The body, in effect, is constantly ingesting matter from without and emitting matter from within. In a sense, this means the body is constantly coming together and coming apart in its cell mechanism. The Buddhist concept of the Five Aggregates is not so exact as the scientific study of cells, but it is more profound, because it accounts for spiritual activity and for the inseparability of the physical and the spiritual.

As we have already seen, in the view of modern astronomy the entire cosmos is in a constant state of flux. There are several theories of the development of the universe, but the one most widely accepted today is that it began with an explosion about 20 billion years ago and has been expanding ever since. Proposed by George Gamow and other scientists, this has come to be known as the explosion theory or, more colloquially, the theory of the big bang. An alternate explanation is the oscillation theory, according to which the universe expands and contracts in cycles. Holders of this view agree with the proponents of the big bang that the universe is now in a phase of expansion.

At one time a number of scientists were attracted to the steady state theory, which rejected the big bang and oscillation theories and held instead that the universe is in a state of equilibrium made possible by the constant creation of matter. The steady state theory did not argue that the universe is unchanging, but simply that in spite of the constant changes going on inside it, it remains relatively stable. This theory presented a number of difficulties, and it has few proponents today.

If we accept an expansion theory, the constellations visible now did not exist during the early stages of the universe, which is to say 20 billion years ago, when all the elements of the cosmos were crowded together in an unbelievably dense mass. The appearance of these stars was the result of later evolution extending over billions of years, and it is certain that with the passage of a few more hundred million years, these constellations will change or disappear.

From the Buddhist viewpoint, the constellations, like human beings, are going through the four stages: birth, maturation, destruction, and latency. At present, for example, astronomers can see an explosion going on in the Crab Nebula, but since this nebula is 4,200 light years away, the explosion must have taken place 4,200 years ago. We shall have to wait another 4,200 years to find out what is going on there now. We can, however, conjecture that similar stellar transformations are even now going on throughout the universe.

Our five-billion-year-old earth is at present in a mature state of stability, but eventually it too will be swallowed up by the sun or destroyed in some other manner. In the case of stars, interstellar gas condenses to form them, they go through a period of stability and then die in an explosion of great brilliance and energy. It is ironic, I think, that stars in this last stage are known as supernovae—a name implying they are new—though the idea fits in well with Buddhist theory, for their death signifies the beginning of a new form of life.

By comparison with the stars, the life-span of a human being is infinitesimal. Indeed, the whole history of mankind is a very recent occurrence in the evolution of organic life on this planet. If the history of the earth were condensed into one twenty-four-hour day, the history of man would be equivalent to the ticking off of the last forty seconds. Such figures underscore one fact: reality as we know it is only a temporary coming together of various components.

At the micro end of the scale, the life-span of elementary particles is so short as to defy the imagination. There is some variation among the types of particles, but the duration is on the order of one thirty-millionth of a second.

The fact is that the more deeply we go into the physical aspects of the cosmos, the more convincing is the evidence of unceasing change and flux everywhere. It is the same with individual personalities as well.

In Buddhist writings, there is an admonition to ascetics to the effect that in order to avoid being tempted by a woman, they should imagine how she would look as a skeleton. The idea has the typical rigidity of Hinayana Buddhism, but it nevertheless succinctly reveals an understanding of the transitory nature of human life as it goes through the cycle of birth and death.

For all its impermanence, life is magnificently harmonious. Molecules and atoms are essentially inorganic, and elementary particles lack even individuality, but they combine into increasingly complex compounds until they become the genes that determine the personality of human beings. A single human being is said to have some 5 billion genes bearing the information necessary for his individual existence. Thanks to these genes, our bodies grow into marvelously precise complexes, we possess consciousness, and we experience happiness, anger, and the other emotions. A certain configuration and interaction of billions of particles determines how we will live and how we will react to our surroundings. Who can say the Buddhist concept of the Five Aggregates coming together temporarily to compose a human being is not an excellent metaphor for this phenomenon? The earth in turn is a superorganism, and the cosmos, with its endless rhythmic movements, is the supreme organism, which with its infinite harmonious fusions gives life to everything within it.

TIME, SPACE, AND LATENCY

Central to the philosophy of Buddhism is the concept of *kū*. *Kū* is frequently expressed in English as "the Void," as "emptiness," or as "nothingness," but none of these terms is very satisfactory, since they all suggest a philosophy of nihilism, whereas Buddhism is not in the least nihilistic. A few Western students of Buddhism have begun calling *kū* "relativity," which is closer, but this tends to associate *kū* with the science of physics and consequently with the physical world.

It is generally said by Buddhist thinkers that *kū* transcends existence and non-existence. If you try to think of it as existent, it does not exist; if you try to think of it as non-existent, it does exist, albeit on a different plane from ordinary reality.

In discussing the Ten Factors of Life, Nichiren Daishonin wrote, "Nature refers to our spirit, which is also called the Buddha of Reward. This refers to Perception of the Latent (*kūtai*)," and it is clear *kū* refers to our spirit or our psyche.

In a broader sense, *kū* means the nature and spirit of all things—what is sometimes called the noumenon. That the concept is so frequently misunderstood and misused is perhaps only to be expected, because it is impossible to explain in simple terms. It is probably the one Buddhist idea which more than any other causes Western thinkers to shake their heads and wonder what Buddhism is all about. But Western thinkers are not alone; there are not many Orientals who have a proper understanding of *kū*.

Josei Toda, the second president of Soka Gakkai, used to tell a story of a certain Japanese Buddhist scholar who tried to explain *kū* to a Western student by taking a folded-paper crane and crumpling it up in his hand, the idea being that *kū* was the crane that was no longer there. I doubt this approach was of much assistance to the student, for it comes perilously close to the dualism of existence and non-existence. This dualism appeals to contemporary man, but to understand *kū*, we must start from the idea that there are things, like dreams, which cannot be placed neatly into the categories of existence and non-existence.

Our everyday criteria for existence or non-existence are based on our concepts of space and time. Kant, for one, said that man perceives the exterior world in a spatial and temporal framework. And as far as Kant went, he was right, for we do normally use time and space to recognize, to measure, and to calculate.

If we add time to the three spatial dimensions of length, breadth, and height, we have the means of describing the world we see, which is to say, the physical world. Our spiritual nature goes beyond the framework of space and time and consequently cannot be confined within the ordinary limits of existence and non-existence.

If we try to search out our spirit, we can find neither form nor substance, and yet the idea spirit does not exist is contradicted by countless physical manifestations of its action. Perhaps one should consider existence and non-existence to be two aspects of a single concept. In one aspect of being, the physical world, the framework of space and time is applicable. In the other, which is *kū*, it is not.

Kū is not simply the spirit of human beings. It is the character and essence of all things. To offer an example, diamonds and coal are both composed of carbon, but because of the difference in molecular structure, diamonds are spectacularly different from coal. *Kū* is the fundamental nature making diamonds diamonds and coal coal.

Pres. Toda sometimes used the concept of anger to explain *kū*. We possess anger at all times, but we cannot see it until it is provoked and causes surface manifestations. Anger is, then, an innate potentiality, it is normally dormant, but it can cause overt actions under certain conditions. Similarly, *kū* is a continuing substratum that has the power, under proper conditions, to cause activity in the visible superstratum.

Expressions such as "neither existent nor non-existent" are numerous in Buddhist writings. A classic example is in the Sutra of Infinite Meaning

(*Muryōgi-kyō*), where there is a passage saying, "Its entity is neither existence nor non-existence, neither cause nor condition, neither itself nor something else, neither square nor round, neither long nor short . . ." The complete statement lists no less than thirty-four negations in its efforts to explain the Buddha. This process of repeated negations strikes me as being one of the main reasons why *kū* is so difficult to understand: although it is specifically stated that *kū* is not non-existence, the repetition of negations seems to give the impression that it is something close to non-existence.

The main reason for the negative mode of expression is that *kū* defies positive description. A second reason is the desire to overcome preconceptions and avoid conventional value judgements. If you try to explain such things as the subconscious mind or the inner spirit, the temptation is to talk in terms of material greed, or sexual impulse, or brain cells, or some other ready-made concept. This may suffice in some instances, but when we talk about the spiritual realm of *kū*, no ready-made concepts exist to fit the situation. It is therefore necessary to explain by telling what *kū* is not. This is no doubt the reasoning behind the long string of negations in the Sutra of Infinite Meaning. This is a blanket negation of ordinary conceptions, one might even say a negation of conventional negation.

If you tell someone for the first time about the Buddha, one of the first things he will want to know is what the Buddha looks like. But since the Buddha is life itself, words will not give a proper description. This is why the ancient Buddhist writers resorted to telling what the Buddha did *not* look like.

When people conceive of the physical world as temporary or transitory, they are almost inevitably moved toward pessimism. The ascetics of Hinayana Buddhism, for example, were strongly inclined to regard this world as mere nothingness. They knew the concept of *kū*, but they took it to mean complete emptiness. Mahayana Buddhism may be viewed as a movement to sweep away this idea and establish a new concept of *kū*.

Since the world of *kū* is essentially spiritual, I should like to return for a moment to the subject of psychology and our subconscious minds. In exploring the subconscious, we are in a similar situation, because the world of the subconscious cannot be described in terms of time and space or of existence and non-existence. Psychoanalysts use the word *id* to refer to the innermost reservoir of unconscious drives and impulses in the subconscious mind. Prof. Takeo Doi, in his *Psychoanalysis* (*Seishin Bunseki*), explains id as follows: "In the first place, id is completely without organization. It has no direction, and it knows no logic. It is what might be called 'pre-moral.' Within it is a hodge-podge of impulses that neither cancel out each other nor separate themselves one from the other. There is chaos, but with no inconsistency. It may be considered that there is no passage of time within the id."

In other words, id cannot be defined in terms of time and space. It is chaotic, but without being self-contradictory. It is not immoral, but it is in the primitive state preceding the imposition of morality by the environment.

I think we could say id contains man's primordial instinctive urges—the basic vital energy in human life. It lies outside the framework of such value judgements as good or evil, and it is too primitive to be affected by logic. It is pure drive, the constant motivation and energy that makes people live. Perhaps we could call it the primitive spiritual energy necessary for human life. It is only natural for id to have neither order nor organization, even though the various impulses it contains do not conflict with each other. Despite the chaos, there is harmony and unity in the urge toward life. There is a "coming together" or "fusion" of urges. Id gives rise to the actions of a human being in his contacts with the outside world. Id, in a word, is nothing other than *kū* as it applies to individual human beings.

We could also regard the information contained in DNA molecules to be *kū*. A human being, as we have noted, has in him some 5 billion DNA particles that impart to him a tremendous amount of inherited information. There are so many of these particles that no one could use all of their information in a lifetime, and it is thought that most people use only a small fraction of it. The information conveyed by the DNA genes might be said to be what Jung spoke of as the accumulated wisdom and experience of mankind. As an example of accumulated wisdom, it may be that the widespread human fear and dislike of snakes is an inherited memory of a prehistoric age when human beings had to battle against reptiles for control of the earth.

The information passed on in genes goes largely unused. Even in the greatest geniuses, two thirds or more of the cerebrum is dormant throughout life. A lifetime is not long enough to fully use all the brain's potential. If it were actually used to the maximum, people would have far greater intellectual capacity than they do.

This is much the same as saying that within a human life there are limitless potentialities. What we must remember is that man is endowed by nature with a capacity for both good and evil. He can become truly wise, or he can become cunning and devious. Even if we were able to use our inborn information to the maximum, there would still remain the question of whether it is used for good purposes or bad.

Only the information contained in DNA is *kū*. The particles themselves belong to the physical world, as do the manifestations caused in a human being as he comes into contact with the external world.

It is interesting to consider the idea of *kū* in connection with modern theories of physics. Until the twentieth century, to say that something neither existed nor did not exist was to challenge the basic principles of physics. It was precisely by measuring and examining the visible world that Isaac Newton and the classical physicists sought to deduce the laws and principles of the universe. With the coming of Einstein, Niels Bohr, and other modern giants, with their fields and electrons and elementary particles, there have developed concepts of the ultimate that are very close to *kū*. (Whether these theories will prove to be the final answers of science remains to be seen, but that is another question.) The traditional approach of physicists was to examine things and the way they acted and then draw conclusions as to their nature or condition. Now, however, it is not unusual for a quality or characteristic to be hypothesized theoretically, and physical proof to be found later.

A case in point is the theory of fields, which was developed in the course of the search for the medium by which light is transmitted. In classical physics, it was postulated that there had to be some medium of transmission for all energy in wave form, such as that of sound and light, but the famous Michelson-Morley experiment (1887) proved light could be transmitted in a vacuum. This was an earth-shaking discovery, but it was soon found that electric and magnetic waves could also be transmitted in a vacuum. This gave rise to the theory of fields, which, in effect, hypothesized a condition and called this condition a field. Subsequently, electric fields, magnetic fields, and gravitational fields were recognized.

It was evident from the transmission of electric impulses and from magnetic lines that there is something electric or magnetic in the character of space. In the case of magnetism, we can see where the lines of force are by making the simple classroom demonstration with a magnet and iron filings. The point is this: when it is specified that a quality in space itself affects all matter, then this quality, now called a field, is of the same character as what we call *kū*. Today, physicists speak of the presence of fields in space as the "curvature of space."

The idea of a gravitational field was first presented by Einstein. This concept altered our ideas of why things fall to the ground when we drop them. According to the old idea, they fall because of the pull of gravity. This is correct as far as it goes, but in the concept of the gravitational field, it is held that the object follows a gravitational line, which, by traditional mathematics, is not absolutely straight.

In other respects, scientists seem to be arriving at theories in which the lines between existence and non-existence in the traditional sense are breaking down. The general trend, it seems to me, is toward a physical concept of the universe compatible with Buddhist ontology.

I spoke above of light as a wave phenomenon, but in modern times, it has come to be considered that light displays the characteristics not only of waves, but of particles as well. Although this defies traditional ways of thought, it has been demonstrated in actual experiments. In effect, light has two distinctly different characteristics: its photoelectric effect can be explained only on the assumption that light is composed of particles, but the interference effect demands that light consist of waves. The dual characteristic of light led to the development of the quantum theory; this in turn upset many long-held views on matter and radiation.

Dr. Shin'ichiro Tomonaga, who received the Nobel Prize for Physics in 1965, in his "Trial of the Photon" sums up the difficulty of explaining how the photon could be both wave and particle by offering an analogy with a criminal court case. The photon is a burglar who can prove he has entered a house by two different windows simultaneously. This would cause difficulty at a court trial, and indeed the dual character of light has caused much difficulty among physicists. Actually, however, the quantum theory suggests to some scientists that all matter might, like photons, have the properties of both particles and waves. The French physicist Louis de Broglie, for example, postulated in 1924 a wave theory of matter.

Einstein attempted to develop a unified field theory. The electric field and the magnetic field had by then already been synthesized as the electromagnetic field. To this Einstein added the gravitational field and attempted to explain the cosmos in terms of one great unified field. His theory is not necessarily perfect, but it seems to me to be headed in the direction of Buddhist cosmology. Einstein's idea, stated simply, is that great concentrations of energy are perceived by us to be matter and small concentrations to be fields.

If Einstein is correct, the traditional absolute dichotomy between matter and field is wiped out, and we arrive at the conclusion that they represent two manifestations of the same thing. If such is the case, space itself could be said to be neither existent nor non-existent and its properties such that it has infinite capacity to produce matter.

In the largest sense, then, the essence of the cosmos itself can be regarded as being in the state of *kū*. As for the elementary particles of matter, they were discovered only a few decades ago, but since then microscientists have found several hundred different types, and a search is now going on for the really ultimate particle. Indeed, some scientists are beginning to suspect that the ultimate might not even be a particle. The physicist and Nobel laureate (1949) Dr. Hideki Yukawa postulated a new elementary domain theory. Put simply, his idea is that it is not possible to conceive of the ultimate in terms of points or physical bodies. We must instead conceive of a domain, which he often speaks of as a "circle."

And so we find the ultimate form of matter and physical being drawing closer and closer to the concept of *kū*. Similarly, among the most advanced depth psychologists, the innermost core of the human mind is also being described in terms suggesting *kū*. It would appear that in the most fundamental considerations of matter and mind, it is impossible to avoid such a concept. However that may be, the idea of *kū*—that is, the idea of breaking through the traditional distinction between existence and non-existence—can no longer be described as "vague." Or if *kū* as a concept is vague, then that vague state of chaos in which there is yet order and harmony is itself the true nature of the cosmos, and scientists are beginning to recognize it as such.

THE CONSTANT AND IMMUTABLE SELF

We have discussed the temporary and constantly changing physical aspect of life and the concept of *kū*, which transcends the dualistic distinction between existence and non-existence. But even these two aspects of life together are insufficient to give us a complete view of the true nature of things. To arrive at the ultimate truth, we must take up *chū*, the *mean* or the *middle way*, for this is the essential entity of life. As a word of caution, let me say that the term *middle way*, or *chūdō* in Japanese, is very frequently misinterpreted. Sometimes it is considered to be even vaguer than *kū*, and superficial students occasionally confuse it with the Confucian idea of the ethical middle way (*chūyō*).

In one of his writings, Nichiren Daishonin says: "The third [of the Ten Factors], entity, is this body of mine. This is also called the Buddha of the Law (*hosshin nyorai*), or the middle way, or the nature of the Law, or nirvana."

In this passage, "this body of mine" does not mean the physical body; it refers to the essential entity of life, which supports the physical aspect and the spiritual aspect, *ke* and *kū*, and contains them both. The fundamental properties of our lives are, in the physical world, our tangible form and figure; in the world of *kū*, our wisdom, feelings, and individual character. But these two worlds do not represent the whole of life, for there is an essential source sustaining them both. This is what we call the middle way, or *chū*. While our physical bodies and our spirits are in a state of constant change, there runs through them this immutable and essential entity of life.

Let us take a particular human being, Mr. A. Mr. A's body, composed of tens of billions of cells, undergoes continual transformation in the process of metabolism. In the world of *kū*, his mind and feelings change with varying conditions and at times are aroused from their dormant state and bring about physical manifestations. Since Mr. A's spirit may grow and become richer, it can be said that *kū* also is constantly in movement. Because of this continual change, Mr. A at forty is quite different, both mentally and physically, from what he was at twenty. Despite this, he is still Mr. A; some consistency, some continuum, preserves his individual being. Furthermore, this continuum is deeper than the physical or emotional resemblance of Mr. A at forty to Mr. A at twenty. There is an unchanging reality, and it makes Mr. A Mr. A and keeps him from becoming Mr. B.

In Occidental terminology, this would be called the self or the ego. Since it is at the core of life, one might even use the expression *essential self*. It seems to me that among the Western philosophers, the existentialists have perhaps come closest to the Buddhist concept of the middle way in their search for the roots, the fundamental essence, of the self as it exists in this world, though in the final analysis, their view is partial and superficial. Kierkegaard's "man, the individual," Nietzsche's "superman," and the "coming-back-upon-ourselves" of Jaspers or Heidegger are all similar in some respects to the essential entity Buddhism calls *chū*.

The general trend in existentialist philosophy, I think, is toward the idea that we ourselves must seek out the path we are going to follow. There are those who recognize a god of the Christian type and those who do not, but one sees a general striving for self-conversion for the sake of leading a better life or of overcoming death or uncertainty or despair.

Although Kierkegaard arrives in the end at a god very like the Christian god, we see in Kierkegaard a man who is struggling alone against uncertainty and disappointment. The self in this kind of life is a solitary self. Nietzsche, for his part, denied God outright, but in his place apotheosized man. The ideas of Jaspers and Heidegger are different one from the other, but both men thought that the essential man, or the essential self, lives in defiance of death and doubt.

These thinkers all maintained that one must not be deceived by the vicissitudes of life to the extent of forgetting one's original self. In sum, in the existentialist philosophies, one recognizes an effort to look directly into the essential self and thereby to deepen one's understanding of it.

Without doubt, by looking deep within ourselves, we can discover the origins of our actions and the direction in which they are leading us. The materialists take the temporal world as their substructure and regard it as fundamental. The idealists, on the other hand, regard the mind to be a more basic feature of the universe than matter. And yet one wonders whether either materialism or idealism is as powerful as the idea of self as a motivating force for action. There are many youths in Japan today who, while accepting the materialistic principles of *Das Kapital* in their economic thinking, take Existentialism as the driving force for their conduct and action.

There is a distinction between the self we have been talking about and the self as it is conceived of by modern psychologists. In psychology, the self, or ego, is inextricably linked with the mind and consciousness and is a part of a human being's mental or spiritual makeup. Freud analyzed the human psyche into three elements, the id, the ego, and the superego, with the ego including not only the conscious mind, but the unconscious stratum as well. The Buddhist concept of self expressed in "this body of mine" in the passage above not only encompasses the self of the existentialists and the ego of the psychologists, but goes beyond these to include the fundamental and total entity of life. The existentialists and the Freudians consider self as the ego in an individual sense. They are talking about one individual life as distinguished from all other individual lives. But in the Buddhist concept of self in terms of the middle way, or *chū*, a self is one with the cosmos. It is the core of life and remains immutable even if all external conditions and circumstances are eliminated.

Pres. Toda explained self or ego by reference to dreams. When we are dreaming, something inside us experiences happiness, sadness, or some other emotion. Pres. Toda thought that this "something" offered a hint as to the true nature of self. Often when we are dreaming we are somehow conscious that what we are seeing is a dream, which means that some part of our consciousness is telling us that what is going on could not happen in ordinary daily life. I think Pres. Toda meant for us to gain a better insight into the ultimate reality of our deeper selves by watching ourselves in action during the course of dreaming.

We have been discussing so far the three aspects of life, *ke*, *kū*, and *chū*. These three terms, which lie at the core of Buddhist philosophy, are often referred to as the Three Perceptions, *santai*. It is extremely important, however, to understand what we are talking about, namely, one reality viewed from three different standpoints, not three separate entities. The middle way sustains the tangible and the intangible, *ke* and *kū*, but that is not the whole story of the nature of life. The middle way appears in the tangible, and it exists in the *kū*. The three work together to produce a single life. The complete interexistence and interfusion of the Three Perceptions into one is the ultimate principle of the Lotus Sutra.

In relation to the life of the Buddha, the Three Perceptions become the Three Bodies (*sanjin*). On the temporal, phenomenal level, there is the Manifest Body of the Buddha. On the level of *kū* is the Body of Reward. On the level of the middle way, there is the Body of the Law.

It is possible to understand all of the entities of life in terms of the Unified Three Perceptions (*en'yū santai*). By taking a proper total view of life—not only that which does not change, but that which changes and that which is dormant—we can develop our lives and bring about our own human revolution. The wisdom of Buddhism is profound, and among its most profound points is the idea that all things must be viewed from several different standpoints. In attempting to understand such fundamentals as life and the cosmos, one must not be strapped down to a single viewpoint or framework. Instead, it is essential that one be flexible and examine things in a variety of ways or contexts. Otherwise, one can only arrive at half-truths or untruths.

THE RIDDLE OF TIME

PHYSICAL TIME

The flow of time is curious. There are times when one feels one year has lasted for ten. At other times one year seems to have passed in an instant. Whatever the clock or the calendar says, this is the way people's minds and feelings respond to time. Voltaire said, "Of all the things in the universe, time is both the longest and the shortest, the quickest and the slowest; it can be divided into the most infinitesimal parts or stretched out into eternity."

This strikes at the essence of the phenomenon. Insofar as our senses are concerned, time is relative. Spent happily, it goes quickly; spent in sadness or pain, it goes slowly. I think it is important to try to understand what makes time seem so different in different circumstances.

Aristotle said time is "the criterion for measuring the movement of all things in the universe." If a train is moving along a track, its location is different at one point from what it is a second later. We can measure its motion in units of time and give its speed in terms of so many meters per second or so many kilometers per hour.

Kant believed our sense of space and time is an innate part of human consciousness. I think he was right: this sense or ability on the part of human beings leads us to feel the passage of time and to devise means of measuring it. What we do, in fact, is select a body moving in a regular fashion, such as a heavenly body or a pendulum, and use the movements to measure off segments of time. Without measuring time, it would be difficult to carry on our daily lives. In trying to understand the ultimate reality of time, however, we must take into consideration not only measurable time, but our sense of subjective time.

We are inclined to regard time and space as separate entities existing independently of each other, but everything we think of as existing is moving or changing with the passage of time. Time and space together form the framework for all movement and change, whether it is the movements of the cosmos, the transformations of matter, or the flow of human life. We must therefore conceive of time and space as being fused into one. Though we can conceive theoretically of time without space, or space without time, the concepts are of no value in the physical world.

One reason for the importance of physical time in our lives is that it accords with the movements of the universe, and much of our daily living is governed by the rhythm of these movements. The changing of the seasons affects our lives considerably, as does the passing of days, months, and years. And yet, while we live in and are a part of physical time, each human being has a distinct sense of time—perhaps we could call it a time-rhythm—of his own.

One might draw an analogy to the fish in the sea. They live in salt water and their body fluids contain saline compounds, but these fluids are by no means identical with salt water. The salt that fish absorb from their surroundings is recomposed within their bodies into a variety of life-supporting fluids. Similarly, people live in a framework of physical time, and to a large extent they accommodate themselves to it, whether consciously or unconsciously, but within their minds, time changes do not necessarily correspond to changes in physical time.

SUBJECTIVE TIME

Scientists call the flow of human life in response to the rhythm of nature human biorhythm. This is a sort of built-in clock, and it governs the periodic movements within our bodies. There are, of course, all sorts of rhythmical or cyclical movements in life, ranging from the beating of the heart to the cycle of birth and death. Some of these are directly related to the movements of the universe, some are not. An example of biorhythm is the cycle of sleep, which in most people is adjusted to the twenty-four-hour day.

Babies, we might note, are not attuned to the twenty-four-hour cycle. After they are fed, day or night, they go to sleep. A newborn baby usually goes through the cycle of sleeping and waking about seven times a day. After the baby is about four months old, his ears can hear, and his eyes sense light and darkness, with the result that he begins to acquire the adult pattern, but this is not firmly established until after the child has reached the age of ten or so. Excepting adults who work and sleep unusual hours, the pattern of human life, generally speaking, is to arise when the sun shines and sleep when it is dark.

According to a report written in 1960 by Dr. Theodor Hellbrügge of the University of Munich, the rhythm of a newborn baby's heart, which is to say the periodic changes in his heartbeat, is not identical with its mother's. As is normal for adults, the mother's pulse is faster in the daytime than at night, but a baby's pulse remains very much the same throughout the twenty-four-hour day. When the baby is about three months old, its heartbeats also begin to distinguish between hours of light and hours of darkness.

In adults, body temperature, kidney function, and the secretion of hormones show an increase in the daytime and a decrease at night, a variation which does not appear in children until between the ages of one and five.

Biorhythm also includes changes having an annual cycle instead of, or in addition to, a daily cycle. Changes in pulse, body temperature, blood pressure, and hormone secretion, for example, follow a daily cycle, but they also follow an annual cycle. Normally, an individual's pulse is highest in the summer and lowest in the winter, as is also the case with body temperature. There is even a rhythm in the growth rate of hair; one study reported that a man's beard grew only 0.305 millimeters on a day in January, as opposed to 0.538 millimeters on a day in August. We might note, however, that these annual changes are also absent in babies.

Simply stated, the flow of life in the human body adjusts itself to the rhythm of nature. It is as though human life were immersed in a great natural movement, vibrating in tune with the changing universe.

But some changes in our bodies cannot be explained by reference to nature alone. We can find no connection between the movement of celestial bodies and the process of growing old, except insofar as the longer the celestial bodies continue to move, the older we grow. Human aging, however, is only relative, for some people are old at fifty and others are young at eighty.

Here we are dealing with an irreversible process, rather than a cyclical one. Unfortunately, hair that has turned gray in the summertime does not return to its original color in the winter. In the process of aging, however, over the years a human being's biorhythm does undergo changes. Blood pressure, while varying to some extent from day to night and from season to season, tends gradually to increase as a person grows older, whereas pulse rate and respiration are higher in children than in adults. A child's body temperature also tends to be higher than an adult's. These phenomena suggest that though the human body may be attuned to the rhythm of the external world, each individual human being undergoes changes peculiar to himself.

There is, in other words, a flow of life in the human body that is unrelated to the rhythm of the exterior world. Each person's own life-rhythm brings together the energies of all the functioning parts of the body and unifies them into a single personality. This might, I think, be described as the *somatic rhythm* of an individual life. The somatic rhythm changes as a person lives out his time, and the rate of change varies with the individual, but I believe it is safe to say that the rhythm is fastest when a person is young, and that it slows down as he grows older.

Some scientists attempt to measure somatic rhythm in terms of what they call *physiological time*. This is based on the bodily changes undergone by human beings from the time of their conception until the time of their death. While the human body is always changing, the rate of change is far more rapid in the young than in the old. There are measurable differences in the composition of the body fluids between youth and old age, and the healing of wounds is slower in old people than in young people. One physiological year in childhood can be equivalent to ten years in old age in terms of the rate of bodily changes.

Of course, there is more to human life than this, for we embody the principle that the body and the mind are one, and we consequently have what could be called *psychological time* as well as physiological time. For a person who leads a full spiritual life, a year has greater substance than it does for a person who is spiritually empty. Physiological time and psychological time together make up what we have spoken of as subjective time, but it is important to take notice of human perception. In this respect, psychological time is by far the more important.

Goethe wrote in his diary, "I think I must be more careful to distinguish between good days and bad days as they occur within myself. Emotions, love, desire, courtesy, creativity, activeness, truthfulness, joy, stamina, fatigue, stubbornness, and agreeability all seem to come and go on a schedule of their own."

This is a very observant statement. Regardless of what goes on around us, there are days when we feel full of energy and life; on other days we are just not with it. Everybody experiences a slump from time to time, whether there is any obvious reason or not. We go along feeling down for a few days, and then inexplicably the clouds seem to roll away, and everything is all right again. The frequency with which this occurs varies greatly with the individual, but certainly there is a recognizable rhythm in all individuals.

One group of scientists explains this phenomenon in terms of what they call the *PSI rhythm*, P standing for physical condition, S for sensitivity, and I for the intellectual condition. The idea is that these three elements undergo cyclical changes. Physical energy peaks every twenty-three days, while sensitivity to external influences peaks every twenty-eight days, and intellectual power, as indicated by the strength of memory, peaks every thirty-three days. This theory is not widely accepted, and it is indeed questionable whether a human being's physical and spiritual rhythms can be measured in terms of a definite number of days and weeks. But this is not to deny some kind of rhythmical movement in the working of the mind and spirit, as well as in that of the body.

Just as there are peaks in our somatic rhythm when the physical movements within our bodies are most rapid, there are peaks in our spiritual and psychological rhythm in which we understand things more clearly and feel them more deeply. It is important to remember that our life-rhythm is affected by our experience and our environment. We can be feeling splendid one minute, but be plunged into deep grief the next by the arrival of some piece of dreadful news. Conversely, a pleasant experience can stimulate and speed up the life-rhythm. The experiences we absorb into our inner selves reemerge in the form of our life-rhythm. The speed of our life-rhythm, therefore, depends to a great degree on what sort of experiences we receive and absorb into ourselves. There are experiences that add substance to our lives, and others that sap our vital energy.

Some psychologists speak of substantial time and empty time. In general, substantial time is time spent in absorbing activities, time when our minds are occupied with something interesting, time when we are taking an active and creative role in what is going on around us. By the same token, empty time is time spent in boredom, in inactivity, in grief, or in pain. Substantial time gives us a sense of fulfillment. Empty time does not.

In a sense, we could say substantial time passes quickly, empty time slowly, but I think this would be oversimplifying. This is a key point in my concept of time, and I would like to go into it a little further.

We sometimes say, "I was so interested in what I was doing that I forgot all about the time." In situations like this, what has happened is that a great deal of life activity has been compressed into a comparatively short period of time. The clock may indicate the passage of only an hour, but during this interval, one may in terms of life-rhythm have lived ten hours. On the other hand, if one has put very little activity into the same physical hour, that hour will seem long. What we sense is the flow of our life-energy. When it is flowing rapidly, physical time seems short, but when it is flowing slowly, physical time seems long. But even when we are faced with grief, if we try to do something about it, time passes much more rapidly than if we sit back and allow it to overwhelm us. In short, whether our life-flow is active or passive is a governing factor in our psychological grasp of time.

From the psychiatric viewpoint, to a person incapacitated by shock, grief, or uncertainty, an hour can seem like years. One doctor noted that a patient suffering from severe depression was genuinely convinced that the doctor had kept him waiting for six months, when in fact it had been only five minutes. Another patient seriously told the doctor his sick mother had to live 2,000 years in anguish and torture.

Drugs can have a similar effect on people. One person taking mescaline reported, "The second hand on my watch seemed hardly to move at all. I felt one night was an eternity never before experienced by anyone." Isn't this precisely what we call Hell—a state in which we have lost our inner life-force, and our flow of life has stopped? How sad that so many young people today are entrapped in this Hell, whereas if their life-flow were active and healthy, they could look forward to being young in spirit and in mind even at an advanced age!

ETERNITY IN AN INSTANT

At this point I would like to turn to another basic question, the relationship between past, present, and future.

Since ancient times philosophers have likened the passage of time to the flow of a river. Heraclitus, who is known for holding that all things are in constant flux, is one example of a Western thinker. In the Orient, the Buddhist word for transmigration, which in Sanskrit is *samsara*, is thought to have originally meant the flowing of water. By analogy with water, people speak of the flow of time, though it should be noted that in Heraclitus's theory, as well as in the Buddhist theory of transmigration, what was referred to as "flowing" was "all things in the universe" rather than time. Still, the framework of the flow of things is formed by time and space, and it can be said that these ideas presuppose a flow of time.

From observing change, we arrive at the concept of past, present, and future. If we adopt the metaphor of the river, the future is constantly flowing into the present, and the present instantly becomes the past. The past stretches out downstream and the future comes from upstream. The present is only momentary. Some might be tempted to liken it to a geometric point, which is to say a position that occupies no space and has no mass. I do not think the analogy is valid, because a geometric point has no substance whatever, whereas the instant of present time is brimming with substance. Indeed, when you consider it, this instant in our lives contains all the memories of the past, including both the spiritual and the purely physical memories. Furthermore, this instant includes all the hopes, expectations, desires, and potentialities of the future. Indeed, at any given instant, our bodies contain all the physiological information that we will use in the future.

The Japanese philosopher Seiichi Hatano has written a book called *Time and Eternity* (1943), in which he says, "The present is by no means equivalent to a simple point. It has a finite duration and a fixed internal structure." This may not be the whole truth, but it is a step in the right direction, because a single moment does have an internal structure. I do not mean, of course, that this is a spatial structure.

Psychologists say all our experiences, no matter how small or insignificant, are contained somewhere in our memory apparatus. Our physical experiences are engraved upon our cells and organs. Spiritual experiences, and in this I include all memories of feelings both conscious and unconscious, are stored in the brain. Cerebral physiologists identify the areas of the cerebrum involved as the temporal lobe and the hippocampi of the old cortex. Our vocabularies, our knowledge, and our thinking experiences are in the temporal lobe; emotional experiences, such as joy, fear, and sorrow, are retained in the hippocampi. These repositories of memory absorb all impulses coming to them, just as a blotter absorbs ink.

We often hear that when a man is just about to die, his past experiences pass before him instantaneously in kaleidoscopic fashion. This may very well be true; it may be that when a person faces immediate death, the doors of the repositories of memory suddenly open, and everything comes to the conscious level at once.

Earlier I mentioned the presence in human beings of an inner memory core in which the whole experience of mankind, lasting over a period of a million years, is retained. I suspect this memory goes even farther back to the experience of the mammals from which man descended, or possibly even to the amoebic stage. Our hunger instinct, conceivably, might have originated with amoebae, because even an amoeba displays hunger of a sort. If a nourishing substance comes within range, the amoeba senses it and approaches to eat it. In effect, our momentary present may very well contain, in the form of memory, the entire history of the earth. The more we consider a moment in our present, the richer it becomes in terms of heritage from the past.

The present is connected not only with the past but with the future. As mentioned in our discussion of *kū*, our bodies contain something like 5 billion DNA molecules carrying the information we need in order to live. We use only a relatively small amount of this information during our lives, and it may consequently be said that we contain a large quantity of information that, unexpressed, remains in a state of potentiality. From a positivistic viewpoint, this suggests we have at this very moment untold potentialities for the future.

The momentary present is always creating and developing paths into the future, so it is unwise to underestimate the potential inherent in any given moment. I am reminded of what has been called "the miracle of Louis Pasteur." Everyone knows about Pasteur's great accomplishments and contributions to mankind, but surprisingly few people know that the more important part of his work was accomplished after he was partially paralyzed by a stroke at the age of forty-six. At the time, the French government, considering his condition hopeless, halted construction of a research institute designed for his use. This news caused Pasteur's illness to become worse, but a friend of his persuaded the government to resume construction, and Pasteur's health began to improve. He carried on his brilliant work for another twenty-seven years, achieving results that might not have been realized for several more decades had he allowed his illness to cause him to lose hope. His ability to see beyond the present to the future made possible what seemed a medical impossibility.

Our hopes, desires, and ambitions are powerful forces existing within us for the manipulation of the future. They are the generating forces that create the future. To lose hope or give up one's goals because of the evils of the moment is to reduce one's own life potential.

Dr. Viktor E. Frankl, professor of neurology at the University of Vienna, was among the many Jews who were thrown by the Nazis into the concentration camp at Auschwitz. Afterward, Dr. Frankl wrote a book in which he made the following statement: "Any man who was unable to believe in his own future was destined to be destroyed in this camp. Lacking a future, he had nothing to hold onto, and he collapsed inside, sinking lower and lower both physically and spiritually."

Doubtless Dr. Frankl's confidence in the future was what enabled him to survive, for hopes, dreams, faith, and a sense of mission are forces enabling us to open up our future. They are our inner support and the manifestation of our powerful life-flow.

Our life-flow at this very instant contains all of the experience of the past and all of the infinite potentialities of the future. The life of this present moment is a force that summons up the remembrance of all things past and sets forth hopefully into the future. The life of the past is concentrated in this moment, which is itself the foundation for the future. For this reason, it cannot be argued that the momentary present exists apart from the past or the future. Nor is there any past or future not concentrated in the momentary present.

In the *Orally Transferred Teachings* (*Ongi Kuden*) of Nichiren Daishonin, there is a passage on the Japanese word *irai*, which usually means either "from now on" or "from then on." The passage says, "*I*, literally 'already,' means the past, and *rai*, literally 'to come,' means the future. *Irai* includes the present moment." The meaning clearly is that the present moment encompasses both the past and the future and is the necessary continuative link between them.

The more we probe into our inner lives, the more we see the past and the future inherent in the present. As we look from the surface to some point deeper within ourselves, we see the stream of life broaden, become more abundant, and swell into a great tide. The ultimate source of this stream embraces the lives of all mankind, the formation of the earth, and the endless pulsations of the universe. It is the source of universal life. As the stream of life flows from this source, it divides itself into our individual lives. The Mystic Law is identical with the source of all life-flow.

The Mystic Law contains all life from the infinite past and all life of the eternal future. Within the Mystic Law, the phenomenal classifications of past, present, and future do not exist. The past and the future are fused with the momentary present into one great unity. Eternity is a succession of momentary presents; the Mystic Law is at once momentary and eternal.

Nichiren Daishonin wrote, "Although we speak of the past, the future, and the present as three, they are actually indivisible, because they belong to the ultimate essence of every life-moment." Here we must interpret the "ultimate essence of every life-moment" as being the Mystic Law itself.

According to Bergson's theory of time, the division into past, present, and future is the product of human consciousness. I think this idea is close to Buddhism. Bergson considered the true nature of consciousness to be in flux, and he spoke of "flowing time." Time perceived from the physical, objective viewpoint is time past. In contrast, "flowing time" is the flow of consciousness or of life itself. In essence, there is no distinction between past, present, and future, since they are created by the flow of consciousness. What is inseparable becomes separated in our minds.

Accordingly, the universe, including nature, is a cosmic life entity created by a cosmic life-flow. If our individual life-flow is strong, we respond actively to nature, in the sense that we possess a life-force completely in harmony with the workings of nature.

Presumably animals and lesser living beings have their own time, just as human beings do, but no other being has as rich a life-flow. Only humans can transcend the state of harmony with the rhythm of nature and go on to create new and diverse currents in the realm of the mind and spirit.

Unfortunately, it appears that in our everyday lives, people do not usually give adequate expression to the life-flow with which they are blessed. They are prone to weaken and by their own conduct hold back the flow. While possessing the potentiality to feel and enjoy a strong, rapid flow of subjective time, we all too often deny ourselves this privilege.

It is most important in our daily lives to draw on the life-force of the Mystic Law in order to strengthen our own lives and fulfill each moment of the present. If we used the infinite treasure encompassed in one moment of life, our lives would be incomparably richer. In order to do this, we must open up and draw on our repositories of memory.

I am convinced that the key to these repositories is the practice of

Buddhism. Through faith and through actual conduct, men can bring to life the infinite past stored within any given moment of the present. As we have already seen, this past transcends our personal experience. It goes back to the beginning of all things.

It must not be forgotten that even if the infinite treasure is called forth, it is the individual who must use it to build for himself a full and creative life. The raison d'être for all humans lies in crystallizing and utilizing the past for the sake of the future. The future, I believe, contains infinite possibilities, but I cannot help feeling people are always trying to reduce the range and scale of these possibilities. We must not forget that a hopeless, resigned, pessimistic view of the future can produce a bleak future, whereas hope, determination, and optimism can, with the aid of the infinite treasure that is the past, open up a future of unlimited brightness. We must also keep in mind that the future opened up by the past and present becomes the present for a moment and then is past, but by flowing into the past, this future is not lost. On the contrary, it is now a part of the past and together with a new present moment will work once again to create a new future.

People with determination and hope use the past and the future to fulfill the momentary present, thus speeding the flow of life within them. To put it another way, a rich past and a rich present guarantee a rich future; a rich present and a rich future guarantee a rich past. It goes forever in a circle, and the starting point on the circle is the single moment of life called the present. If we live each present moment meaningfully, the infinite past and the infinite future will enrich our lives with a constant flow of the cosmic life-force. One moment in our lives will become a manifestation of the Mystic Law, which includes all time, and in that sense this one moment in itself becomes eternity, our life-flow fusing indelibly into the life-flow of the cosmos.

But the necessary factor is determination, a determination compounded of hope and optimism, a determination as large as the cosmos and as long as time itself, a determination to follow the fundamental workings and principles of the universe. In a concrete sense, we must have the will to achieve eternal peace and prosperity for mankind and for all things. We must be resolved to eliminate suffering and sorrow. We must be conscious of the mission to live and let others live as genuine, complete human beings.

Our lives are rooted in the past, but we must not live in the past. Nor should we allow our enthusiasm for the future to make us lose sight of the present. We must set ourselves a lofty goal for the future and live each moment in such a way as to achieve its full potential.

THE ESSENCE OF THE COSMOS

CONCEPTS OF THE UNIVERSE

Let us turn now from the discussion of time to a consideration of space, which is a little easier to visualize, because it is always around us and does not involve such difficult concepts as past, present, and future. Space is related to things we can see and touch, and for this reason people began to examine it in comparatively early times, as can be seen from the development of geometry among the ancients.

The universe, as the totality of space, was conceived of at an early stage, and each of the various civilizations of the world developed theories concerning its form and substance, which became a part of their philosophies and ways of life. Even in ages long before men learned to fly, they developed the science of astronomy to discover more about the unknown. Today, thanks to our huge telescopes and rockets and moon and interplanetary probes, we have little by little unveiled many secrets of the universe—and encountered more undreamed-of mysteries.

The greatest turning point in the history of cosmology in the West was the development of the heliocentric theory, as proposed by Copernicus and confirmed by Galileo. The idea that the earth was not the center of the universe had revolutionary repercussions in philosophy and theology, as well as in astronomy and physics. Copernicus's discovery has been matched only in modern times by the postulation of an expanding universe.

Even Einstein accepted for a time the idea of a static cosmos, but he was forced to change his views by Edwin Powell Hubble's (1889–1953) demonstration of what is called the red shift. Hubble's discovery, briefly stated, was that as the distance of a nebula from the earth increases, the light spectrum of the nebula becomes redder. To explain this he hypothesized that the nebulae were moving away from the earth at a speed such that the Doppler effect would cause a lengthening of the light waves emitted from them, thus making their spectrums redder. Hubble theorized that the speed with which nebulae are moving can be calculated by measuring the extent of the shift toward red.

The Doppler effect, as originally posited, explains why the sound of approaching objects is higher and of retreating objects lower than it is when the source of sound is stationary. There seems to be no reason why the same principle would not apply to light waves as well, and indeed without reference to the Doppler effect, it is difficult to explain why the spectrums of nebulae would grow redder in proportion to their distance from the earth.

The important point is that the galaxies, so long thought to be hanging staidly and quietly in the sky, are actually becoming more and more distant from each other at a tremendous rate of speed, and the logical inference is that the universe is expanding. This idea gave birth to the two most widely accepted cosmological theories of our time. According to one, if we reason backward to the beginning of this expansion, we arrive at the idea that at one time the entire universe was concentrated into a very tiny ball, which contained all matter and energy in existence. For some reason, this ball exploded, and there began an expansion which continues today. According to the other theory, the steady state theory, the demonstrable expansion of the universe is counteracted by the continual creation of new matter in the form of hydrogen atoms.

According to the explosionists, the universe exploded approximately 20 billion years ago, and all the basic elements of the universe took form within the first thirty minutes or so. When it comes to such questions as what existed earlier than 20 billion years ago, and what caused the explosion, the proponents of this theory are unable to answer, but the somewhat later oscillation theory furnishes an answer of sorts. The oscillationists believe the speed of expansion will gradually lessen, and eventually at the outer edges of the universe, a contraction will begin. This will continue until the universe, once again concentrated into a tiny ball, explodes and the whole process repeats itself. The main difficulty with this idea of a rhythmic expansion and contraction is that at present we have no evidence that a contraction has begun.

The steady state theory, for its part, has not found acceptance because the idea of the endless creation of new matter is contrary to all our traditional ideas of physics. And yet I find this theory interesting. The basic idea is of a continuous creation of new matter, which spreads out in waves so that the universe expands, without changing its fundamental consistency. There is no beginning and no end. This is an idea which coincides nicely with Buddhist philosophy.

When you get down to it, of course, neither the evolution theory nor the solid state theory can be proved. For a time, it was held that empirical observations made the steady state theory untenable, but today this has become doubtful. Doubts have also been cast on the calculations involved in the evolution theory.

The most distant stars we know are 20 billion light years away; our observations of them are as they were 20 billion years ago. Perhaps there are stars even more distant, receding at speeds approaching that of light. It may, indeed certainly will, prove impossible ever to study these. All we can say now of the physical universe is that so far as we know, it has a diameter of some 20 billion light years and is about 20 billion years old. These are immense figures, but they are at least finite, and they constitute the physical limits of the cosmology of our time. Beyond these limits, we can rely only on imagination. It could even be, as I have said before, that our cosmos is only one part of a much larger supercosmos, or perhaps there is a companion cosmos composed entirely of antimatter. In fact, we know only the limits of what we know, not the limits of what may exist. One is reminded again of the Buddhist idea that the cosmos is limitless.

When the Buddhist philosophers of the past spoke of the dimensions of the universe, instead of using the word "infinite," they often strung out numbers as large as those used by modern astronomers. And so we now have the well-known concept of the "Three Thousand Major World Systems." A full explanation would carry us too far afield, but briefly the idea is that each single world consists of a sun, a moon, an earth, and six planets. A thousand (or some say ten thousand) of these worlds make up one "Minor World System." A thousand "Minor World Systems" make up one "Intermediate World System," and a thousand "Intermediate World Systems" make up one "Major World System," or "Three Thousand Major World Systems." In the Juryo chapter of the Lotus Sutra, mention is made of $5 \times 10^2 \times 10^3 \times 10^4 \times 10^5 \times 10^{12} \times 10^{52}$ Three Thousand Major World Systems.

Fantastic numbers aside, the general idea fits rather well into present-day astronomical theory. One world corresponds to a single star, such as the sun, and its satellites, while a Minor World System corresponds to the galaxy, an Intermediate World System to a galactic nebula, and a Major World System to the whole of the cosmos. Even more important is the implicit assumption that the universe is not chaotic, but ordered. One world is a unit in a larger entity, which itself is a unit in a still larger entity, and so on. This accords in a general way with what today's scientists tell us about the composition of the universe. That there was little or no scientific background for the Buddhist concept does not detract from the fact that it is an exceptional display of intuition.

Interesting, too, is the contrast to the strong geocentricism of most Occidental philosophy, for Buddhism has always regarded the earth as only one of many worlds. One example is the concept of the "Buddha-lands of the Ten Directions," which means simply a very large number of Buddha-lands. The implication is not only of the existence of many other worlds like our own, inhabited by sentient beings of some sort, but also that they are spread out over three-dimensional space, for the "Ten Directions" are the eight points of an ordinary compass (north, northeast, east, etc.) plus up and down. A passage in the Sutra of the Benevolent King (*Ninnō-kyō*) says, "Know thou, O King, that I am manifest in 10 billion worlds with 10 billion suns and moons, and in each world there is a Mt. Sumeru and around it are four continents."

It should also be kept in mind that all these worlds and Buddha-lands are thought of as constantly going through the stages of birth, maturation, destruction, and latency. In the overall concept, an infinite universe consisted of infinite ordered parts, all in a state of rhythmic change. It is almost as though the early Buddhist philosophers had anticipated the science of our times.

It does not require much imagination to conceive of the stars as eternal lights in an otherwise empty sky, but it is remarkable that in a prescientific age the Buddhist philosophers conceived of them as being born, maturing, beclining, and then passing into a state of emptiness. Emptiness, it should be noted, is *kū*, and what is meant is not utter obliteration, but extinction from the phenomenal viewpoint. The whole process, including *kū*, is a manifestation of the cosmic Law.

To come closer to home, scientists today agree that the earth is in the mature stage and is relatively stable. They also agree that the sun will eventually explode in a dying gasp and carry the earth away with it. Similar phenomena will occur even on the galactic level. It seems to me extremely significant that Buddhism considers such cataclysmic changes to be inherent in the cosmic Law.

What most clearly distinguishes Buddhism from other religions, especially the Judaic-Christian religions, is that Buddhism sees the cosmos itself as being the Law. A Buddha is someone who has recognized his identity with this cosmic Law. This is much different from postulating an absolute deity who creates and dominates the Law, and the differences between the two types of religion are evident in their cosmological theories.

I might mention here, in connection with what was said about the destruction of the earth, a passage in one of Nichiren Daishonin's writings where he speaks of the "world" as "the eternal pure land, impervious to the three calamities and the four stages of change." This seems inconsistent with the idea of a life cycle for the earth, but the passage in question does not refer to the planet earth. It is speaking of the Mystic Law inherent in the earth's existence. The earth itself may undergo physical catastrophe and destruction, but the Mystic Law continues to operate throughout the universe.

With respect to other worlds in our universe inhabited by intelligent beings, many people have wondered how these intelligent beings might resemble or differ from ourselves. Most people who believe such worlds exist think that the creatures on them might well have developed natural sciences and mathematics in the same way as earthlings have, but that their politics, economics, art, and social systems would be entirely different. I wonder myself, however, if we would not find that beings on other planets had also developed or were developing a philosophy like Buddhism that gives the highest priority to life itself.

I have no doubt but that Buddhism is a completely universal philosophy and would be applicable in other worlds as well as in our own. Indeed, it is my firm belief that Buddhism *must* be completely universal, and that eventually all beings everywhere will discover it. From the practical viewpoint what we ourselves are concerned with at this point is how to create here on this planet the completely peaceful society advocated by Buddhist philosophy and religion.

SUBJECTIVE SPACE

Writers rather often refer to Pascal's concept of a man as a "thinking reed," but comparatively few people seem to know the context in which this idea was put forward. It occurs in sections 347 and 348 of the *Pensées*, as follows:

> 347. Man is but a reed, the feeblest creation of nature, but he is a thinking reed. The universe has no need to arm itself to crush him: a vapor, or even a drop of water, is sufficient to destroy him. But even if the universe were to annihilate him, man would still be greater than his adversary, because he knows he is dying and realizes the advantage which the universe holds over him. Yet of this, the universe knows nothing. . . .
>
> 348. *Thinking reed.* It is not in space that I must search for my dignity as a human being, but in the ordering of my thought. Though I may possess property, it is as naught. Through space the universe seizes me and engulfs me like a mote; through thought I seize the universe.

Though emphasizing man's insignificance in comparison with the universe, Pascal asserts that by means of thought, man can grasp and absorb the universe. The idea is both well stated and profound.

We customarily think of the space occupied by the human body as being just the space contained within our skin, but the well-known American anthropologist Edward T. Hall has pointed out that the spatial boundaries of the self extend beyond the body itself, because we all require a certain amount of space in which to live. The point is well taken. One cannot talk with someone unless there is a certain amount of intervening space, nor can certain of the senses function properly unless there is open space around them. So even in the physiological sense, the space required by the body is larger than the body itself.

Hall speaks of *visual space* and *auditory space*. Since, in general, our eyes are our most sensitive sense organ, we tend to rely on visual space for our bearings. Dogs, on the other hand, rely largely on their olfactory sense. For animals as well as humans, the size of the space sensed differs with the particular sense organ. In human beings, visual space is the largest, and auditory space the next largest. The space limits within which we can sense things with our noses or skin are much smaller.

We must also consider space required in connection with our activities or our consciousness of what we are doing—space such as the house, the office, the schoolroom, and so on. Perhaps we should class this separately as *life-space*, because although related to our sensory space, it has a separate identity of its own.

The more we think along these lines, the more evident it becomes that the space occupied by our lives is much larger than the space occupied by our bodies, and that living space expands in proportion to our movements and activities. Over and above this the space that can be encompassed by the mind and spirit is potentially limitless.

In addition to his own physical sphere of action, each individual has various worlds created by the mind. We create worlds of our own in our jobs, our studies, and our hobbies, and we create still different worlds in our relationships with others. We create a world of friendship through discussions or through sports; there is a world of beauty created by our appreciation of nature. There are worlds of faith we create through our passion for religion, philosophy, and poetry.

There are, unfortunately, too many people whose worlds are desolate expanses filled only with ambition, jealousy, or megalomania. Just as people's faces differ one from another, so do the scope and content of their spiritual space, that is, their life-space. Each person's life-space is a reflection of his ego. Schizophrenics aside, each person amalgamates his various physical and spiritual spaces into one unified world, which for him is the full extent of space in any sense. When the spiritual world is well integrated with the self, life and the life-space become sufficiently free and substantial to exert an effect on the outside world. As the life-space broadens, there is an increase in the individual's power to think and act, and he himself leads a more rewarding life.

The self, seeing more and more, rejoices in the wider scope opening up around it and in the new meanings and dimensions being added to the realm of life. With joy and lightness of heart, it seeks its own way to self-perfection.

Encompassed in an ever-expanding life-space is a well-lighted future, one which can be contemplated with hope and confidence. This space spreads beyond the self to enrich the lives of others, to inspire familial love, to create a richer social environment. It grows into a love for mankind, sympathy for all living things, and oneness with the cosmos.

Expanding spiritual space increases our life-force and makes us feel light in body and mind. When life is full of vitality, energy spreads to every part of the body, and one ceases to feel the heaviness of the flesh. Because of the unity of physical and spiritual elements, the changes taking place in the mind are in a mysterious way reflected in the body. When the mind has ample spiritual space, the body feels free to move about at will, lightly and with joy.

SPACE-TIME

From the time of Sir Isaac Newton until only a few decades ago, people thought an apple fell because of the pull of the earth's gravity. Now scientists tell us it is because of the curvature of space in the vicinity of the earth. The idea is that space is greatly curved near large masses such as the earth, and that the falling apple is simply following the lines of this curvature. On a practical level, it does not seem to make much difference whether we attribute the effect to gravity or to curvature, but to scientists their image of the universe itself hinges on the difference.

The idea of curved space is a part of Einstein's general theory of relativity. According to Einstein, the curvature of space increases near the earth and increases still more in the vicinity of larger masses, such as the sun. In effect, Einstein was saying that what we call gravity is not a direct pull, but rather an indirect result of the spatial curvature, or gravitational field, that the earth causes in the space surrounding it.

The curvature theory has been demonstrated in an experiment having to do with light. Until the end of the nineteenth century it was generally accepted as immutable fact that light travels in a straight line, but if space itself is curved, one would expect the path of light also to be curved, and if this is the case, there should be a recognizable curve in the space near the sun. In 1919, during a total eclipse of the sun, the British astronomer Sir Arthur Stanley Eddington made the crucial discovery that light coming from distant stars does indeed curve around the sun, to the extent that stars which by the straight-line theory ought to be hidden by the sun are in fact visible.

This result meant also that space is curved around stars other than the sun, and that there are countless complicated curves in cosmic space as a whole. It follows that with the movement of the stars, the complex of curvatures is constantly changing, and the cosmos itself, like a living body, is in a state of unceasing transformation.

The curvature of space also affects the passage of physical time. The curvature near the sun being greater than that near the earth, the passage of time on the sun is slightly slower. Specifically, one second on the sun is about 1.000002 seconds on earth. In the vicinity of heavenly bodies larger or denser than the sun, the passage of time is even slower.

In recent years we have been hearing a good deal about black holes, which seem to be stars around which the curvature of space is very pronounced, and all light in their vicinity is entrapped, so that we can see nothing at all of the stars. It may be that on such heavenly bodies there is virtually no passage of time at all.

A thousand years on earth is perhaps a half-day less on the sun in terms of earth time. In a black hole, it might amount to only a day or less. On the other hand, there may be places in the universe where a thousand years on earth are a hundred million years. In short, time varies with the location within the universe.

Einstein's theory of relativity upset the very foundation of our ideas about time and space. Confined as we are to our little planet, we are prone to think in terms of Newton's absolute space and absolute time, since they work reasonably well in this one corner of the universe, but Einstein showed that neither space nor time is absolute. Since changing curvatures in space caused by movements of the heavenly bodies affect time, we can no longer think of space-time as being separate from matter.

This is more fully explained in the special theory of relativity, according to which the curvature of space slows the passage of time. There exists, then, a direct interrelation, or fusion, between space and time. This is called the *space-time continuum*. Since there is constant interaction between this continuum and the celestial bodies, sun and earth included, we can say that space, time, and stars function as one entity within which the infinite changes and transformations of the cosmos are taking place.

I am reminded of a passage in a poem by Li Po, saying, "Heaven and Earth are an inn where all things stop briefly; time is the eternal accumulation of guests." I have mentioned this because it seems this passage played a part in the development of Hideki Yukawa's theory of the elementary domain.

Einstein did much to clarify the relationship between the space-time continuum and massive astronomical bodies, but he said little about the relationship between space-time and the elementary particles. Dr. Yukawa's theory is an attempt to explain this relationship.

In Li Po's poem there is an inn where travelers stay temporarily. In Dr. Yukawa's theory, the travelers are the elementary particles, and the inn is space, wherein the elementary particles exist for an infinitesimal length of time. Time itself is an eternal traveler and is always passing by. Dr. Yukawa has called his theory the "concept of the inn."

I am very often astonished at the frequency with which the insight of great poets coincides with later scientific theory. In Dr. Yukawa's theory, the fusion of space-time and matter is applicable in the microcosm as well as the macrocosm, but what is most striking is that he drew the idea from Li Po (701–62), who had no scientific knowledge of either.

I would like to go beyond the realm of the purely physical. We exist, it is true, in the space-time continuum, but simultaneously we have our own subjective space-time. Our lives create a subjective life-time. Furthermore, our life-time is measured by, and our life-span contained within, our life-flow.

Conversely, the flow of our life-force cannot be considered separately from our life-time or our life-space. Our life-time and life-space are born of the fact that our life-force is moving and pulsating. At the same time, our life-force is influenced by our life-time and our life-space. One arrives at a fusion of interrelated elements similar to Dr. Yukawa's theory of the inn.

Since physical space and time are fused into a single continuum, it is only reasonable to suppose that at the roots of our life-force, the same is true of subjective space and subjective time. The closer we approach the source of our life-force, the larger our subjective space grows, until eventually it encompasses all human beings, all life, the earth and the stars, and all physical space, becoming one with the limitless cosmos. At that point there cease to be any physical distinctions. Human life, elementary particles, animals, plants, the sun, the stars—all things animate or inanimate fuse into the infinite pulsations of the cosmic life-force. Conversely, this life-force produces and activates all the phenomena of the cosmos. The manifestation of this ultimate existence is called *Nam-myōhō-renge-kyō*. It is also called eternity (*kuon*).

In *On Attaining Buddhahood* (*Issho Jobutsu-shō*), Nichiren Daishonin wrote, "Life at each moment encompasses both body and spirit and both self and environment of all sentient beings in every condition of life, as well as non-sentient beings—plants, sky, and earth, on down to the most minute particles of dust. Life at each moment permeates the universe and is revealed in all phenomena." The meaning is that the entire cosmos is encompassed in the mind that subsumes every life-moment, and every life-moment expands throughout the cosmos and becomes the principle of all elements. It is identical with *Nam-myōhō-renge-kyō*, which is cosmic life and the force behind cosmic movements as they appear in the space-time continuum.

All the elements of the universe are contained in eternal cosmic life, which is the Mystic Law. When the Mystic Law takes concrete action or form, it becomes the life-time and life-space of individual lives. Each self in the universe is a part of the cosmic life, and it draws on the strength of the cosmic life to carry out its functions in the physical world. In its depths the self of each life is identical with the life of the cosmos. Hence the Buddhist phrase, "The cosmos is the self."

Our selves and all other selves partake of the fundamental cosmic energy that creates all phenomena. When this fundamental energy appears in the ordinary world as life-force, the various selves assume their individual identities as stars, planets, humans, or other living beings. The energy possessed by the self pours forth as life-flow, which creates life-space and life-time. The self and the manifestation of its fundamental energy give birth to space and time. There is no space or time apart from life activity. This principle must be understood before one can fully understand the identity of the self and the cosmos or the concept of eternity in every life-moment.

It is not a case of our being set down within a vast previously existing expanse of time and space called the universe or the cosmos. On the contrary, we are an integral part of this expanse, drawing our energy from the single fundamental life-force that creates and motivates all other elements in the universe. All individual selves are fused together in the cosmic self, and the fundamental entity endowing them with the energy to become manifest in the ordinary world as individual selves is eternity, which is the Mystic Law or *Nam-myōhō-renge-kyō*. Everything is included in this; everything proceeds from it; everything returns to it.

The self of universal life spreads out infinitely through time and space. This is the working of the Mystic Law which is the fundamental essence of the universe at this instant or any instant. It is an outpouring of the infinite energy of *Nam-myōhō-renge-kyō*. The existence of this present instant is the existence of the form of the cosmos at this present instant, and since this instant contains all of the cosmos, it contains eternity. The self of the cosmic life, which underlies the cosmos as it exists at this moment, is fused with the selves in all our lives.

When we do not draw on the infinite energy of the cosmos, we run into difficulty, since we are ignoring our identity with the cosmic self. Eternity is implicit in our lives, but we do not make provision for even the coming year. Potentially, our life-space is infinite, but as things are now, it does not even extend throughout our tiny planet. What we must do is find the way to expand, to live an eternity in a single moment, to increase our life-space and life-time until they fill the universe. We must realize our oneness with the Mystic Law.

II

THE BUDDHIST VIEW OF LIFE

THE TEN STATES OF BEING

FROM HELL TO BUDDHAHOOD

After twenty years of massacres and atrocities, the war in Vietnam finally came to an end. Over and above the appalling casualty figures, one wonders how many lives have been twisted and warped by the decades of fighting.

Around the end of 1972, a Japanese correspondent returning from Hue reported that the Vietnamese were "afraid of peace." He meant not that the Vietnamese did not want peace, but that they did not know what peace was, or what it would bring. War they knew. Peace was an unknown quantity. To those of us who have the good fortune of being accustomed to peace, there is something unreal about this. How sad to think there are so few people in Vietnam today who are old enough to have experienced a state of peace.

Having somehow survived a hellish war, these unfortunate people now have to ask themselves, "What is peace?" There is a whole generation that knows nothing but war, bombings, and scorched earth. However much they may have hoped from time to time for a more humane way of life, each time that hope has quickly changed to distrust and despair. In their lives, the only certain thing has been death.

The greatest evil of war, I think, is that it destroys the natural human desire for peace. Everybody hates war. Everybody longs to live out his life in peace. But when war comes, it buries the natural impulse toward peace in the mire of doubt and fear. That is why war is Hell.

When I was a child, I was afraid of Hell. To me, it was a horrible place in the afterlife, populated by vicious hounds and even more vicious devils, and I knew I would go there if I was not good. Today, children laugh at this kind of Hell. The weird monsters they see in comic books and on television seem to be more real to them than the devils and hounds that terrified me.

Hell is by no means a figment of the imagination. It exists in our very lives, right here on earth. Hell, indeed, is the agony we suffer during life, and there is no man-made Hell worse than war.

Hell is the ultimate agony. In his *New Year's Writing* (*Mushimochi Gosho*), Nichiren Daishonin said, "First of all, as to the question of where exactly Hell and the Buddha exist, one sutra reads that Hell exists underground and another sutra says that the Buddha is in the west. However, closer examination reveals that both exist in our five-foot body."

In Buddhism it is always important to look within one's inner self, to examine one's own feeling toward life. One may be able to deceive others about one's true feelings, but one cannot ultimately deceive oneself. If one is tortured by unrelieved agony, one is in Hell. If one is completely happy both within and without, one is experiencing a touch of Buddhahood. Each of the 3.7 billion people in the world is different from the others, but we all have some things in common. We all understand happiness, sadness, grief, joy, fear, and other basic emotions. Our common qualities, which transcend questions of race or color, are part of our sense of self. The sense of self is, in other words, the common foundation shared by all mankind.

Though self is a common denominator, the inner condition of the self varies with the individual. Buddhism recognizes ten states or realms in which the individual self might exist. In the universal sense, these are ten categories of existence into which at any given time all living beings fall. We speak of them as the Ten Worlds, or States (*Jikkai*), and they are (1) Hell, (2) Hunger, (3) Animality, (4) Anger, (5) Humanity, (6) Rapture, (7) Learning, (8) Realization, (9) the Bodhisattva Nature, and (10) Buddhahood.

Most of the people I talk to about the Ten States tend to regard them as ten different worlds. This is no doubt because they have interpreted the traditional names for them too literally. The second state, for example, is written in Japanese and Chinese with characters meaning the "World of the Starving Souls," and the third state with characters meaning the "World of Beasts." These terms suggest places apart from our own world inhabited by creatures different from ourselves. In reality, each of the states can and does exist within a single human being as the ever-changing condition of his self. Put simply, we do not have to die and go to another world to be in Hell or to become a beast or a starving soul.

Nichiren Daishonin explained the Ten Worlds as they apply to human beings in the clearest possible terms. In *The True Object of Worship* (*Kanjin no Honzon-shō*), he wrote of the first six states: "When we look from time to time at a person's face, we find him sometimes joyful, sometimes enraged, and sometimes calm. At times greed appears in the person's face, at times foolishness, and at times perversity. Rage is the world of Hell, greed is that of Hunger, foolishness is that of Animality, perversity is that of Anger, joy is that of Rapture, and calmness is that of Humanity." I think this passage is an excellent illustration of Nichiren Daishonin's insight into the human self. He saw that no matter how well a person presents himself to others, he may actually be in Hell, and no matter how self-possessed he may seem, he may be in a state of spiritual starvation. The traditional names for the Ten States are vivid representations of the state in which the self may be, whether it is a self controlled by impulsive passion, a self absorbed in egoism, a self uncontrolled by intelligence or conscience, or a self full of joy and life. The Ten States are abstract in the sense that they are generalities drawn from human experience. Having taken into account all of the various conditions in which the self might exist, Buddhist philosophers concluded that there are ten basic conditions.

The number is not accidental, nor was it chosen because ten is the basis of the decimal system, or some such thing as that. It was chosen so as to be all-inclusive on the one hand and on the other to find the smallest number of categories. Eight categories would have meant combining two essentially different states; twelve would have meant dividing what are essentially two single states to make four.

I assure you the whole thing has been well thought out, and would like to give you an example or two. Suppose we consider the condition of agony, which corresponds to the state of Hell. There are many kinds of agony—the agony of a person suffering from an incurable disease, the agony of a wife whose husband drinks too much and is unable to provide for his family, the agony of a mother who has a delinquent son, the agony of a father whose daughter plays around with men. The situations are different, and each has its own particular nuance, but the people who are affected are alike in that they lead lives of suffering, and the suffering is recognized by others for what it is. A person who has somehow managed to recover from what was considered an incurable disease *feels* the agony of someone who has such a disease. A mother who has lost a child *feels* the agony of a parent who has to send a son off to war. Vicarious suffering may not be as painful as personal suffering, but there is something deep in the human self that recognizes and understands suffering and agony as such. Agony is a condition we can all experience and comprehend.

The state of Animality, or in traditional terminology the "World of Beasts," is the condition in which the self lives by instinct alone. Here again there are numerous types of instinct—the sex urge, the instinct to eat, the instinct to sleep, and so on. There are people who live to eat, people who would be happy to sleep the rest of their lives, people who cannot control their sex drive, people who cannot bring themselves to give up drugs. They are all different, and they lead different lives, but they form a group in that they give themselves over mindlessly, like animals, to their instincts.

Each of the Ten States, you will find, has a universality of this sort. On the other hand, the states do not overlap to the extent that they can be combined. The agony of constantly wanting food is not the same as the agony of suffering an incurable illness. No more the same are the realms of Hunger and Hell, for in Hell not even desire is left—only helplessness and dull anger at the self for being helpless. In Hell you do not scream for what you want, you groan because you know it is useless to want. But in the state of Hunger, there is constant, insatiable desire, for it is the desire that creates hunger. You might notice, too, that there is a difference between the hunger whose source is voraciousness and the hunger that comes from normal instinct, and this is the difference between those in the state of Hunger and those in the mindless state of Animality.

One can go from one state to another. A person who has no appetite because he is running a high fever, or because he has a horrible toothache, is not in the state of Hunger. We would be closer if we said he was in Hell. But if his fever goes down, or if his tooth gets better, only to find that he is not allowed to eat solids, he is apt to leave the state of Hell and enter that of Hunger.

Agony and insatiability, helpless anger and sheer greed, are different one from the other, and we know and feel them to be different. The states characterized by these feelings are qualitatively different and therefore cannot be combined. On a purely practical level, people simply do not get hungry when they are suffering true agony, and they do not get angry at themselves when they are being greedy.

Before going further into the idea of the Ten States, I should like to point out that what we are dealing with is simultaneously subjective and objective. The Ten States are based on the subjective sense of self that characterizes human life, and in this sense they are subjective categories. At the same time, the standards for describing these categories are distinctly objective, and the concept develops on both levels, objective and subjective.

From the objective viewpoint, we should first analyze the substance and content of the self. What characteristic does the self take on in each of the Ten States? Is it desire, or reason, or compassion, or egoism, or what? In the second place, we should think of the Ten States in terms of life-space and life-time. Finally, we must consider to what extent life in any state is fulfilled, and whether it is active or passive, subjective or objective, free or shackled.

It is even more important, by examining the Ten States, to discover ways to help people live more humane lives, ways to avoid war, pollution, and social evils, ways to lead individuals to improve their own karma. The Ten States can furnish a basic philosophy on which a more humanistic culture and society can be built.

We need to know what state or condition the self is in when it causes wars and destruction of the environment, as well as when it works for peace and friendship. This, I believe, is a first step toward uprooting the evil causes that bring on disrespect for human life and the denial of the right of every human being to live. We must find ways to revolutionize the lives of people who have been so tormented by war that they have to ask, "What is peace?" We must try to show them how to draw on the fundamental life-force that can enable them to live as genuine human beings.

The philosophy of the Ten States is a pragmatic philosophy. It enables the self to rise above agony and despair to lead a life truly worth living. We must try to develop the concept of the Ten States into its more universal and cosmic forms, which are the philosophy of the Mutual Possession of the Ten Worlds and the theory of Three Thousand Possible Worlds in Every Life-moment. In short, we must show the way from the pragmatic Ten Worlds to the sublime total life philosophy that can serve as the basis for a new human civilization and culture, in which people will have to ask, "What is war?"

THE EVIL PATHS

Whenever I think of Hell, I recall the horrifying devastation of Hiroshima on August 6, 1945, after the dropping of the first atomic bomb. Here is a description written by the novelist Yōko Ōta, who was one of the victims:

> The days came and went, shrouded in confusion and nightmare. Even on a cloudless clear day in the fall, we were sunk in a deep twilight of gloom and muted chaos. There was no escape. Every day, all around me, people just like myself were dying. . . .
>
> When death would come to me, I could not tell. Every day I pulled at my hair several times and counted to see how many hairs had come out. Time after time I squinted at the skin on my hands and feet to see whether the dreaded spots had begun to appear. . . . My mind was perfectly clear. I knew that no matter how horrible the sores, there would be no pain, no burning. The weirdness of this atomic-bomb disease, its lunatic aspect, was a new Hell for the victims. Writhing together inside me, like two great snakes, were the dread of being called to a death I did not understand and a screaming hatred of war itself. However gloomy the day, the snakes writhed and screamed within me. [From *A City of Corpses* (*Shikabane no Machi*)]

This is not merely vivid writing. These are the words of a person who has gone through the excruciating experience of hanging helplessly between life and death, a person who has been deprived of the freedom of life, the freedom to act. This is precisely what we call Hell. There is no strength left to change things around one, no hope for the future, no freedom for the self.

The powerful life-force inherent in our lives furnishes us with the urge to live, with instinctive desires, and with the mental capacity to lead a humane existence. We learn to love, we thirst for knowledge, we are overcome with passion. Or we might be moved in the opposite direction, toward aggression, destructiveness, or jealousy. In either case, there is a life-force moving within us and weaving the patterns of our lives. In the realm of Hell the energy coming from this life-force is almost completely nullified, and we experience nothing but indescribable anguish.

People suffering from atomic sickness never know when they are going to die, and modern medicine is still in many cases powerless to prevent death. Another of our modern terrors, the *itai-itai* disease, which is caused by pollution, is perhaps even more dreadful. In the advanced stages the pain is so severe that the patient can neither eat nor sleep, and as often as not he dies screaming in physical agony.

It is noteworthy that the characters used to write the Japanese word for Hell, *jigoku*, mean "the lowest" (*ji*) and "to be bound or imprisoned" (*goku*). The root meaning of *jigoku* thus contains the idea of being unable to move or act freely.

Hell is, in short, the condition of being crushed by agony and unable to do anything about it. In this state, no matter how long life goes on, it cannot be fulfilled.

And yet, our life-force never completely disappears, no matter how severely it might be constrained. Even in the face of death, people will attempt desperately to find some ray of hope. Often a person whose disease is pronounced incurable will hang on in the slender hope that some new medicine or treatment will be found in time, or that his doctor's reading of an X-ray was wrong, or the disease might somehow heal itself naturally.

In *The Cancer Ward*, by the Russian novelist Solzhenitsyn, there is excellent insight into the psychological effect on patients of the suggestion that a natural recovery from illness is possible. A patient comes across a passage in a book on pathology saying that cancer has been known to cure itself. It is said to happen very seldom, but the patient was immediately convinced that he himself would be one of the rare cases of natural cure, and other patients also quickly convince themselves. In Solzhenitsyn's words, "It was as though an iridescent butterfly called 'Natural Recovery' had leapt from the pages of the great textbook." The patients must have realized in their hearts that the butterfly, the crystallization of their hopes, was a fleeting thing, but they treasured it nonetheless.

Some people would call this clinging meaninglessly to life, but the same people, in their own way, are clinging to life—they just do not happen to be sick. The inner life-force, the source of the urge to live, can change into violent anger against those who say there is no hope, and as a result, the patient can experience severe emotional turbulence. The fight to continue living is natural, and yet if it engulfs the self in an emotional storm, it can sap a person's vital energy and bring death even closer. This is the special cruelty of Hell.

Anger can be the anger and hatred one feels against war, pollution, incurable illness, poverty, or family strife, but it can also be the debilitating anger one feels against one's own helplessness to do away with these evils. It is this latter anger that characterizes the state of Hell.

In *On Revealing Slanders* (*Kenhōbō-shō*), Nichiren Daishonin described the horrors of eight levels of Hell, of which the worst was the Great Hell of Abi. He speaks of the wailing coming from Abi, which I interpret to mean the pitiful groaning of the self as it sees its life-force cut off, and of an appalling odor emanating from the ground, which I suspect is nothing other than the stench of death.

People everywhere think of Hell as being under us. Perhaps this is because the self, when in agony, feels as though it is sinking. In talking about the aftermath of Hiroshima, Yōko Ōta mentions being "sunk in a deep twilight of gloom," and in the sutras there are passages saying that Hell is many thousands of kilometers under the earth. This is figurative, of course, because we know that Hell lies within the human being himself. I do not think, however, that it would be idle to conceive of Hell in terms of subjective time and space. I suspect, for example, that the space occupied by a life in a state of agony is in a subjective sense very small indeed. It is no joke to say that when you have a terrible toothache, the life-space you are occupying is likely to be confined to your tooth, because you are simply unable to think about anything else. The life-space of a person who does not know where tomorrow's rice is coming from is likely to be confined to the rice bin. The "cloudless clear day in the fall" Miss Ōta wrote about was no part of her life-space at that time, because she was totally absorbed in the surrounding twilight of gloom. When the self is in Hell, it can find no room to rest.

As for the passage of time in Hell, the sutras say that life there lasts an astronomical number of eons, which fits in with our ideas about subjective life-time. We have already talked about how slowly time seems to pass when we are in grief or pain. The life-force weakens, and the life-flow is almost cut off, so that there is little passage of life-time. Such being the case, the time required to escape from Hell seems interminable. The sutras give tremendous figures for the amount of time a person must remain in the Great Hell of Abi.

One level above Hell is the state of Hunger, the second of the Three Evil Paths. This state is traditionally called the Realm of the Starving Souls, and it is also spoken of as the state of starvation or rapacity or voraciousness. Nichiren Daishonin said succinctly, "Greed is the state of Hunger."

The mark of the self in this state is greed, a seemingly unending greed, burning strongly, consuming body and mind. We are all susceptible to it, because greed is only an extreme form of desire, and we are born with many instinctive desires, including the most vital one, which is the basic desire to live. In addition to the desires involved in our instinct for self-protection, we are either born with or acquire more complicated forms of desire, such as self-assertion, possessiveness, the urge to dominate, aggressiveness, and so on. These desires are connected with the states of Hunger, Animality, and Anger, but human beings also have various spiritual desires.

Since desires are necessary to the maintenance of human life, they are in that sense beneficial. But to pursue desire with no higher aim is to become a slave of desire, and this can lead only to misfortune for oneself and others. Herein lies the true nature of the state of Hunger.

In Nichiren Daishonin's *On the Bon Observance* (*Urabon Gosho*), a passage describing the mother of the disciple Maudgalyayana (in Japanese, Mokuren) as she appeared in the Realm of the Starving Souls, says: "Mokuren opened his heavenly eyes and saw the entire universe clearly, as in an untarnished mirror. He was able to look through the earth and view the Three Evil Paths as clearly as we can see fish swimming under the ice on a pond. He saw the Realm of the Starving Souls, and there within it was his mother. She had nothing to eat or drink. Her skin was like a plucked fowl's, and her bones like so many rocks. Her head looked like a large globe, her neck was as thin as a thread, and her belly was swollen like the vast ocean. With her mouth open and her hands together, she was begging for something, and she reminded him of a starved leech sucking blood from a man's face." The text goes on to say that when Mokuren tried to give his mother a bowl of rice, the rice went up in flames.

The state of Hunger is characterized by a painful yearning for something just beyond reach. The life spent in a fruitless search for honor and power revolves about a self that burns with perpetual dissatisfaction. But if what is desired is somehow achieved, or if the urge to dominate triumphs, the self enters the state of Humanity or even that of Rapture.

A passage in the *Risse Abidon-ron* says, "The way of the Starving Souls communicates with all of the other states and can be good or evil."

When a person has eaten all he wants of his favorite food and then is content to lie down and sleep, he is in the state of Animality. If his desires and impulses conflict with those of others, he may enter the state of Anger. If the food he eats or the water he drinks is poisoned, his self may enter the state of Hell.

The desire of the person in the state of Hunger can work for good or evil. Indeed, the frustration born of this desire has been the driving force behind the creation of much of our material civilization. To give just one example, the mechanized production of foodstuffs has largely put an end to famine in the developed countries.

I do not think it is a mistake to say that one of the main reasons most of us work is that we want good things to eat and a comfortable house, or want to go places and do things when we are at leisure. People work overtime in order to buy something, and a husband may endure under terrible working conditions because he wants to see his wife cured of an illness. There is no doubt but that our wants and desires furnish the motivating power for much of our action. In society as a whole, the desire for a better life can bring about better politics and greater economic development.

We must not forget, however, that it is also desire, or greed, that brings about war and the destruction of our natural environment.

It is as described in the *Risse Abidon-ron*—the desire inherent in the state of Hunger can work for good or for evil. Those who allow themselves to be controlled by desire, however, are confined to this realm and lead miserable lives. That is why the state of Hunger is counted among the Three Evil Paths. Fundamentally, it is a state of constantly wanting something, but not being able to do anything about it.

This inability to find satisfaction distinguishes this state from that of Animality, in which the self is constantly following its instinctive desires. If the self in the realm of Hunger is a vegetable, the self in the state of Animality is a beast.

In a sense, we are all animals, for we have instinctive desires in common with the lower animals. Still, certain animal instincts cannot be denied without peril. The most enlightened of men have to eat and sleep, just as dogs and cats do, in order to keep themselves functioning properly. To be sure, from the animals' viewpoint, some people have rather strange desires. In many women, for example, the desire to remain svelte is so powerful that they will literally starve themselves to achieve this goal. Some sort of record was set by a housewife in Los Angeles, I am told, who fasted for 117 days. She brought her weight down from 308 pounds to a mere 188, but then she had to stop to keep from dying, even though she apparently had the will to continue.

From the scientific viewpoint, we all belong to the order of primates; to survive we must fulfill the instinctive desires of primates. That, however, is not the same as saying we must act upon every instinctive impulse. On the contrary, as the most highly developed of the primates, we have mental and spiritual capacities not shared by our fellow creatures. Along with instinctive desire, we, and we alone in the animal kingdom, have intelligence, conscience, the ability to love, and the sense of compassion. It is the ability to use these powers to satisfy our instinctive desires, while yet keeping them under control, that makes us human beings rather than animals.

Nichiren Daishonin said, "Foolishness is the world of Animality." He meant, no doubt, that a state in which action is not controlled by intelligence or conscience is bestial.

There is further explanation in a sentence in Nichiren Daishonin's "Letter to Niike" (*Niike Gosho*), which says, "Beasts are cruel, and they kill each other." Another statement, in the "Letter from Sado" (*Sado Gosho*), says, "It is the nature of beasts to threaten the weak and fear the strong." The actions of the self in the state of Animality are thus governed by the principle that in the everlasting struggle for existence the strong devour the weak.

It is commonly said that animals do not tell lies, but this does not seem to be true. Obviously, while animals do not lie as cleverly as people do, zoologists say that within the animal kingdom, lies and deceit are rampant. Animals of the same species are likely to band together to protect themselves, but when they attack a different species, they are comparatively treacherous. In making surprise attacks, they aim at the weak, the sick, and the aged among their victims. To be sure, this is not a conscious resort to foul play, but a matter of instinctive self-protection in the struggle for existence. We must not be too harsh on the animals, for it is not as though human beings abided by the rules of fair play in killing or capturing animals. With the animals, the fight to fulfill the instinctive urges is the same as the fight to survive.

When the instinctive desire of the self in the state of Animality has been fulfilled, it experiences that combination of satisfaction and sluggishness that we usually feel after eating our fill. But I think it more a matter of simple happiness. Not an ethereal joy, or even the quiet satisfaction of having accomplished something, but what we might call a biological sense of fulfillment. Perhaps satiety is the word.

There are many people today who do not see anything wrong about the strong winning out over the weak. This is the Law of the Jungle, but I think such an attitude is foolish because it is mindless. As in the world of animals, it involves no wisdom, no reasoning, no will.

Although instinct is blind, it is necessary in that it enables living beings to adjust to their environment—to find food, to find a place to sleep, to evade enemies. But instinct alone enables neither people nor animals to adapt to changing conditions, and it is virtually powerless in the face of higher intelligence.

In the "Letter from Sado," Nichiren Daishonin wrote: "Fish want to survive; they deplore their pond's shallowness and dig holes to hide in, yet tricked by bait, they take the hook. Birds in a tree fear that they are too low and perch in the top branches, yet bewitched by bait, they too are caught in snares." We see, then, that in a world where higher intelligence operates, to act solely on instinct is to invite disaster, and those who can do no more than follow their instincts have no control over their fate.

This seems to be true of whole species as well as of individuals. According to zoologists, a species that multiplies too rapidly at the expense of other living beings is doomed to extinction. One of the most spectacular cases of mass self-destruction occurred at the end of the Cretaceous period, about 70 million years ago, when the age of the dinosaurs came to an abrupt end. Until then, the dinosaurs had held sway over the earth as mankind does today. In an astonishingly short period they passed into oblivion. This was due in part to cataclysmic geological changes, but another important cause was the animals' inability to adjust to new surroundings. The herbivores apparently lost the plants they thrived on, and the carnivores died when they had eaten all the herbivores. The large-scale destruction of living beings on this earth has been repeated many times. Creatures feed on other creatures until they have destroyed the basis of their very existence. Many scientists believe that that is exactly what the human race is doing today, and that mankind faces certain destruction if it does not discard the principle of the strong devouring the weak.

"Foolish" is an apt word for the self that is so immersed in instinctive pleasure that it happily eats away at the bases of its own existence.

Until now, we have been considering the Three Evil Paths, which are the states of Hell, Hunger, and Animality. In all of these states the self is controlled by helpless agony, desire, or other emotions or factors that do not involve volition. The fourth state, that of Anger, is often grouped with the first three, but there is one important difference: in the state of Anger, there is self-consciousness and thus an element of humanity. This is what is traditionally called the Realm of Ashura, Ashura being the name of a class of monstrous superhuman beings.

Nichiren Daishonin said, "Perversity is the state of Anger." In this state the self is centered about itself. It takes no cognizance of other living beings, but works exclusively for its own benefit and for the realization of its egoistic purposes.

Nichiren Daishonin also wrote: "The first volume of *Great Concentration and Insight* (*Maka Shikan*) says, 'The person in the Realm of Ashura has an irresistible urge to win out over everyone else. Like the hawk flying high in the sky in search of prey, he looks down upon others and respects only himself. He makes a superficial show of benevolence, righteousness, propriety, wisdom, and faith, and he may even display a primitive form of moral integrity, but inside he is a monstrous Ashura.' "

This is an excellent description of the complete egoist—the man who is determined to win at all cost, the man who "looks down upon others and respects only himself."

I cannot help thinking of the "education mothers" we used to hear so much about, the women who were going to put their children through prestigious schools and colleges come what may. One doesn't read so much about them any more, but there was a time when they were a menace to most educators. They got all excited about getting their children even into kindergarten, and when the time came for the children to go to college or medical school, they were prepared to make huge donations to the schools or to individual teachers to see that their offspring were admitted. Numerous instances of bribery were reported in the press.

What was so horrible was that in most instances the ultimate purpose was to bolster the ego of the parent. The children, as a rule, were innocent victims. No one can blame parents for taking a lively interest in the education of their children, but they can certainly be blamed for pushing the children along relentlessly, without regard for the children's own abilities or aptitudes. The education mothers and their spouses were not really interested in their children's education; they were interested in themselves. When their children did well in school, they regarded it as their own accomplishment and an enhancement of their own self-esteem. Japanese teachers have frequently been treated to the spectacle of mothers consumed with hatred for children whose grades were better than their own children's.

There are many other cases in which jealousy or a sense of superiority is a defense mechanism against a deep feeling of inferiority. The self when insecure is apt to bluff its way through or create delusions of grandeur. It may be that the consuming urge to win out on all occasions results almost entirely from the need to camouflage inner failings.

It is certainly true that what is inside is often not apparent on the outside. There are men who appear under normal circumstances to be perfect gentlemen in complete control of themselves, but who from time to time fly into a rage over practically nothing. They have what is called an "explosive personality," a psychological abnormality surely, but one which, unfortunately, is none too uncommon. People with this affliction usually do not themselves know when they are going to explode, and it is of course impossible for anyone else to tell in advance, particularly since the dynamite inside is so often concealed by the outward appearance. For that matter, I might mention that to the unpracticed eye, the education mothers are as a rule guileless womanhood itself.

This is what was meant in the passage saying that people in the state of Ashura, or Anger, were able to put on a show of great virtue. We have here something different from the self moved entirely by instinct or desire. In this case, the self is performing stunts to attract the acclaim of others and thereby acquire a sense of superiority. No doubt it is all unconscious, but the self that exists in this state must live in a perpetual turmoil of emotions and frustrations.

Desires in the state of Anger are much more exclusively human in character than the purely instinctive desires. In this state, the instinctive desires, including the urge to live, are more or less satisfied, and there is a new element of self-consciousness, which, though egocentric, is on a higher level of intelligence than the mindless state of Animality. It is because there is self-consciousness that there can be the desire to win out over others, the urge to achieve glory, and other such egoistic qualities as aggressiveness, exhibitionism, and destructiveness. The inner turmoil of emotion appears on the surface as anger, hatred, animosity, or jealousy.

The anger we spoke of earlier as being a quality associated with Hell is different. The anger of Hell lies beneath self-consciousness. Existing in the innermost depths of life, it is aimed not at others, but at the self. Its nature is such that it works toward the destruction not of outside antagonists, but of the self within which it exists. The anger of the state of Anger, on the other hand, is directed at others. It is self-conscious, and it seeks to destroy real or fancied antagonists in order to protect the self.

The life-force in the state of Anger then, is stronger than in the Three Evil Paths, even though it operates in a fundamentally insane fashion. A statement made by the twenty-sixth High Priest of the Nichiren Shoshu, Nichikan Shonin, in his *Threefold Secret Teachings* (*Sanjū Hiden-shō*), says, "An Ashura is 84,000 *yujun* tall [one *yujun* is thirty kilometers], and the four seas do not even come up to his knees." I interpret this to be a reference to the life-space of someone in the state of Anger. We speak, after all, of "towering rages," and it is beyond doubt that when we are extremely angry, or when we are being arrogant, we persuade ourselves that we are very large indeed. Needless to say, our antagonist seems very small.

Though people in a state of Anger often seem more than life-sized, I doubt whether this is a true picture of their life-space. In the "Letter from Sado," it says, "An arrogant man will be overcome with fear when he meets a strong enemy, just like the haughty Ashura who shrank and hid himself in a lotus flower blossoming in Munetchi Lake when reproached by Taishaku."

Taishaku is mentioned in the Lotus Sutra as one of the gods who safeguard Buddhism. In contemporary terms I think we can consider him as being a person who is able to perceive the truth. Perhaps we may also take Munetchi Lake to mean a place where a hothead can cool off. What Nichiren Daishonin's statement means, is that a big blustery brute encountering a person with enough intelligence to see through him will shrivel into insignificance. Thus we have a more accurate indication of the true life-space of a being in the state of Anger.

The apparent size, or importance, of someone in the state of Anger is an illusion. His true self occupies very little life-space, but dissatisfied with this area, it expands itself by auto-suggestion into a huge apparition. Often we are fooled into thinking this is real. The person in this state, for his part, does not doubt its reality, and he makes what use he can of his illusory strength to cause mischief wherever possible.

All in all, the state of Anger, like the Three Evil Paths, is one of unhappiness, frustration, and self-deception, and it is easy to see why it is often included with the other three states as one of the Four Evil Paths.

HUMANITY AND RAPTURE

The famous riddle of the Sphinx is, "What is it that walks on four legs in the morning, two legs in the daytime, and three legs in the evening?" The answer is man, for such are the aspects of man in infancy, adulthood, and old age. A more difficult riddle would have been, "What is man?" To this, there are no easy answers.

As mentioned before, Pascal at one point described man as a "thinking reed." Other definitions have been "a reasoning animal," "an animal that can use tools," "an animal that enjoys social life," and so on. Linnaeus used the term *Homo sapiens*, meaning "an anthropoid who thinks," to devise a means of distinguishing contemporary man from the less intelligent anthropoids. The late French pathologist and physiologist Charles Richet (1850–1935), who was the recipient of the Nobel Prize for Physiology or Medicine in 1913, thought *Homo sapiens* was too flattering. He proposed instead *Homo stultus* (man, the foolish), which he felt was more in accord with the facts of history.

Although man can be defined from several different viewpoints, in Buddhism the state of Humanity is a state of tranquillity in which man is at peace both with himself and with the world. The Sanskrit for the state of Humanity is *manusa*, which means "a being who thinks." A passage from the *Risse Abidon-ron*, mentioned above, says: "The path of Humanity is called *manusa* because it has eight qualities: intelligence, excellence, acute consciousness, sound judgement, superior wisdom, the ability to distinguish truth from falsehood, the ability to attain enlightenment, and a good karma from the past." Nichiren Daishonin was including all these characteristics when he said, "Calmness is the state of Humanity."

The state of Humanity is indeed a tranquil realm. The Four Evil Paths are realms of struggle and hardship; the state of Rapture, which we shall consider presently, is filled with joy and delight, but is nevertheless active and dynamic. But the natural state of human beings, which is to say the state of Humanity, is calm. In our own lives, we experience many emotional ups and downs, but we also have periods of peace and quiet, such as those wonderful moments when we return home and relax after a hard day's work. It is at times like that that we really feel human, and it is this feeling that characterizes the state of Humanity.

The trouble is that in the environment in which we live, tribulations can easily pull us out of the state of Humanity into one of the Four Evil Paths. To remain in the state of Humanity, it is necessary also to reflect calmly upon ourselves, to analyze our social surroundings, and to make decisions befitting the state of Humanity. Beyond this, it is possible in this particular state to develop one's natural potentialities and rise to higher states. Perhaps the reason the state of Humanity is nearly in the middle of the Ten States of Being is that it is a basically neutral state from which one may go to any of the other states. It is possible through the practice of Buddhism for those of us in the state of Humanity to refine and polish ourselves, and thereby to advance to a life condition that is always enlightened by the brilliant sun of wisdom.

In one sense, it is tremendously difficult to remain calm and composed, to form an accurate view of life and society, and to conduct oneself properly. For many, it seems easier to live by impulse or thrash about in a turbulent sea of emotion, even though this "easy way" can only lead to greater suffering.

The "easy way" is the path to lower realms of existence. In order to lead a tranquil life in the state of Humanity, one must be able to use one's reasoning power and one's wisdom. One must have a conscience and distinguish accurately between good and evil, and one must have the will power to overcome difficulties and temptations. Above all, one must have the determination to lead a good life.

Being born human does not mean that one will continue without effort to live in the tranquil state of Humanity. It merely means one has the capacity to do that. The self in this state must make use of the human qualities of reason and conscience to exercise control over instinctive desires and emotions that give rise to greed, animosity, jealousy, and other evils. Only in this way can we lead fruitful, responsible, and broad-minded lives.

Controlling the passions is like riding a runaway horse. If you relax the reins for an instant, you may well be thrown. The objective is to be able to control and utilize forces and energies so that horse and rider move as one.

In the summer, I see the young people waterskiing. The good skiers glide around like magic, but the beginners are soon flailing their hands and legs in the water. The human self is like these young people, for the self must skillfully maneuver over a sea of desire, passion, and impulse just as the skiers maneuver on the water. If the self makes a misstep, it may drown in a sea of passion. Or perhaps a head representing sheer egoism might bob above the waves.

We should not dwell too long on the dangers of falling into the Four Evil Paths, even though they are ever-present, for the state of Humanity also presents the self with the opportunity to increase in stature, to gain greater wisdom and light, and to become stronger in judgement, insight, and compassion.

As we saw, the *Risse Abidon-ron* mentions as one of the properties of Humanity the possibility of achieving enlightenment. This means, among other things, that if the human self refines its nature, it has the potentiality of living in a state of complete peace and happiness. This potentiality is what distinguishes the state of Humanity from the Four Evil Paths. In the world of our times, the Four Evil Paths lead to such evils as war and pollution of the environment, but the state of Humanity offers the self the ability to achieve peace and prosperity, while at the same time enjoying considerable personal freedom and individualism.

Regarding the location of the state of Humanity, the *Threefold Secret Teachings* says, "Humans dwell on the earth."

All the individual selves in this state share a common dwelling place. The common-sense explanation would be to take "earth" to mean simply our physical planet. In my opinion, however, the point here is that there is a common spiritual foundation which supports all mankind. This foundation includes the will to live and the other impulses needed to sustain life, but that is not all. In order to live as true men, we must have such things as the love of parent for child, the love of husband for wife, mutual trust between neighbors, and ideals we can believe in.

We need social conventions and ways of thought upon which we as human beings can agree, and above these, we must have a certain control over human desire. All these things, I think, are part of the common dwelling place, or "earth." The human self inherits a sense of values from society, decides upon its own goals for living, and attempts to achieve these goals. And in this way the human self finds meaning and satisfaction in life, as well as a standard for judging values and a sense of mission.

The foundation for human life rests on faith and a sense of values. It is in one's concept of life and of the world. Only by sharing in this common foundation for human life can we stand up against the trials confronting human beings and enjoy complete peace and tranquillity. In a very real sense, residing on earth means having one's feet on the ground.

One cannot maintain life in the Buddhist state of Humanity without having a foundation in this wider "earth." There may be all sorts of differences in individual views of life and the world at large, in individual aims, and in individual value standards. Indeed, the world we live in is one in which values are becoming ever more diverse. And yet, the self in the state of Humanity must have the sort of basis and foundation for existence that I have been outlining. When the self plants itself upon this foundation, it can lead its life in peace. The flow of life is smooth, and subjective time passes steadily and peacefully.

In the state of Humanity, the energies of life are under considerable control. Unless something goes wrong, for example, we are virtually unconscious of the workings of our bodies. On the spiritual level, it takes a good deal of pent-up emotion or desire to disturb our composure greatly, and most of us are able to put up with a certain amount of discontent or dissatisfaction. Humanity is, on the whole, an admirable state.

The state of Rapture has traditionally been called the Realm of the Gods. When we enter this condition, we become lighter all over. We walk with lighter step and feel as though we could soar up in the sky. What we experience is not so much conscious pleasure as it is a deep sense of overall good—all's right with the world, and we feel that nothing can disturb our well-being.

In *The True Object of Worship* (*Kanjin no Honzon-shō*), Nichiren Daishonin said, "Joy is the state of Rapture." To be happy is to experience a kind of general exaltation, a sense of exhilaration coupled with a strong feeling of satisfaction. A person in this condition is in every sense happy to be alive. According to the *Threefold Secret Teachings*, "The state of Rapture includes the six realms of the World of Desire (*yokkai*), the eighteen realms of the World of Form (*shiki-kai*), and the four realms of the World of Formlessness (*mushiki-kai*)." As this suggests, there are many gradations in this state of Rapture, but the happiness experienced by the self in the World of Desire is different from the happiness experienced in the World of Form and the World of Formlessness.

According to Buddhist scriptures, the World of Desire includes the first five of the Ten States and a part of the state of Rapture, that is, all those states in which desire or impulse is a driving force. The states of

Hell, Hunger, Animality, and Anger are all centered upon the desire for life, upon instinctive desires, emotional urges, cravings for social or physical well-being. In the state of Anger, there emerges a certain self-consciousness, and in the state of Humanity, a truly humane self comes into being, but even in these states there are underlying currents of desire. The state of Rapture is the condition in which these various desires are satisfied.

One is experiencing the state of Rapture when one is happily eating food one likes, but there is no need to limit it to the instinctive desires. The happiness of Rapture also comes from the satisfaction of the desire to rule, of the desire to be honored, of the desire to possess things. These are all pleasures of the World of Desire.

In the World of Form, the state of Rapture is what we feel when our somatic rhythm is in good condition and our life-force is strong. This happiness is more profound than that resulting from the satisfaction of ordinary desires. It makes one feel healthy and vigorous and aware of the life surging up from within one. The somatic flow, merging with the environment, produces a strong urge to create and to make the most of life. This urge can bring profound happiness to the human self.

As for the Rapture of the World of Formlessness, perhaps we would call it a spiritual flow, or a surge of psychic energy. It is the joy of leading a full life, the joy of broadening the scope of one's freedom, the joy of self-realization and creativity. The happiness of the World of Desire and the World of Form is fulfillment of a kind, but the Rapture of the World of Formlessness is more, for it pervades one's whole being.

The scriptures say that a day in the state of Rapture is equivalent to several hundred years in the state of Humanity, and a lifetime in Rapture lasts several hundred Rapture years. In his writings, Nichiren Daishonin said the life span of the Four Heavenly Kings, who represent the state of Rapture is 500 years, in which each day is the equivalent of 50 years of human life. The thirty-three gods on the summit of Mt. Sumeru live a thousand years, in which each day is a hundred human years, and the gods in the Sixth Heaven live far longer than that.

One can understand the real meaning of these figures if one thinks in terms of the life-time we discussed earlier. Life-flow in the state of Rapture is extremely fast, and its influence on the outer world is very great. The self in this state feels that physical time is flying by at a tremendous rate.

When we are happy and our lives are fulfilled, physical time seems short, because much life-time is compressed into it. The life-fulfillment in a single day in the state of Rapture may be equivalent to that of several hundred years in the state of Humanity.

In the state of Humanity, subjective life-time passes at very much the same rate as physical time. Life goes on quietly and smoothly, and when the earth has turned around once on its axis, one feels oneself to have lived a day. In the state of Rapture, the self may note that physical time has passed very quickly, but it will realize from recalling events that a much greater life-time has gone by.

The important life-experience of a day in the state of Rapture can indeed be as full of substance as a hundred years of ordinary life, and a self that has lived its life in this state may in terms of subjective time have lived thousands of years, even though the physical time elapsed is less than a hundred years.

In speaking of the state of Rapture, the *Threefold Secret Teachings* says, "Deities reside in palaces." From the viewpoint of the life philosophy, this means people in this state reside in the environment best suited to the workings of the human self. In the light of the principle that the self and its circumstances are inseparable, we may take the "palaces" to indicate an environment in which there are no hindrances to the flow of life-energy. In this environment, all desires can be satisfied, and the self can enjoy a life of intelligence, conscience, and love.

There is a difficulty, however. The palaces of the state of Rapture collapse easily, and it is characteristic of the state that people tend to fall back from it into one of the Four Evil Paths. That this is true is mentioned in the Nirvana Sutra, wherein are described five types of decay into which deities—which is to say, beings in the state of Rapture—tend to fall. For all its magnificence, the state of Rapture is impermanent.

Why, some may ask, does the palace in the state of Rapture tend to vanish like a dream? Why does the self begin again to suffer? To answer these questions, we must consider the states of existence that transcend those of Humanity and Rapture.

THE SIX LOWER STATES

I think it was a little over ten years ago when I first heard of campaigns initiated by businessmen to stimulate waste. One strategy was to urge people to throw things away even though they were still serviceable. This has since led to the production of many goods into which an element of obsolescence is deliberately incorporated and to numerous model changes in what are normally thought of as durable goods. People with perfectly serviceable automobiles, refrigerators, or television sets are pressured into buying "newer and better" models.

A second strategy is to persuade or force people to use more of a product than they need. All aerosol dispensers, for example, dispense more soap or shaving cream or what-have-you than is necessary at one time, and once it is out of the can, it cannot be put back in. Still another ploy is to urge people to buy a second this or a second that. Conspicuous or unnecessary consumption has become the fashion of the times.

We live today in a world where desires beget more desires, and this is true not merely in the commercial sense. As individuals and as members of society, we all have the fundamental desire for self-preservation, but over and above that, modern society is a vortex of desires for fame, wealth, authority, power, and mere convenience. Vanity and desire are rampant, and they color the whole of contemporary life. Powerful egoists pursue their own purposes with disdain for the welfare of the little people, and many little people, because of some foolish desire, allow themselves to be taken in by advertising and commercials. Ultimately, desire is the motive force behind contemporary civilization.

We must, of course, take into consideration that the desire for material well-being motivated many of the genuine advances in our culture and civilization.

In looking back over the postwar history of Japan, it is interesting to see how the things people most wanted changed about every five years. In the hungry years just after the war, the main thing people wanted was enough food. This was also a period in which attitudes toward sex changed drastically.

By around 1950 there was enough food to go around, and the sex liberation movement had achieved most of its immediate goals, so people turned their attention to clothing. This was about the time when nylon and vinyl compounds appeared on the market. By about 1955 the sights were lifted, and we went through half a decade when what everybody aimed at having was a washing machine, a vacuum cleaner, and a refrigerator. These came to be spoken of in those days as the "three sacred regalia," a wry reference to the sacred regalia of the Imperial family.

After 1960 high-level economic production had raised the standard of living to the extent that people's attention turned to the problem of what to do with their free time. So-called leisure stocks enjoyed a boom on the Tokyo Stock Exchange, and the spirit of hedonism was implanted more deeply in the popular mind.

The desire was primarily for material goods and possessions, and a good deal of vanity and pride were involved. It was, naturally enough, at about this time that there began the concerted campaign to go beyond legitimate consumption and create artificial needs—a campaign, you might say, to create greed and acquisitiveness—and it is still going on today.

In a way, then, the postwar history of Japan reflects a development from the primal desire to keep alive through the desire for food and sex, the desire for clothing, and the desire for modern conveniences, to the present state, in which there is a complicated pattern of desires for all sorts of material possessions, including many that are not really needed. It would not be generalizing too broadly to say that in our time the desires of the Japanese people as a whole have shifted from the state of Hell or Hunger to a state of Animality or Anger.

It could also be said, I should add, that in this age when we have reached a fairly high level of affluence, it has become easier for people to enter the states of Humanity and Rapture.

In progressing from the age of hunger that followed the war to a point where people are being urged not only to consume, but to overconsume, it seems likely that there are now more people whose selves display the characteristics of the state of Rapture. From the Buddhist viewpoint, we might say material culture which encourages the proliferation of desires has as its aim the creation of a state of Rapture. Certainly many people, though perhaps unconsciously, regard the state of Rapture, represented by material affluence, as an ideal condition.

To carry on the analogy, the aim of Western materialistic culture appears to have been to employ all the means of science and all the resources of the earth to build palaces for this state of Rapture. In the days when the futurologists were still predicting a rosy future for mankind, it seemed almost as though this was being accomplished, but now we are beginning to see that the palaces were built on sand. Today, they seem on the verge of collapse, along with the civilization that built them.

What it amounts to is that we have traded spiritual affluence for material affluence. We find that the threat of nuclear war is still with us, that pollution, along with uncontrolled use of resources, has thrown nature out of balance and that not only nature, but society, culture, and humanity are all threatened with extinction.

Having enjoyed prosperity for a short while, we seem destined soon to find ourselves standing amid the ruins of our palaces. When our vision of paradise has faded, the agonies of Hell and the sufferings of Hunger, which we so lately left behind us, will still be there waiting. So long as people remain small-minded and prone to conflict, our future looks dismal indeed.

Our material culture has aimed at satisfying everybody's desires, but it threatens instead to pull us all back into the Four Evil Paths. What is the reason for this? Is there some basic evil inherent in our civilization?

In order to answer these questions, I shall have to refer once again to the Buddhist attitude toward desire. We have seen already that in Buddhism the first six of the Ten States of Being are included in the World of Desire. This is as much as to say that there are six fundamental categories of desire.

In Buddhist demonology, at the very peak of the World of Desire sits the Devil of the Sixth Heaven. It is not without significance that devils dwelling in the Sixth Heaven enjoy the life of supreme Rapture by controlling and making use of others. Indeed, it is the very act of controlling and utilizing others that is the source of this Rapture. The anthropomorphic aspects of this concept need not trouble us unduly, for the point is that there is an intrinsic evil in desire of any sort.

In our own lives, the happiness we derive from asserting our control over nature and over other people has a certain diabolic quality. There is a demon residing in all desires, but the utmost manifestation of this evil being in human life is our urge to control and dominate others.

In this connection, it is interesting to recall Nietzsche's view, wherein the desire for authority is at the root of all human desire. From the psychoanalytic viewpoint, Adler was also interested in the human lust for power. Both views are close to Buddhism. Most people think of Freud in connection with his emphasis on the sex urge, and indeed this is a vital element in his system of psychoanalysis, but in reference to what we have been saying about desire, I think it is pertinent to note that in his late years Freud was concerned not only with the instinct to live, but with the instinct to die, which is to say, the instinct to destroy life.

The essential character of the Devil of the Sixth Heaven is that he deprives other beings of life. He destroys life, saps the strength of others to survive, and drives living beings into the agony of Hell. This is the essence of evil. Confronted with such phenomena as the desires for authority, dominance, or possession, Buddhism looks into the inner depths of human existence to discover the true form of the Devil of the Sixth Heaven, who is manifest in these various types of desire.

In *On the Curing of Disease* (*Jibyō-shō*), Nichiren Daishonin says, "The benighted quality of man's original nature is manifest in the Devil of the Sixth Heaven." This means, in effect, that the demon of desire is inherent in life itself. I believe that the "benighted quality" in man's original nature is identical with the element of egoism that resides within the self. We might call this the demon of life.

This demon of life, manifesting itself in the form of the demon of desire, assumes control of the self and causes it to work exclusively for its own benefit. The self, unless liberated from its own benighted quality, manifests itself in egocentric ways. If this benighted quality gains strength, even the intelligent, conscientious self in the state of Humanity or Rapture can be transformed into a self-centered, self-righteous being.

As we have noted, the world has made use of science and technology to create an environment in which our wants and desires would all be fulfilled. Thanks to this effort, many people have felt we were creating a society in which people could live as true human beings, no longer deprived of their basic right to live or forced to suffer hunger. We fulfilled our basic desires and then set about fulfilling our emotional desires, and then we found social and cultural desires involving authority and possession. Now we discover we have unleashed the demon of desire inherent in human life and we ourselves are its victims.

The maneuverings of this demon threaten to destroy both nature and human existence. The root of our problem is in the selves of contemporary men, men who abuse authority, who seek power and glory, and who have lost their sense of humanism. Such intelligence as these men have is used for diabolical purposes, rather than to sustain and support mankind's wisdom and creativity. Such wisdom as they have is employed for the purpose of destroying others.

The benighted quality in human life has been allowed to transform desire, the self, and intelligence into forces for evil, and it is now securely in control of government, capital, business, and science. Perhaps this quality even rejoices at its ability to bring about wars, pollution, and the destruction of nature.

Lives corrupted by the evils of contemporary civilization are destined to fall helplessly into the state of Hell or one of the other evil paths, for they continue to repeat what we call the Transmigration in the Six Lower States (*rokudō rinne*). So long as people remain in the World of Desire, they pass ceaselessly from one of these states to another. These states are the realm of the Devil of the Sixth Heaven, which is to say the benighted quality of man's original nature. Even the self in the state of Humanity is powerless before this original egoistic force.

The self has much more freedom in the states of Humanity and Rapture than in the Four Evil Paths, but even so, it is a freedom, an independence, that on further analysis can be seen to be granted to the self from without. It is conferred upon the self by nature, or by heredity, or by social environment, and it can be revoked as easily as it is bestowed.

It is true that the self in this state lives by its own will. But it is a creature of the miraculous workings of the universe and our earthly surroundings. Without these, the self would not appear in this world. Therefore, the process whereby we are born on this earth as human beings—human selves—demonstrates the unfathomable beauty and compassion of the cosmic life-force. We should be eternally grateful for the potentiality we as human beings have been given. Having been born in this state and with the potentialities of Humanity, it behooves us to polish the intelligence and goodness within us so as to procure for ourselves true independence and freedom. We must live in such a way as to express our gratitude for the compassionate nature of the cosmic life that has given us our being. We must work hard for our own improvement and remain constantly on guard against the demon of desire and the evils of our benighted quality, for it is by overcoming them that we may escape from the limitations of the first six states and enter the provinces of the Four Noble States. I do not mean by this that we can separate our lives entirely from the Six Lower States. On the contrary, we continue to live and work in the midst of our demon-possessed culture and society. But by raising ourselves to the higher states of existence, we enable them to lead others toward these states and gradually to break down the destructive forces of greed and egoism. The path to the Four Noble States is the revolution and reformation of the human being. This is also the path leading out of our current cultural dilemma.

LEARNING AND REALIZATION

The Four Noble States of existence are those of Learning, Realization, the Bodhisattva Nature, and Buddhahood. Of these, the first two are ideals of Hinayana Buddhism. Traditionally the state of Learning is the condition of the *shrāvaka* (in Japanese, *shōmon*), a disciple who has acquired understanding by listening directly to the teachings of the Buddha. The state of Realization is the condition of the *pratyeka-buddha* (in Japanese, *engaku*), a being who has experienced a type of enlightenment by recognizing the Twelve Links of Dependent Causation. Mahayana Buddhists, while recognizing these two states as noble, do not class them among the most sublime forms of existence. They are states of partial, or specialized, enlightenment.

These two states are definitely more advanced than the first six. In *The True Object of Worship* (*Kanjin no Honzon-shō*), Nichiren Daishonin says, "The fact that all things in this world are transient is perfectly clear to us. Is this not because the worlds of the two vehicles are present in the world of Humanity?" This points up the distinguishing characteristic of the self in the states of Learning and Realization, which is that it recognizes the impermanence of all phenomena. This recognition does not exist in the state of Rapture, for in that state we are prone to have an abnormal sense of our own well-being, power, or importance. Rapture comes from having achieved something for which we have hoped and prayed, and we are apt to be so overcome with happiness that we are deluded into thinking our happiness is permanent. When it slips from our hands, as it always does, we sink once again into the evil paths.

Not that it is impossible for a person in the state of Rapture to go on to the next two states, but in order to do so one must not be too distracted by the changes going on about one. To enter the state of Learning or Realization, one must look back and reflect on the path one has followed. If one reflects long enough, it soon becomes evident that all existence is constantly changing and consequently impermanent in nature. I consider the self in these two states to be a reflective self—a self that stops, looks back, and tries to understand the meaning of things. This process may often involve introspection, which is the process of reflecting upon one's own innermost life and its relationship to the cosmos. While the self in the states of Humanity and Rapture typically focuses its attention on its surroundings, the self in the states of Realization and Learning turns its eye to its own inner life and to the deeper meaning of human life as a whole.

When the light of true wisdom is focused on the inner life, the strength of this light is such that it also illuminates the external world to some extent. If the self has a deep knowledge of one instant in life, it also understands the past and the future and the principle of Three Thousand Possible Worlds in Every Life-moment.

In discussing the state of Humanity, I used the analogy of the self floating in the great sea of life that gave birth to it. The self in this state may have spiritual qualities and desires, such as intelligence, goodness, determination, and compassion, but it lacks the strength to fix its attention on the undercurrents and the depths of the sea of life. It is too busy trying to stay afloat on the waves. Without knowing the undercurrents and the depths, the self is likely to be sucked under.

If we continue this analogy, the self in the state of Learning or Realization is able, while coping with the rough waves of life, to direct its intelligence and the light of its insight down into the depths of the sea. This is a reflective self which becomes a source of light on the surface casting a ray down into the depths. This light is composed of wisdom, goodness, love, and the will to know the truth. Its strength and color vary with the individual.

I might offer as another analogy the efforts of the astronomer, who by probing with his rationality deep into a distant sector of space discovers facts that lead to the hypothesis of an expanding universe or other theories of the cosmos as a whole. Again, intensive scholarly research into particular fields, such as economics and politics, throws light on human culture in general. Most important, perhaps, is that when the reflective self looks in upon its own inner nature, it sees the never-still waves of desires and emotions and energies constantly at work there. Its light may even enable it to see within these things to the ultimate workings of the cosmos. When it does, the self will naturally understand the impermanence of all things and the futility of becoming absorbed and lost within this impermanence. In the states of Learning and Realization, the self first acquires true independence from the transient worlds about it. As it comes to understand the sea of life and the greater cosmic sea of which the sea of life is a part, it learns to move independently but in harmony with the motions about it.

The ability to enter the states of Learning and Realization is not necessarily present in everyone. There are selves from which no amount of reflection or introspection can elicit light. And even when the light of intelligence or wisdom appears, it may vary greatly in strength and quality. There are children, for example, who have an immediate insight into mathematical problems or a natural talent for music or art, but can cast little light on other activities. And there are many adults who have strong analytical talents, but not a trace of human compassion. In the latter case, of course, the self is more likely to be in one of the Three Evil Paths, rather than in the state of Learning or Realization.

Education and rich experience can strengthen the light given off by the self. The original designation for the state of Learning, after all, referred to disciples who had listened to the teachings of Shakyamuni and were thus educated in the Buddhist Law. It is important for us to try to absorb learning and wisdom accumulated by those who went before us, for such knowledge can be an important part of the light we wish to cast. It may well be that scholars and students are in a better position to enter the state of Learning than other people, but the state is also open to anyone who tries sincerely and humbly to understand the experiences and the wisdom of others. The factor preventing so many students and scholars from entering the state of Learning is undue pride in their own superior knowledge. For all too many, the purpose of acquiring knowledge is self-aggrandizement, and when this is the case, the true state of the self is not that of Learning, but that of Hunger. The person who has genuinely entered the state of Learning is concerned instead with enriching his spirit.

In the everyday world, the person who does what is required of him in his work, but nothing more, is not likely to enter the state of Learning for this state belongs to the people who regard their work as an opportunity for inner growth and development. Learning does not derive from putting in time and drawing a salary; it comes from applying oneself and increasing one's spiritual stature, whether by learning from others or by acquiring personal experience. The time-server, whether he works in an office, a factory, or a research institute, is usually not far from the state of Animality or Anger.

In addition to the state of Learning, we must look here more closely at the state of Realization. Realization is a type of enlightenment that suddenly comes to one in connection with some phenomenon observed or experienced. The phenomenon might be anything: the splendid workings of the universe, a flower blooming in a field, a bright star in the sky, a small item in the newspaper, the evil odor of a polluted river, the sting of photochemical smog, in short anything at all that brings one insight. Realization is the sort of inspiration that often comes to artists, scientists, or great leaders, and it is likely most of the great pioneers of human civilization have experienced this state. An almost perfect illustration is furnished by Descartes, who while sitting before the hearth on November 10, 1619, suddenly received the insight embodied in his famous statement "*Cogito ergo sum.*" This moment of enlightenment led to the development of the philosophical foundation underlying most of Western science.

Kierkegaard is also said to have changed his whole outlook on life as the result of an insight he had one day in 1835. He wrote in his diary that a sudden, frightening upheaval had taken place in his mind, forcing him to view all phenomena in a new light. He called the experience his "great earthquake."

We all have similar experiences. We can pass by the same scene day in and out for weeks and months without paying much attention to it. Then one day we suddenly see new meaning in it. In the case of Descartes and Kierkegaard, a sudden inspiration changed their whole concept of life. This is a typical example of Realization. Suddenly the light from their selves shone on what had been a world veiled in darkness, and a new territory of the spirit spread out before them. To describe this as a "great earthquake" is no exaggeration.

But these sudden revelations would not have come to Descartes or Kierkegaard if their earlier studies and efforts to understand the universe had not prepared them for the moment of truth. The state of Realization is achieved through one's own strength, by virtue of studying and pondering over the life of the cosmic entity. After one has prepared oneself to receive the truth, it may be revealed in the simplest, most commonplace object or experience. And then it spreads out through one's whole life, enabling one to participate creatively in the total life-existence.

Revelation or inspiration of this sort may be more common to artists and thinkers than to ordinary people, but it is by no means theirs exclusively. By studying and by refining the self, anyone can prepare himself for the instantaneous insight that reveals the truth. I do not exclude from the state of Realization the housewife who after struggling against the seemingly endless rise in food prices suddenly sees a way to make ends meet, or the husband who having been nagged for years by a jealous mother-in-law suddenly figures out the right thing to say to her, or the businessman who suddenly sees exactly how to handle a project he has wanted for years to undertake. One may even see an element of Realization on the part of the victims of the Minamata disease in Kyushu, who, despite the long wranglings of the university professors over the causes, knew instinctively from the beginning that the disease came from poison in the water they were using. Among everyday ordinary people, the polishing and refining of the soul that leads to Realization can produce peace and happiness within the home as well as important changes in social, political, and economic structure.

Even in that part of the state of Rapture that lies within the World of Formlessness the self experiences the happiness of fulfillment, expansiveness, and creativity. But this depends largely on the external condition. In the state of Learning or Realization, the level of happiness ascends to bliss because of their own efforts to attain it.

The happiness of the person in the state of Learning comes from learning to apply the truth one has learned from books and other people to one's own life. The happiness of the state of Realization is greater than this, because it is essentially achieved or created by oneself. The degree of happiness depends not so much on the amount of effort spent in the search as on the extent to which the self has been polished, disciplined, and refined.

From a different viewpoint, we may say that the self which casts light on the world has as its life-space the entire area that it illumines. When the light is strong, the person in the state of Learning or Realization has a whole world of his own. This is as true of the wage-earner in his company and the housewife in her home as it is of the great scholar in his ivory tower. The scope of the life-space will vary with the individual, but it is much greater in these two noble states than it is in the first six states, and the influence of the self on others is correspondingly broader.

It will doubtless seem curious to some that although the states of Learning and Realization are full of wisdom, happiness, and a type of enlightenment, they are condemned by Mahayana sutras. In *The Opening of the Eyes* (*Kaimoku-shō*), Nichiren Daishonin quoted sutra passages which place these two states below the Three Evil Paths. What is the meaning of this paradox?

Basically, there are two explanations. One is that people who have arrived at these lofty states tend to become infatuated with their own importance. The other is simply that these people have not yet advanced beyond the level of selfishness. The two states are arrived at by the path of arduous study or by contemplation, and this in itself implies the person who has reached these states has strong ambitions and strong determination. The power of a strong will can indeed produce a kind of enlightenment, replete with intelligence and spiritual riches. It is all too easy, however, for people who have experienced this kind of enlightenment to assume that it is the highest enlightenment of all, that they themselves have arrived at the source of life and the cosmos. But at the moment they forget their own limitations, the evil element of life lying deep within them comes once again into action. The situation is much the same as in the state of Rapture, where at the moment of fulfillment, the demon of desire asserts itself.

We often see such things happen. There is, for example, the medical research scholar who discovers an important scientific truth and proceeds to try to make it his own personal property. As likely as not, he will try to conceal his discovery from his fellows, who now seem to him merely a collection of dullards. Foolishly forgetting the whole purpose of medicine, he guards his secret until the day when he can present it to an eminent scholarly society to rounds of thunderous applause. His revelation has produced within him not true enlightenment, but vanity and selfishness.

This is the path so often followed by those in the states of Learning and Realization. Actually, in these states there still remains in the depths of life an element of delusion, and even if the self attempts to put its superior intelligence to work for good causes, it cannot without further enlightenment overcome the evil of desire and the passion for self-aggrandizement. There is no final escape here from the "benighted quality of man's original nature," which lurks much deeper than reason, conscience, or compassion. The self in these states emits light, but it is spotty and imperfect light, confined within definite limits.

At best, the aim of the person in these states is the development of his own character and the improvement of his own personality. In a sense, he may enjoy success, but the aim is essentially selfish, and the enlightenment he achieves does not carry him to the true source of life.

Partial enlightenment leads to pride and the loss of humility. To the partially enlightened one, only his vision is correct. He is thenceforth deaf to other ideas, no matter how perspicacious they may be. He tends to criticize for the sake of criticizing or simply to bolster his own self-satisfaction. When this happens, he may well block the path to happiness for others as well as for himself.

The second reason the states of Learning and Realization may be considered inferior to the Three Evil Paths is the sheer power people in these states so often possess. As a rule, they have superior knowledge, intellect, and insight, and though these qualities may enable them to do more good than others, they also may enable them to do more evil. If people in these states become possessed by the evil within the self, they can cause far more destruction of life in the cosmos than can lesser mortals. The difference is like that between an ordinary gun and the hydrogen bomb. The analogy is not chosen at random, because nuclear weapons and the sciences upon which they are founded are the results of revelations on the part of immensely learned scientists. An ordinary man possessed by evil may inflict a gun or a sword wound, but the great scientists of our time have made it possible to destroy all of mankind in one swift stroke. It does not help matters that people in the states of Learning and Realization are typically more independent-minded than ordinary people, for this means that if they set forth on the wrong course, it is difficult to lead them back to the right one. A small change in the surrounding circumstances may lead ordinary people from one to another of the first six states, but the people in these two states are not so easily influenced. They "stick to their principles" and are not shaken by the criticism of others. All too often, it has been such people who have led us into the tragedy of war.

We have then the paradox with which we began. Learning and Realization, in the abstract sense, are sources of knowledge, wisdom, and intellectual power. They may enable a person to shed much light, both intellectual and spiritual, upon his surroundings. They may even lead him close to the understanding of the true cosmos, but at the same time they do not of themselves relieve the self of the innate "benighted quality of man's original nature." For that reason, they can in some circumstances lead ultimately not to the essence of cosmic life, but to its antithesis, to suffering and destruction. The road to the ultimate truth of the universe lies in the two noble states of Mahayana Buddhism, the Bodhisattva Nature and Buddhahood, to which I shall now turn.

BODHISATTVA NATURE AND BUDDHAHOOD

Recently I read a book called *Rediscovery of Man* (*Ningen no Saihakken*), which was the record of a symposium held by Dr. Hideki Yukawa, Prof. Kikuya Ichikawa of Dōshisha University, and Mr. Takeshi Umehara. Among other things, these three learned gentlemen talked about the Buddhist concept of compassion (*jihi*).

Dr. Yukawa observed that the word contains an element meaning "sorrow," which sets it apart from the Christian "love thy neighbor," the Confucian "benevolence," and the common concept of philanthropy. Prof. Ichikawa suggested sorrow meant sharing someone else's sorrow. Dr. Yukawa countered that in order to share someone else's sorrow, one must of necessity experience sorrow oneself. Mr. Umehara concluded that compassion was a special kind of recognition involving identification with the fundamental state of another person's life.

At this point, Prof. Ichikawa asserted that compassion of this sort is completely lacking in the modern world, but Dr. Yukawa made the following reply: "I cannot at all agree that it does not exist. You yourself told us about the baby chick you had. With me, it was a baby granddaughter. Before the child was born, I had never considered how it would feel to be a grandfather, but the minute she came into the world, I realized what strange and mysterious feelings people are capable of. . . . As far as I was concerned, my granddaughter was completely without fault. The feeling may be illogical, but it is nevertheless real. Somewhere inside me, this feeling had always been present, but I had been unaware of it until the child was born. You should understand because of the baby chick."

Prof. Ichikawa's baby chick was one his daughter had bought as a pet. It seems that the chick became very sick, and the whole family was so concerned about it that Prof. Ichikawa, who is the president of his university, was calling up from school to ask how it was. Eventually the bird died, and Prof. Ichikawa observed that his family was nearly as shaken up as they had been when his mother had died a year earlier.

Here are two homely examples indicating the extent to which even a great scholar might become emotionally involved in the affairs of a child or a small animal. In my opinion, the absorption they experienced is the essence of Buddhist compassion.

Nichiren Daishonin wrote in the *Orally Transferred Teachings* (*Ongi*

Kuden), "Great compassion is like the empathy of a mother for her child; it is the compassion of Nichiren and his disciples." Perhaps the most important similarity between Buddhist compassion and motherly love is that both are completely unconditional, as was Dr. Yukawa's affection for his granddaughter. True motherly love is selfless—nothing, not even the life of the mother herself, must stand in the way of the child's growth or happiness. There is almost perfect empathy. When the child is happy, the mother is happy; when the child is troubled, the mother is troubled; when the child is ill, the mother suffers the most.

But notice that I said "true motherly love," because counterfeit forms exist. We all know cases of the domineering mother whose ostensible concern for her child is really concern for her own ego. And we also know mothers whose obsessive concern for their own offspring leads them to adopt hateful attitudes toward the children of other people. But the existence of counterfeit forms does not alter the basic similarity between Buddhist compassion and maternal love.

As Dr. Yukawa suggested, we are all born with the propensity for compassion, though we often do not become aware of it until some particular occasion arises. In *The True Object of Worship* (*Kanjin no Honzonshō*), Nichiren Daishonin wrote, "Even a heartless villain loves his wife and children. He too has a portion of the Bodhisattva world within him." This means simply that everyone is by nature capable of compassion.

In the state of the Bodhisattva Nature, the whole of life is sustained by the strength of compassion. By strength of compassion, I mean a strong energy that flows from the inner depth of human life. This includes intelligence, goodness, wisdom, and a host of spiritual desires. The self is in the state of the Bodhisattva Nature when all of its better qualities—wisdom, love, determination, and valor—are fused together with the energy of compassion for the sake of doing good to others. The character of the Bodhisattva is completely altruistic, and the essence of the Bodhisattva's compassion is to deliver others from suffering and grant them happiness.

Altruism is the most effective means of self-realization and self-perfection. Doing good for others is the best way to improve one's own character and to find greater happiness for oneself. In order to relieve another person of suffering, one must become identified with that person and share his suffering. As Mr. Umehara put it, this is a case of "identification with the fundamental state of another person's life." This very identification is the means of practicing compassion, and the acts of relieving others of suffering and giving them happiness lead to the perfection of the self. The Bodhisattva plunges into the midst of his fellow human beings and attempts to take their sufferings and sadness upon himself. His compassion is an active, practical force. This is the essential difference between the Bodhisattva and the sages who have not gone beyond the states of Learning and Realization. The Bodhisattva is capable of deep thought and sure insight, but these are inseparably joined with practical action.

Nichiren Daishonin's *Causality within the Ten States of Life* (*Jippōkai Myōinga-shō*) says: "The Bodhisattva, moving among the common people within the Six Paths, humbles himself and exalts others, attempting always to direct evil against himself and good toward others." In other words, the realm of the common people is the scene of the Bodhisattva's action, and his attitude is one of humility and self-sacrifice.

The Bodhisattva must have the courage to challenge the very sources of evil. Without courage, he cannot hope to overcome the diabolical elements within himself and others, and unless he defeats these evil forces, he cannot give happiness to others. One Buddhist scripture, the *Butsuji-kyō-ron*, goes so far as to say that the meaning of the word Bodhisattva is "courage."

By helping others, the Bodhisattva qualifies himself, for the act of doing good to others suppresses the latent egoism within him, enabling the light of wisdom within his self to illuminate the evil darkness in the world around him.

The word Bodhisattva is composed of *bodhi*, meaning "the wisdom of the Buddha," and *sattva*, meaning "sentient beings." I shall go into the meaning of sentient beings more thoroughly later, but for the moment, suffice it to say that the term refers to living things, and particularly to human beings. The wisdom of the Buddha is the wisdom the Bodhisattva gains by devoting all his actions to the benefit of others. The self in the state of Realization lacks this ultimate wisdom, because its efforts are self-centered, and there consequently always remains the possibility that egoism will assert itself. With the Bodhisattva, the struggle to help others is in itself a frontal attack on the egoistic self.

The fundamental life-energy flows out as wisdom and compassion, and the self, which is all too inclined toward egoism, gradually assumes a more altruistic character. It grows in wisdom, judgement, and conscience, and its spiritual desires grow stronger.

The chief Bodhisattvas written about in the scriptures are Monju, Kannon, Yakuō, Fugen, Miroku, and Myōon, each of whom represents a particular ideal. Monju stands for wisdom, Kannon for mercy, Yakuō for medicine, Fugen for learning, Miroku for compassion, and Myōon for music and the arts. Although their attributes and the activities in which they engage are different, they are alike in that their every deed is directed toward the benefit of others.

Nichiren Daishonin regarded these Bodhisattvas to be provisional Bodhisattvas. The scriptures prescribe for them fifty-two stages of practice, the last of which is Buddhahood. To attain each of these stages requires an immensely long time and tremendous effort and steadfastness. It is doubtful whether this path of austere practice can be followed by ordinary mortals. To attempt the ascetic path and then fall by the wayside does not lead to a realization of Buddhahood.

The way for the ordinary person to accomplish the ultimate goal of Buddhahood is to cultivate himself through altruistic deeds, thereby causing the energy of compassion to gush forth from the innermost source of life. One must reform oneself both outside and in. The continued performance of actions that benefit others will evoke the life-force necessary for a full and happy life.

In contrast to the provisional Bodhisattvas, Nichiren Daishonin spoke of the Bodhisattvas of the Earth (*jiyu no bosatsu*) described in the Lotus Sutra. Manifestations of the ultimate Buddha, they spring forth from the earth to spread the Buddhist Law throughout the universe. They are the people who in the everyday life of this world challenge the forces of evil by devoting themselves wholeheartedly to promoting the good of others, at the same time causing the infinite energy of compassion to well up within themselves.

The four leaders of the Bodhisattvas of the Earth are Jōgyō, Muhengyō, Jōgyō, and Anryūgyō.* Of them a passage in the *Orally Transferred Teachings* says: "In explanation of the Four Great Bodhisattvas, the ninth volume of the *Fushōki* [a commentary on a work by Chih-i] states, 'The Four Leaders spoken of in the Lotus Sutra represent four virtues: self, eternity, purity, and happiness. Jōgyō represents the self; Muhengyō represents

*Jōgyō, who represents self, is Viśiṣṭacārita in Sanskrit. Jōgyō, who represents purity, is Viśuddhacārita. Muhengyō and Anryūgyō are, respectively, Anantacārita and Supratisthitacārita.

eternity; Jōgyō represents purity; Anryūgyō represents happiness."

This cryptic statement calls for further explanation. In my interpretation, the virtue of self means the strengthening of the self to the point where it can withstand challenges from without and turn difficulties into opportunities for growth. Eternity means a firm belief in eternal life, together with an effort, founded thereon, to press forward ceaselessly toward the goal. The sense of eternity strengthens one's confidence that through compassionate action one can change one's neighbors, one's surroundings, one's country, or even the whole world.

Purity means a clean and brilliant life, in which evil or egoistic instincts are powerless to sway one. A life devoted to helping others, rather than pursuing one's own advantage, sheds the light of true wisdom and intelligence. Happiness means the joy of living on an unshakable foundation rooted in the life-force of the cosmos.

In *The True Object of Worship* (*Kanjin no Honzon-shō*), Nichiren Daishonin writes, "Jōgyō, Muhengyō, Jōgyō, and Anryūgyō represent the world of the Bodhisattva within our lives." This means we can create for ourselves the life condition of the Bodhisattva. We can be Bodhisattvas of the Earth, confident of ourselves, full of the infinite life-force, and dedicated to helping others. The life of a Bodhisattva of the Earth is a truly humane, compassionate, and joyful life.

The Bodhisattvas of the Earth are described in the sutra as "welling up" out of the ground. "Ground" here is figurative for the ultimate foundation of life, which is the Mystic Law. The Mystic Law, which is the cosmic life-force, is identical with the life of Buddhahood. It is because Buddhahood manifests its power in tangible form in every activity of our daily lives that we are able to act as Bodhisattvas of the Earth and dedicate our full energies to achieving happiness for other people. When we become Bodhisattvas of the Earth, we manifest the Buddhahood that is within us. Furthermore, the life condition of the Bodhisattvas of the Earth, unlike that of the provisional Bodhisattvas, is exactly the same as that of Buddhahood. It is only the Buddhahood within ourselves that can make possible the four virtues of the Bodhisattvas of the Earth.

This brings us to the highest of the Ten Worlds, Buddhahood, a state which cannot be described completely in words. Nichiren Daishonin wrote, "Buddhahood is the most difficult to demonstrate. But since you possess the other nine worlds, you should believe that you have Buddhahood as well." The fact is that Buddhahood must be experienced to be understood, and the best description possible must of necessity be only a partial discussion of the Buddha's attributes.

There are ten traditional titles for the Buddha, and they try to express the infinite wisdom, power, and compassion of Buddhahood. The name Buddha itself means the "enlightened one," whose wisdom encompasses the fundamental principles of the universe and all life within it. Another title is Nyorai, or in Sanskrit, Tathagata, which implies that the Buddha's every word or action is in unity with the cosmic life. This means understanding the eternity of life, hence enlightenment.

Titles such as Shōhenchi, Jōgojōbu, Zenzei, and Myōgyōsoku emphasize the Buddha's understanding of people. Shōhenchi in particular means the Buddha's wisdom to understand all things of the whole universe impartially and regard them with equal compassion. Jōgojōbu suggests strength sufficient to lead all men to happiness and to triumph over any diabolical element lurking in the depths of the self. The word literally means a titan who "harmonizes and controls." By controlling evil impulses, he harmonizes all elements in the universe, and by constantly performing acts of compassion, he revolutionizes his own life.

Zenzei, literally "going to the world of enlightenment," originally meant extinguishing all desires and attaining nirvana, but since desires cannot really be eradicated, we must interpret this to mean that they are sublimated—made sublime—and directed toward the benefit of others. The Buddha, possessing the strength to control desires, causes them to seek satisfaction in altruistic acts.

Myōgyōsoku, "one who sees the eternal truth clearly and walks the way satisfactorily," emphasizes the unity of wisdom and practical conduct. Perception of the eternal truth comes from actual experience. The Buddha explores all spheres of life, including man's activities, his society, culture, politics, economics, and education. The Buddha knows why the price of commodities soars, why our educational system is not functioning properly, why there is difficulty over land prices. Another name for him is Sekenge, "he who understands the ways of the world." This emphasizes that the Buddha is not an utterly remote being, but one who understands all aspects of real life here and now, and one who knows how to solve current problems.

This gives rise to the name Tenninshi, "leader of gods and men." In this case, we can interpret "gods" to mean "leaders," and "men" to mean "ordinary people." The Buddha is able to lead all men, whether they are leaders or ordinary people. He captures their hearts with his wisdom, his strength, and his compassion. His actions receive their approval and support, so that he may be described by the name Ōgu, which means "worthy of oblation." Obtaining donations indicates that one has won admiration and support from the people. This is emphasized by the name Seson, the "world-honored one."

In the world of today, a person in whom the Buddha nature is expressed is at first glance a man with good sense. He is a well-integrated person, with a strong sense of responsibility and strong faith, friendly toward others and able to think flexibly. Above all, he is rich in compassion, wisdom, and creativity.

People in the state of Buddhahood may not seem very exceptional at first glance. Their activities are those of the Bodhisattvas of the Earth, who are able to lead benevolent lives because they are supported by the life-force of the Buddha, by the Earth that is identical with the Mystic Law. The Bodhisattvas of the Earth understand all aspects of life in the universe and the principles underlying them. They understand too the society around them and the trends of the times. By drawing on the cosmic life-force, they find their own life-force increasing limitlessly. And their freedom extends throughout the universe.

Their joy is the joy of joys: an indescribable ecstasy welling up freely and spontaneously from the innermost essence of life. There is joy in living, joy in the earth, joy in the trees and flowers, joy in the faces and movements of people—everything is colored with joy. Each breath, each wave of the hand, each step brings joy and gratitude and a love for life. Birth, old age, illness, and death are no longer sufferings, but a part of the joy of living.

The light of wisdom illuminates the entire universe, destroying the innate benighted nature of man. The life-space of the Buddha becomes united and fused with the universe. The self becomes the cosmos, and in a single instant the life-flow stretches out to encompass all that is past and all that is future. In each moment of the present, the eternal life-force of the cosmos gushes forth as a gigantic fountain of energy. In the life of Buddhahood, each present moment contains eternity, for the entire life-force of the cosmos is compressed into a single moment of existence. A person in the state of Buddhahood is hardly conscious of the passage of physical time, because his life is full and happy at each instant, as though he were experiencing the joy of living throughout eternity.

The provisional Bodhisattvas attempt to draw on the immense power of the Buddha by engaging in self-discipline and self-sacrifice, but the ascetic practices of these beings, as outlined in the sutras, is too severe and impractical for ordinary people. Nichiren Daishonin's Buddhism teaches that the only way to evoke the Buddhahood inherent in all men is "to believe." To believe, that is, in the Mystic Law, which is itself the cosmic life-force. According to the *Orally Transferred Teachings*, all forms of life in the universe, regardless of their temporal condition, are essentially directed toward the Buddha nature. In other words, the most fundamental urge in life is an aspiration for Buddhahood—the impulse to combine with the cosmic life-force and to return to its essence. This urge, which is stronger than love, hate, reason, desire, or even the wish to live, is at the innermost core of each individual life, and often it is veiled by the workings of desire and ignorance. Still it is there, in all beings, and it is the most basic human craving of all. I call it *religious desire*, or the *instinct for the ultimate truth*.

This impulse can be given full play only by following the practice expounded by Nichiren Daishonin, which is based on an understanding of the Buddha nature in all beings, and which is aimed at achieving oneness with the universal life-force. In the religion of Nichiren Daishonin, every person can become a complete realization of the Buddhahood within his own self.

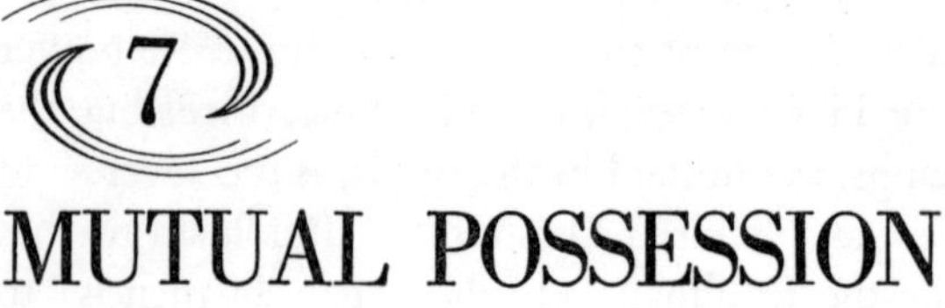

MUTUAL POSSESSION

EXAMPLES FROM LIFE

Let us consider for a moment what happens when a moving picture film or a video tape is stopped at a given instant, as it often is in replays of sports events. From seeing the action stopped at the critical moment in a sumo wrestling match or a horse race, we may decide which wrestler or which horse won. Though not the whole story of the race or the wrestling match, this is extremely important information.

If you could suddenly stop time at precisely three o'clock this afternoon, you would find people caught in all sorts of attitudes and conditions—men walking on the street, women about to give their children a mid-afternoon snack, children about to eat the same, a scholar in the middle of writing a word, a gymnast in the middle of a flip, a driver seemingly about to run a red light.

This is the kind of picture we get of people's lives when we look at them with respect to the Ten States. A dejected-looking man on the sidewalk might at that moment be in the state of Hell; a cheerful-looking one, in the state of Humanity; the children waiting for their snack, in the state of Hunger; the scholar, in the state of Learning; the gymnast, in the state of Rapture; the driver, in the state of Anger. We can even anticipate to some extent what will happen when time starts moving again; the children will probably eat their snack; the scholar will probably finish writing the word; the gymnast will probably complete his flip. But this is only a matter of probability, for we cannot be completely sure of what will ensue. The driver may run the red light, but he may brake to a sudden stop. The gymnast might fall on his face; the scholar may decide he is writing the wrong word and mark through the part of the word he has written. There is no way of knowing, just as there is no way of knowing but that any of the people might instantaneously change from his present state of being to another.

The theory of the Ten Worlds can be used to describe the condition of a human being at a given point in time, but we have to keep in mind that this condition is constantly changing. No matter how slow the life-flow becomes, it does not cease completely. Accordingly, the state in which the self exists can and often does change from moment to moment.

If a person in Hell goes to a different state, will it be the state of Hunger, or Animality, or some other state? If we could find some rule or formula for determining this, we would have a principle of life. Such a principle exists in Buddhism in the form of the theory of the Mutual Possession of the Ten Worlds, *Jikkai Gogu*, which states that each of the Ten Worlds contains all the others. Even if one state dominates at a given moment, the others are nevertheless present, and any of them might be dominant in the next moment. Thus the whole realm of existence is potentially available to the self at any time.

I think it would be best to illustrate this with examples from real life. In selecting these examples, I have tried to avoid both the bizarre and the drab, for cases of excessively rapid change would seem too remote from ordinary human experience, and cases of little or no change would hardly illustrate my point. Too, I have had to consider the privacy of the persons involved.

The first instance that came to mind was the case of Dr. A, who has a clinic in a small country town. I first learned of Dr. A about ten years ago from the newspapers. At that time the Japan Medical Association decided to call a strike and refuse for a stated time to treat patients. Dr. A, however, ignored the strike order, went right on taking care of the sick, and was written up in some of the newspapers. Personally, I do not think doctors should allow anything to take precedence over their duty to their patients. In some ways I sympathized with the doctors' claims, but I feel basically that when medical men go on strike, they reveal a serious character defect. Dr. A, it seemed to me, was doing no more than what was right.

Still, it required courage for him to defy the majority, and it is even more remarkable that he was extremely embarrassed by newspaper articles praising him for his stand. Most people would have had a satisfying sense of vindication, but Dr. A felt he had done nothing to be proud of. As he explained it, he lives in a place where in the winter he sometimes has to wade through several feet of snow to visit a patient. There were times in the past when he failed to visit some of the more distant houses. He still felt guilty about this, though he had by this time found in the philosophy of Buddhism a way of overcoming his weakness. Dr. A has since written, "It now makes me happy to forget about myself and work for the sick." It is apparent that his early struggle with himself led him to a philosophy that enabled him to win out over his baser instincts and, when the occasion arose, to reject the medical association's call for a strike.

Perhaps an even more striking story concerns an athlete whom I shall call B. B went to the Helsinki Olympics on the Japanese gymnastics team, but while he was there, through no fault of his own he injured his Achilles tendon seriously and was forced not only to retire from the Olympic Games, but to give up gymnastics altogether. His whole life had been wrapped up in the sport, and after this horrible blow, he lost all hope. He took to drink and was constantly getting into brawls with the ruffians into whose society he had drifted. Before long he began taking sleeping pills, and eventually his addiction landed him in a mental hospital. After a while, he was released, but in no time he was back on the pills and had to be rehospitalized. This process repeated itself until B happened to learn of the teachings of Nichiren Daishonin. He decided to turn to Buddhism for support. Then, bolstered by his new faith, he resolved to kick the habit, and for six days he went through the torture of withdrawal. Later he wrote: "On the seventh morning, I woke up surprised. The sun was streaming in through the window. It was almost blinding. I thought, 'I've been asleep!' I got up and opened the window wide. A soft breeze blew in. I took a deep breath, and the air was delicious. It was early summer, and I saw green leaves on the trees, cabbages growing in a nearby field, a little dog running down the muddy road. I had won! I had survived withdrawal!"

He learned what true happiness is. Since that time, he has found a new life and a new mission for himself training younger people in gymnastics. Far from regretting the fame and honor his accident cost him, he now feels training young people is an activity really worth devoting a lifetime to.

My third example is neither as dramatic as the story of B, nor as involved with personal ethics as that of Dr. A. It is the story of how a girl and her mother suffered through years of bitterness and sorrow to a happy ending.

The girl, whom I shall call Emi, contracted infantile paralysis when she was two years old. This was just after the war, and practically no Japanese hospital was able to offer proper treatment for the disease. For four years, the girl underwent acupuncture, massage, and hot-spring treatments. By the time she was old enough for school, she had learned to walk but she remained badly crippled. Walking for her was a process of moving the right foot forward and then dragging along the helpless left leg. Her mother, painfully watching the girl struggle along, was afraid the handicap might give her a warped attitude toward life, one that, as frequently happens, would grow worse as the girl grew older. Fortunately, the mother's fears did not come true. The girl grew up with a singularly happy and cheerful disposition.

When Emi finished high school, she found a job in a nursery, but after only two months she was fired because she could not walk well enough to be sent out on errands. Despite this cruel blow, the girl bravely found herself another job and stayed with it until her marriage five years later. During this time she so impressed the president of the company that he resolved to employ more people with physical handicaps. He now has quite a few working for him.

Each of these three persons attacked his own problem in his own way, but the three are alike in that they all found happiness through their own efforts. They carried out for themselves a human revolution, and their stories strongly suggest that if the self is sustained by confidence and a sense of mission, the goddess of fortune smiles. Let us now consider these stories in connection with the theory of the Mutual Possession of the Ten Worlds.

I can picture Dr. A in the days just after he started practicing medicine in his little country town. He has just finished his day's work and is beginning to relax when someone arrives and asks him to go out on an urgent call. What changes occur in the state of Dr. A's existence?

Since he has just finished work and is relaxing, the chances are that he is in the tranquil state of Humanity. Or if his last case that day was a sick child who is responding beautifully to his treatment, he may even be in the state of Rapture. All this changes after the urgent call, however, and the state he enters depends on how he reacts to the call. Perhaps in those days Dr. A was angry at the person who had the lack of consideration to get sick at just this time. Unable to blow off steam in his caller's presence, he retreats to the kitchen and says a few sharp words to his wife. He is in the state of Anger.

But maybe he keeps everything to himself and suffers in silence, cursing himself for being unable to do anything about the situation. If that is the case, he is in the state of Hell. Or perhaps he is hungry or thirsty or sleepy, and the necessity to go out prevents him from satisfying his instincts. He is then in the state of Hunger. Let us hope he does not tell the caller to come back tomorrow and then sit down calmly to dinner, for that would mean he is in the state of Animality.

Suppose he was in Rapture and the call threw him into Hell, but before he started out, someone else arrived to say that the patient was much better, so that there was no need to come after all. In a flash, Dr. A is in Rapture again.

The question is where was Rapture while Dr. A was in Hell? Did it cease to exist? No, because it was back minutes later. Did it take a trip somewhere? No, again because it was back too soon. Did it move into some other person? No, because it is unthinkable that the state of one's self can be transferred willy-nilly to another. Then what happened to it?

The answer is that it was there all the time. The state of Rapture is inherently present in Dr. A's life, even though he may be in the state of Hell, or the state of Hunger, or the state of Anger. It is there in undiminished form, but Dr. A has lost sight of it for the moment.

The state of Rapture cannot be perceived by the five senses and is therefore not a part of what we would normally describe as "existent." At the same time, it is palpably not "non-existent," for the self experiences it. One can only solve this paradox with the Buddhist concept of *kū*. The state of Rapture, having dominated Dr. A's self for a time, retires as it were to a latent, potential state of *kū*, from which it can emerge again at such time as the proper circumstances prevail. No time at all is required for either change. Indeed, "change" may not be the proper word, for the state of Rapture is always there, and the only question is whether it is in a manifest state or a potential state.

What is true of the state of Rapture is true of the other states as well. In the case of Dr. A, for instance, we have seen that after experiencing the state of Rapture, he was capable, dependent on the circumstances, of entering the state of Hell, the state of Hunger, or the state of Animality. That is because these states are dormant while the state of Rapture is manifest. The higher states are also always present. If upon hearing of the urgent call, Dr. A had completely forgotten himself and become entirely absorbed with the need for getting to the patient and healing him, he would have been in the state of the Bodhisattva Nature. Or if he had had a sudden inspiration as to exactly the right treatment for the patient, he might have entered the state of Realization or Learning for a time.

In sum, no matter what state the self is in, the other states are all present in potential form. Even when Dr. A was in the state of Rapture, that state remained partially in the potential, for there was a possibility of further joy becoming manifest at any moment. Potentially, all of the Ten States are simultaneously contained in a moment of Rapture, and the same is true of the other states. To take an extreme case, the potential for Buddhahood is present even in the state of Hell, and vice versa.

The Chinese priest Miao-lo (717–82), the ninth patriarch of the T'ien-t'ai Sect, wrote that "Both the life and environment of Hell exist within the life of the Buddha. On the other hand, the life and environment of the Buddha do not transcend the lives of common mortals." Here Hell should be understood in a broad sense to represent the nine states other than Buddhahood. The meaning is that Buddhahood contains the nine states and each of the nine states contains Buddhahood. The agonizing torture of Hell exists within Buddhahood, and Buddhahood in its glorious entirety exists in one human thought.

In *The True Object of Worship* (*Kanjin no Honzon-shō*), Nichiren explains the theory of the Mutual Possession of the Ten Worlds by reference to the Lotus Sutra: "Chapter two, *Hōben-bon*, of the Lotus Sutra states that the Buddhas appear in this world 'to open the door of Buddha-wisdom to all beings.' This refers to the fact that all the nine worlds possess the realm of Buddhahood. Chapter sixteen, *Jūryo-hon*, states: 'Since I attained Buddhahood, an unimaginably long period has passed. The length of my life is infinite aeons. My life has always existed and shall never end. Men of devout faith, once I also practiced the bodhisattva austerities and the life which I then acquired has yet to be exhausted. My life will last yet twice as many aeons from now.' Here the sutra refers to the realm of Buddhahood which includes all of the other nine worlds." The language of the Lotus Sutra is full of difficult terminology that I do not wish to go into here, but with regard to its exposition of the Ten States, Nichiren Daishonin comments quite succinctly that each of the Ten States contains all of the Ten States.

People have tried to chart the Ten States. In one scheme they are arranged vertically with the state of Hell raising its head above the surface of life, and the other states placed in descending order with Buddhahood at the bottom, rooted in the innermost life of the cosmos. In another diagram, the Ten States are arranged horizontally, like the cars of a freight train. Some conceive of the Ten States as being interwoven like the threads of an intricate brocade.

The interwoven idea is probably the closest to the truth, but ultimately even this is an oversimplification, and the idea of the states succeeding one another in an orderly vertical or horizontal procession is quite wrong. The Ten States are neither linear, nor circular, nor square, nor spherical. As in the case of *kū* (latency), it is impossible to give a complete description; one must fall back on saying what the totality of the Ten States is not. Since the Ten States are in the realm of *kū*, they are free from any limitations. They may be magnified to infinity or reduced to the size of a geometrical point.

In trying to explain the inexplicable *kū*, I sometimes fall back on the analogy of radio waves, which are all around us in great profusion, but can be detected and sorted out only by the use of receiving devices. Under normal circumstances, these waves do not interfere with each other, though they occupy the same space. They show, therefore, that two or more things can be in the same place at the same time, as is the case with the Ten States in the condition of *kū*. The analogy should not be pressed too far, however, for there are cases in which radio waves jam each other or become distorted. It should always be remembered that neither the Ten States nor *kū* can be considered as spatial concepts.

Nevertheless, the idea of the radio waves is helpful as an illustration of innumerable potential forces operating continuously and simultaneously, ready to be made manifest by the turn of a switch or a dial. Over the years I have observed that even when people come to understand the difference between *kū* and nothingness, they tend to think of *kū* as being static, whereas in fact it is filled with dynamic life-flow and charged with all sorts of energy. In the state of *kū*, the Ten States are pulsating constantly as they form the total substance of our lives. One after the other, often with bewildering speed, they become manifest in our overt or spiritual life, each state carrying within it the potential emergence of any of the other states. All states are constantly changing and developing, whether as manifest forces or potential forces.

The constant shifting from one state to another is caused by our fundamental life-force, which makes possible the fusion and interaction of the various states. If the pulsating life-force were artificially halted for a moment, like the crucial moment in the television replay of a sumo wrestling bout, we would see each of the Ten States separate from the others.

Sutras other than the Lotus discuss the Ten States separately, revealing no insight into the principle of mutual possession. Since these sutras expound the concept of *kū*, it seems curious that they do not at least arrive at the idea that the first nine states are fused together, even if the tenth state, Buddhahood, is separate. They do not, however, and the explanation can only be that their view of life is imperfect. They tend, in their efforts to analyze, to stop life for a moment. When this happens, the Ten States fly apart, because it is the continuity of the life-force that fuses them to begin with, and if this is interrupted, even for the purpose of analysis, the reality of life cannot be completely observed. The situation is similar to scientific experiments in which the act of performing the experiment alters the object or process being investigated. To avoid this fallacy, we have recourse to the theories of the Three Perceptions (*santai*), the oneness of matter and spirit (*shikishin funi*), and the inseparability of life and its environment (*eshō funi*), all referred to earlier.

Reading what I shall refer to as pre-Lotus scriptures, one can find only a partial and therefore distorted explanation, rather than a whole and perfect view of life. (I use the term "pre-Lotus" in the developmental, rather than the chronological, sense.) One sees the Ten States only in a hypothetical, non-viable form. Without the sublime teaching of the Lotus Sutra, it is impossible to synthesize the Ten States into a meaningful, living whole.

To sum up, none of the Ten States is separated from the others. They are all fused into one entity of life, eternally in action even though they may be in the potential condition of *kū*. Each of the states contains all the others, and at any time may be supplanted at the manifest level by any one of them. Theoretically, it is possible that the Ten States might manifest themselves in ascending order from Hell to Buddhahood, but that is a matter of accident. The unfortunate truth is that there are far too many people who experience only the Three Evil Paths or the first six states and remain completely ignorant of the states of the Bodhisattva Nature and Buddhahood.

THE HUMAN REVOLUTION

The question of how to live among the Ten Worlds in such a way as to enjoy true happiness can be answered, I think, by analyzing the experiences of the gymnast whom I have referred to as Mr. B and the young crippled girl named Emi.

As an up-and-coming young gymnast participating in the Olympic Games, B was doubtless in the state of Rapture, but in the one instant of his accident—he lost balance in a jump and fell to the mat, injuring his Achilles tendon seriously—he was thrown into the depths of Hell.

As despair overcame him, his only relief from his Hell of drinking, quarreling, and sleeping pills was an occasional moment of Anger, when he fought with those around him. But the energy of Anger soon dissipated itself, leaving him once again in Hell. It was as though he was on a leash that constantly pulled him back into the depths of despair. The palace of his previous Rapture had been replaced by a prison.

Had the ambition of his days as an athlete remained, he might have gradually pulled himself up into a higher state, but deprived of hope, he turned to drugs and eventually had to be placed in a mental hospital. Partially cured and released, he soon relapsed, and by and by it became clear that no matter how hard he tried, and no matter how hard the doctors and nurses tried to help him, he was trapped in a vicious circle.

B was bound to the sufferings of Hell because of a lack of will power, though we should note in justice to him that once a person becomes addicted to drugs, he must have exceptionally strong will power in order to give them up. B happened to have a changeable nature; he lacked perseverance and he tended to be extremely nervous. At the same time, he had good traits, among them a rather strong urge to enjoy life and enough sense to try a hospital cure. Like all other people, B had both good and bad points, but after his accident his over-all personality seemed directed toward Hell.

Personality, which we may define as the totality of an individual's behavioral and emotional tendencies, is closely related to the Ten States of Being as are habits. Personality traits and habits that are on the surface good, can, if the wrong state of being dominates, work for evil. Had B moved into the state of Bodhisattva Nature, as he eventually did, his eagerness to enjoy life would have worked to the benefit of the world, but in the early stage after his accident, before he had discovered Buddhism, the same eagerness led only to drinking, carousing, and otherwise engaging in self-destruction.

There are people who are affectionate, discreet, rich in feeling, strong in will power, modest, clever, able to plan, or able to lead. All of these characteristics are good in themselves, but if the state of the person who possesses them is not good, they can cause great evil to others. A strong will if combined with an overriding ego, can cause much more trouble than a weak will. Similarly, a person with an excellent ability to make plans can, if driven by unbridled ambition, make plans for the conquest and oppression of the world. Or if he is too self-absorbed, he may be satisfied just to make plans and never carry them out.

The various traits and habits a person possesses or forms go together to make up his personality, and most personalities tend to manifest one of the Ten States more often than the others. In the case of B after his accident, the personality was prone to seek Hell. Without Buddhism he would very likely have to live largely in the state of Anger or Animality.

The formation of personality and habit, I think, occurs largely in the vast sphere of the unconscious, but physical constitution and mental disposition also play a part. When a person's body is charged with physical vitality, he can often overcome defects in his character or turn them to good use. In B's case, so long as he was in top physical condition and successful as an athlete, his lack of will power showed up as a rather likable unassertiveness. His personality at that time was directed toward the states of Humanity and Rapture, and even when he fell into the Three Evil Paths for a time, he had sufficient physical strength and spiritual power to return to his normal state. He probably even experienced Learning or Realization at times when he had mastered a new gymnastic technique or worked out a new routine. Basically, he was happy, and lapses from this state were neither frequent nor lengthy.

The basic tendency of one's personality is not limited to one state. There are many people who go through a cycle of Hell, Hunger, Animality, and back again, and many others who rise beyond these states to Anger, Humanity, and Rapture before plunging back into Hell. Some relatively fortunate souls alternate more or less between Learning and Realization, sometimes with the unfortunate result that they lose contact with the world around them. There is a rather famous story about a Japanese professor who was so absorbed in his studies that he failed to notice the Russo-Japanese War (1904–05). One night he asked a student why there was such a ruckus outside. When the student replied, "We won the war, sir," the professor asked, "With whom were we fighting?"

But to return to B, his story illustrates how a relatively minor accident can change the whole direction of one's personality, causing what seemed at worst to be minor foibles to become major defects. B's somewhat retiring manner emerged as a lamentable lack of will power, and his urge to win or succeed led no longer to Rapture, but instead only to Anger. A circumstantial change had altered the direction of his personality, and only through a religious experience was he able once again to direct it toward the higher and happier states. The dramatic human revolution B underwent strengthened his will sufficiently for him to break his drug habit and aspire to happiness by devoting himself to the training of others.

Such a sudden transformation does not occur as frequently as the gradual transformation achieved by Emi, who discovered true Buddhism when she was a child and who was gradually strengthened by her faith.

When Emi was found to have polio, her parents were in that state of extreme distress we call Hell, and so, in a different sense, was Emi. During her childhood, Emi must have experienced all of the Three Evil Paths, and it seems quite possible that after she became fully conscious of her handicap, she lived in the state of Hell, which is understandable in view of the burden she would have to bear throughout her life.

But Emi began at an early age to understand that the Bodhisattva Nature and Buddhahood existed within her, and she was able to overcome difficulties as they arose, thus developing into a charming, happy girl who brought peace and joy to her parents and stood as a model for other polio-stricken young people.

After finishing high school, Emi, like B, suffered a frightening shock. To be fired from her job because of lameness was no less a blow for her than B's accident was for him. Emi, however, was better prepared, because she had been carrying on her own human revolution for many years. The shock was not strong enough to alter the basic direction of her personality. A weaker person, with no faith to fall back on, might well have cursed the injustice of life and turned his back on society, but Emi did not give up. She had spirit and vitality, which came from having early in her life taken Buddhahood as her standard and goal.

When a human being bases his life on Buddhahood, he can do more than just endure suffering. Experiences in the lower states of existence become opportunities for growth. Pain and sorrow become sources of sympathy and compassion for others, for in the last analysis only those who have experienced suffering can sympathize to the full with a fellow sufferer.

Human suffering has a dual nature. It can become either a cause for misery or an incentive for further growth. If we despair in the face of suffering, we are lost, but if we consider it an opportunity for self-development and self-improvement, we find our experience enables us better to lead others to happiness. When we do this we are manifesting the state of the Bodhisattva Nature.

Those who have experienced the state of Hunger acquire deeper gratitude for the resources and the food with which the earth provides us, and they learn greater compassion for those who lack food and for nature itself. Similarly, those who have struggled in a society where the Law of the Jungle prevails and where hatred, jealousy, and conceit are commonplace are all the better equipped to understand the stupidity and vanity of Animality and Anger. Their awareness enables them to help others to confront their egos and recognize the futility of their selfish desires.

This is all part of the theory of the Mutual Possession of the Ten Worlds. When one has taken Buddhahood as the basis for life and has recognized that all the other nine states are contained within Buddhahood, then each of these states, from the basest to the most lofty, can become an impetus for one's personal human revolution. Conversely, it is impossible to make Buddhahood the basis of life without accepting the raging turbulence of the other nine states, for they are coexistent with it.

Let me offer a simple analogy. As human beings, we have the power to digest food and assimilate it into our bodies or convert it into somatic energy. We cannot live without food, but if our digestion is weak or defective, certain foods can damage our bodies badly. Food is like the influences from the nine states; our digestive power is like the Buddha nature. If we are healthy and have a good digestive system, everything we eat is properly assimilated or discarded, and we flourish and grow. In the same way, when Buddhahood is operating inside us, we can even transform experiences in the Three Evil Paths into causes for further growth. These experiences will not weaken us, but will actually strengthen the functioning of our Buddhahood and give it greater stability.

For the person who bases his life on Buddhahood, the agony of Hell is a broadening experience, for it strengthens his identification with other suffering people. Hunger, when satisfied, serves to enhance his gratitude for the bounties of nature, the fruits of the earth, and the life-force of the universe. When he realizes he has been acting on animal instincts, he acquires better knowledge of the means for eliminating such stupidity from the world. When he has experienced and overcome hatred against other men, he learns to direct this hatred against the evils rampant in our society and civilization.

The personality founded on Buddhahood can enjoy the states of Humanity and Rapture without fearing the devil who waits in ambush at the high point of Rapture. Having experienced Learning or Realization, he is able to overcome his own egoism and dedicate his wisdom to achieving happiness for others. And, of course, the altruistic deeds of the Bodhisattva never fail to solidify the basis of Buddhahood in his life. In short, if one's life is based on Buddhahood, all one's activities in any of the other nine states serve to strengthen and ennoble that nature. One accepts all the influences from the outer world and changes them into stimuli for self-development. By helping others to live, one achieves one's own transformation. This is the principle of human revolution based on the theory of the Mutual Possession of the Ten Worlds.

The fundamental way to establish Buddhahood as the basis of one's life is simply to practice Buddhism in everyday life and conduct. Continuous, tenacious practice of Buddhism is the means of absorbing the cosmic life-force and making it flow energetically within one's own life. Actual practice brings out the Buddhahood dormant in the depths of our lives. By this I mean actual practice in the nine states of real life, for they are the field in which Buddhahood operates as an active force.

Buddhahood is endowed with infinite compassion and wisdom. The wisdom of Buddhahood penetrates to the diabolic nature that subverts life and tries to destroy it. The compassion of Buddhahood furnishes the energy to overcome this evil force. In this way, the wisdom and compassion of Buddhahood become manifest in the nine states. And as they act in these states, they themselves are nourished and increased, strengthening the Buddhahood within us.

We must, for this reason, not seek to avoid the difficulties and challenges of the nine states, but rather meet them head on and overcome them, thus turning them into valuable experience. If one attempts to avoid difficulties, one misses the chance to develop and improve oneself. To avoid trouble is no more than to succumb to the illusions of the nine states. The mark of Buddhahood is the ability to meet all challenges and turn them into good.

Indeed, the person who bases his life on Buddhahood seeks out new difficulties and new challenges that need to be overcome for the sake of the world, as well as for his own growth and development.

A person who undergoes suffering of his own volition is manifesting Buddhahood. By plunging into the world of suffering and conflict, he achieves his own transformation and experiences independence in the fullest sense of the word. A person in the state of Buddhahood is willing to give up wealth, high social status, or a brilliant career to confront the Three Evil Paths or live in the midst of the six transmigratory states.

From the superficial viewpoint, happiness is achieved in the states of Humanity and Rapture, and the four lower states hold only suffering and misery. But from the broader viewpoint, so long as Buddhahood is manifest within one, one can find happiness, independence, and fulfillment in any of the Ten States, including the Three Evil Paths.

The suffering undergone to attain Buddhahood is desirable suffering, and the sorrow endured to attain Buddhahood is desirable sorrow. The way to Buddhahood lies in suffering and in sorrow.

THE INFINITE POSSIBILITIES OF LIFE

A movie that made an extremely strong impression on me was *Johnny Got His Gun*, the story of a young man very badly maimed in World War I. Most people would have considered him unlucky to be alive. Caught in a bomb explosion, he had lost both arms and both legs, his eyes, his ears, his nose, and even his tongue. In the middle of his face was a gaping hole, and to all intents and purposes he was nothing but a lump of flesh, kept alive by the marvels of medicine. Although his mind was clear, he had no way of making this known, nor any way of knowing at first where he was or in what condition. Basket case is too mild a description. He was no better off than a vegetable. The question the movie posed is, "What is it to be alive?"

The movie was based on a novel of the same title by Dalton Trumbo, published just after the beginning of World War II. I do not know whether it is true or not. Even if it is not, the question it asks is pertinent to our times, for we have among us many "vegetable people"—some wounded in wars, others damaged by pollution—whom science is able to keep alive, but is unable to cure. Just what is a human being in such a state? What is his life-force?

In the movie, the only sensory perception the soldier retained was tactile. He could tell when someone touched his body, and he could respond by moving his torso slightly. When he first regained consciousness, he had no awareness of time or space, but after a while he acquired a certain feeling for time by becoming sensitive to small changes in the temperature. As the room became a little warmer, he knew it was after sunrise and another day had begun. Gradually, he learned to tell approximately what time it was.

But what a hellish existence! No means of knowing one's surroundings, no ability to express oneself, not the slightest freedom of action. How does the mind cope with a situation like this? Although we are constantly dependent on others, we like to think we are self-supporting. We like to conceive of everything in the universe in terms of its relationship to us. We like to try to manifest ourselves in some ideal form. What happens when the human brain is forced to live almost entirely to itself, as in the case of this soldier?

Life for such a person must be a dreamlike condition, for all activity is mental, as in a dream. In the story, the soldier drifted between memory and fantasy. At first he could only respond passively to external stimuli. When he felt the pain of his wounds he imagined rats gnawing away his body. Later, he was able to analyze external stimuli more rationally. One day it came to him in a flash of comprehension that something he had taken for a rat moving on his chest was in fact a finger drawing letters. He made out the words "Merry Christmas!" and tapped his head against his pillow in Morse code to show comprehension. The nurse who had written the greeting on his chest patted his forehead in response. The soldier had not only reestablished contact with the world, but, as it turned out, begun a warm friendship.

Deprived of limbs, sense organs, and the ability to speak, the soldier still had life. Deep within him the flow of universal life continued, and the energy of his life-force welled up to sustain him. Having found a way to communicate, he began to perceive what his condition was and even in that near-lifeless state to make the most of the little that remained. The movie was in this sense a powerful drama of human victory.

In another sense the soldier's story is a warning to our times. The contemporary age is a mechanized culture, in which the individual human being tends to become no more than a unit in a gargantuan mass society. People think they are free, but more often than not they act in response to a flood of propaganda. Feeling small and powerless inside, they can find no way to express themselves. They talk about "overthrowing the establishment," or "bucking society," or "breaking away from it all," but these ideas themselves usually stem from fads.

From a broad viewpoint, modern man in his industrial society bears a close resemblance to the dismembered soldier. Limbs he has, and even all his sense organs, but he has lost his sense of identity and his independence of mind. More often than not, he cannot even see that his existence is passive and negative. In this respect he is worse off than the soldier. To lose your identity and not even know it is to lose your innate value as a human being.

In our present mechanized society, it is more important than ever to recover the treasure inherent in every human life. An inner human revolution cannot be detected visually, but in the long run it makes itself strongly felt in the external world, gradually transforming the environment.

We must try to understand how a human life can work actively in the external world to which it is inseparably related. How can it influence its environment while at the same time constantly renewing itself? As a clue to the answers to these questions, I would like to move on to the theory of the Ten Factors of Life, which explains how the Ten States become manifest and how their movements are modulated.

APPEARANCE, NATURE, AND ENTITY

The Ten Factors of Life, *jūnyoze*, are enumerated in the *Hōben* chapter of the Lotus Sutra. It says: "The realities of the laws of the universe can be understood and shared only by Buddhas. These laws are appearance (*nyoze-sō*), nature (*nyoze-shō*), entity (*nyoze-tai*), power (*nyoze-riki*), influence (*nyoze-sa*), inherent cause (*nyoze-in*), external cause (*nyoze-en*), latent effect (*nyoze-ka*), manifest effect (*nyoze-hō*), and consistency from beginning to end (*nyoze-hommatsu-kukyōtō*)."

The word *nyoze*, which we render in English as "factor," literally means "thus" or "like this." It is the consistent, unchangeable entity comprising all changing phenomena—the essential nature of life. Our lives are constantly changing from one to another of the Ten States of Being. The Ten Factors offer a way of examining and comprehending any momentary condition of life in its true and exact form, whether that life is in Hell or in Rapture or in any other of the Ten States. The Ten Factors clarify the elements which combine to cause us to change from one state to another.

Of these ten, the first three, appearance, nature, and entity, are somewhat different in character from the other seven, for they are concerned with life itself, while the others are concerned with the functions or workings of life. The last factor, consistency from beginning to end, is also of a different order from the others.

As noted in an earlier chapter, a passage from Nichiren Daishonin's writings that deals with the first three of the Ten Factors says, "Appearance means the appearance of our bodies in color and form." That is, appearance represents the physical aspects of life. In a discussion of the Three Thousand Possible Worlds in Every Life-moment (*Ichinen Sanzen-riji*), Nichiren Daishonin writes, "Appearance is the body. Volume Two of the *Profound Meaning of the Lotus* [*Hokke Gengi*, a work by Chih-i] explains that 'appearance is manifest externally and can be discerned by looking.' " This first factor, therefore, is the tangible, physical aspect of life.

As pointed out earlier (in chapter three), the factor of appearance corresponds to Provisional Perception (*ketai*), whereas inherent nature corresponds to the Perception of the Latent (*kūtai*), and entity corresponds to the true Perception of the Middle Way (*chūtai*). The Three Perceptions (*santai*), as well as the first three factors, are inseparably united, and each contains the other two. We cannot form an accurate view of life until we understand appearance, nature, and entity first separately and then as an interrelated and unified whole.

This is implicit even in the first statement quoted above from Nichiren Daishonin, for to refer to "the appearance of our bodies in color and form" implies there is more to the truth than can be perceived visually. Nichiren Daishonin was hinting at a deeper inner force that causes the phenomena we see.

The expression "can be discerned by looking" should be taken in a broad sense to include that which we can analyze empirically—everything we can see by scientific means, such as the inner workings of the human body. In recent years, medical science has revealed and analyzed to a fine point most of the important elements of the body, including the internal organs, the muscular system, the nervous system, the circulatory system, and even the cells that make up these systems and organs. We know now that the various types of information determining one's basic character are contained in the hereditary genes within these cells, and science has made it clear how these genes retain and transmit information. We know about the fundamental substances called DNA (dioxyribonucleic acid) and RNA (ribonucleic acid), and researchers are now exploring life on the molecular level. All this knowledge is included under the heading of appearance.

It is even possible today to include in this category certain physical aspects traditionally classed as part of the spiritual realm. Brain waves, for example, can be regarded as belonging to the world of appearance, though there are deeper spiritual elements, such as wisdom, disposition, and character, that belong in the realm of what we have called nature.

Of this second factor, Nichiren Daishonin said, "Inherent Nature is our spirit." This statement is expanded in his discussion of the Three Thousand Possible Worlds in Every Life-moment, where he writes, "Inherent Nature is the mind. Volume Two of the *Profound Meaning of the Lotus* says, 'Inherent Nature is eternal and unalterable.' " On the surface, this statement is a little puzzling, because we all know a person's mind and spirit change in response to his experience and environment. Still, patterns of spiritual activity vary with the individual person, and something about each person distinguishes him from all other people. Whether this is called personality or individuality or nature, it is the unchanging element without which a particular person would not be himself.

It is true, of course, that a warped personality is difficult to change, but that is not the meaning of "eternal and unalterable" in this instance. Many adults change their attitude toward life, and all children undergo great physical and mental changes in the course of growing to maturity. Still, each child is the same person when he grows up as he was when he was born, and it is this unchanging quality that is meant here by "inherent nature." This nature is not identical with the "true self," which is the ultimate reality of life, but we may think of it as the temperament, personality, or wisdom of the "true self."

Entity is a composite. It includes and is included in both appearance and nature. In a word, it is the essence of life. Nichiren Daishonin said, "Entity is the entirety of ourselves." Nichiren Daishonin's discussion of the Three Thousand Possible Worlds in Every Life-moment says, "Entity is the combination of our body and our mind. Volume Two of the *Profound Meaning of the Lotus* says, 'Totality signifies principal substance.' "

Entity does not exist apart from our life, but within it. Indeed, it *is* our life, for it encompasses both the physical and the spiritual aspects of our existence. But when Nichiren Daishonin says, "Entity is the combination of our body and our mind," he does not mean that it results from merely putting the two elements together, but rather that it is the function integrating them into one entity. It cannot exist apart from them, nor them from it. The mind and the body are inextricably interwoven within the entity. This is one of the greatest insights of Buddhism.

THE DYNAMICS OF LIFE

If the first three of the Ten Factors comprise the physical and spiritual states of life, the next six may be said to comprise the ways in which life operates. They are concerned, in effect, with the dynamics of life.

Of the fourth factor, power, Nichiren Daishonin's treatise on the Three Thousand Possible Worlds in Every Life-moment says, "Power is both body and mind. Chih-i's *Great Concentration and Insight* (*Maka Shikan*) states, 'Power is the working of endurance.' " The "working of endurance" is somewhat obscure, but I think we can take it to mean using inner strength to cope with life's changes. The inner strength with which life is inherently endowed is the power that a life consisting of appearance, inherent nature, and entity possesses. Power is potential energy and can be directed toward one's surroundings—in short, it is the motivating force of a person's life.

Nichikan Shonin, the twenty-sixth High Priest of the Nichiren Shoshu, states in his *Threefold Secret Teachings* (*Sanjū Hiden-shō*), "Power is the ability to act in each of the Ten Worlds." Power, therefore, is the capacity of life to live. In physics, a distinction is drawn between force applied from without and force inherent in an object. In Buddhism external forces are recognized as "external causes," and power refers only to internal power, the vital energy inherent within human life.

Power is made up of both physical energy and mental energy. In a broader sense, we might say that power includes such factors as economic and political power in society, since such power stems ultimately from the activating energy latent in each individual life. Mental energy includes a wide variety of powers, such as affection, the will to live, the ability to perceive the truth, or compassion, which motivates one to help others. Power varies in form and degree in different states of human development.

In the state of Hell, a person has little motivating force, and such potential as he has is directed largely against his own life. This is not a creative potential, but one working toward death. In the states of Hunger and Animality, physiological energy is conspicuous in the form of instinctive desires; in the state of Anger, force is evident as a lust for power; in the states of Humanity or Rapture, power is apt to appear in the form of conscience or reason, while in the states of Learning and Realization, it manifests itself as superior judgement or intuition. In the states of the Bodhisattva Nature and Buddhahood, all power is charged with compassion.

The life-force manifests itself in ways compatible with the Ten Worlds of our ever-changing lives. In general, it is obvious that power, or motivating energy, increases in strength and improves in quality from the lower to the higher states of existence, and if a person were to progress through these states one by one, he would gradually acquire the energy to resist domination by physical urges alone. In the higher states, he begins to display social, spiritual and psychic energies, and if he advances sufficiently, he acquires the power of compassion, which encompasses all other energies and directs them toward relieving others of suffering and granting them peace. Compassion is the supreme activation of the human life-force and the embodiment of the highest values in human life.

When power is manifest, influence, the fifth of the Ten Factors, is possible either physically or spiritually. Nichikan Shonin's *Threefold Secret Teachings* says, "Influence is the use of thought, word, or deed to create good or evil." Nichiren Daishonin's treatise on the Three Thousand Possible Worlds in Every Life-moment says, "Influence is both body and mind. Chih-i's *Great Concentration and Insight* (*Maka Shikan*) states, 'Influence is creating.' "

Influence, then, is the concrete manifestation or visible influence of power, with which it is inseparably linked. Having said that, however, I must add that, though linked, they are not necessarily always proportional to each other. In some cases, inherent power is great, but the resulting action is small; in others, the inherent power may be small, but the action large. This is no doubt due to the qualitative changes power undergoes from one state of existence to another. Action can be mental as well as physical, and its immediate influence may be apparent only in the innermost depths of human life, rather than in the world of phenomena. The reason Chih-i defined influence as "creating" is that it works to create values or anti-values.

Power, as manifest in influence, can result in either positive or negative values. If we think of it in terms of the physical law that to every action there is an equal and opposite reaction, then the action of which we are speaking is a reaction to some environmental influence. From a practical viewpoint, the important thing is how completely and effectively we manifest our inherent power in some form of influence.

The next four of the Ten Factors are concerned with causality, both latent and manifest. Power and influence are related to spatial concepts, but these four factors are concerned with the concept of time. The Buddhist idea of cause and effect is more subtle, but at the same time more satisfactory, than most other epistemological systems, because Buddhism places tremendous emphasis on the relationship of cause and effect.

Inherent cause, the sixth of the Ten Factors, is explained by Nichiren Daishonin as follows: "Inherent cause is mind. Chih-i's *Great Concentration and Insight* (*Maka Shikan*) states, 'Inherent cause is what gives rise to latent effect. It is also called karma.' " In the *Threefold Secret Teachings*, Nichikan Shonin writes, "Whether a later thought is good or bad depends on whether the earlier thought was good or bad. The earlier thought is the ingrained cause, or the inherent cause, and the later thought is the ingrained effect, or the latent effect." Although the words "earlier" and "later" are used here, they clearly refer to logical sequence, rather than time sequence, for inherent cause and latent effect exist simultaneously at the core of human life in the potential condition of *kū*. Whereas other systems usually connect cause and effect with the concepts of space and time, Buddhism teaches that both are immanent in human life and are coexistent and inseparable.

The *Shinjikan* Sutra says, "If you want to know past cause, look at the present effect; if you want to know a future effect, look at the present cause." Again there is an apparent reference to time, but what the text is saying is that ultimately past cause and future effect are to be seen in the present. A momentary action of one's life in the present automatically leads to the formation of the next moment, and the inherent cause and latent effect are at all times within oneself.

When we observe physical phenomena, there is a certain lapse of time between cause and effect. When we examine the reality of cause and effect within our lives, however, we find that all the causes formed in the past are condensed into the momentary existence of our life, as are their latent effects. This view is unique to Buddhism. The effects, which eventually will become manifest, are entirely our own responsibility. In order to achieve desirable manifest effects in the future, we must form a correct view of our present life and apply ourselves to the creation of causes that yield good effects. This idea of causality is what makes Buddhism a religion of human revolution.

Science pursues causal laws by an analytical and inductive approach. In a sense, then, scientists are concerned with the *how* of things, whereas Buddhism is concerned with the *why*. The two concepts are not mutually exclusive, even though they may be propounded on different levels. Causes and effects perceptible to physicists invariably accord with scientific laws of causality; even the uncertainty theory concerning the movements of elemental particles is a law of sorts, though perhaps one signifying no more than that the causes for the seemingly haphazard movement of the particles have not yet been determined. Causes are, after all, frequently more complex than they seem at first. It is, for instance, impossible to explain human behavior completely in terms of Freud's theories, though his contribution in introducing the principle of causality to the study of the mind was immense. More to the point, it frequently happens that one cannot explain contagious diseases as being caused solely by bacteria or viruses, because not everybody exposed to the germs contracts the disease. In this case, unseen internal factors often cause different people to react differently.

The approach of physicists is to examine perceptible phenomena. Ultimately, so is that of psychologists, for, although they seem to be working in a spiritual field, they are nevertheless basing their studies on observable mental phenomena. Psychology seeks to pursue its study into the subconscious and unconscious areas of human life, but psychologists will admit that there are many cases to which their laws of causality cannot be applied. Specifically, they are unable to explain that element of the human mind that is in the latent condition of *kū*.

Buddhism attempts to cast the light of wisdom into these deeper spheres of life, where the standards used in the study of observable phenomena lose effectiveness. Basically, scientific laws of causation are limited because they involve concepts of time and space, but the realms of the human mind and of human life transcend these limits. Only in the Buddhist theory of causality can we grasp the workings of the mind in the state of *kū*.

The seventh of the Ten Factors, external cause, is the environmental condition activating the inherent cause. It is a sort of catalyst and causes the life-force to move smoothly in response to the inherent cause. Human life never exists in isolation from an environment. Every activity of life occurs as a result of some external stimulus. At the same time, the true cause is the inherent cause within the human being. To give a very simple example, if someone hits you and you hit him back, the first blow is a stimulus leading toward the second, but it is not the ultimate cause. You can maintain that you hit the person because he hit you, but in fact you hit him because you are you. The real cause was inside of you, ready to be activated by an external cause.

The external cause has a dual nature. In one aspect, it acts upon one from without, but in another it becomes a part of one's inner life-force. It is converted into experience, and it conditions later responses to similar stimuli. It becomes, in short, an element in the accumulated inherent cause within one.

External causes can induce any of the Ten Worlds to become dominant in our lives, but, as we all know, not everybody reacts in the same way to the same stimulus. There are people who would not hit back, possibly out of cowardice or fear, but possibly out of benevolence and wisdom. External causes can be debilitating, but they can also be turned into character-building experiences.

Imagine a person who has just been told by his doctor that he is suffering from an incurable form of cancer. Such an external cause is very likely to evoke the state of Hell, and most patients, upon hearing it, would fall into the depths of misery. If, however, a person's life has been cultivated to a very high state, he may be able to say to himself, "This is a great trial. I must overcome it to achieve my human revolution." If he does, the tragic external cause becomes an opportunity for further growth and even further happiness. The manner in which the external cause is assimilated into the ever-changing inherent cause (and consequently the latent effect) is the key point. The principle of human revolution is that we are continually building and changing our inherent cause in reaction to external causes.

As already stated, inherent cause and latent effect exist simultaneously. What, then, is the distinction between them? Essentially, I think we can say that the inherent cause is the tendency that has built up within us until the present moment, and the latent effect is the future direction of our lives at this same moment. Various causes and effects are always present within the depth of human life in the potential condition of *kū*. Since we cannot actually perceive this condition, but see only its manifestations, cause and effect appear to us to be separated by a time interval, but the two are created and exist simultaneously. They are the two sides of the same coin. The instant a cause comes into existence, as it might from the assimilation of an external cause into the well of inherent cause, a corresponding effect takes form in a latent state. To take a concrete example, if you form a dislike for someone, that dislike produces a change in your life. It enters the accumulation of your inherent cause, and simultaneously a latent effect is born. If the person hits you, you are likely to hit him back, since the latent effect of dislike is already there, waiting to be acted upon. There is no way of knowing when a latent effect will become manifest. Once formed, it remains within us until the inherent cause is triggered by an outside stimulus.

This brings us to the ninth of the Ten Factors, which is manifest effect. Of this the *Threefold Secret Teachings* says, "Manifest effect, whether good or bad, is a visible response to inherent cause and latent effect." Thus in considering the manifest effect, we may think of inherent cause and latent effect as the combined cause. There is no need to distinguish between them in describing the manifest effect in the phenomenal realm. One vital point here is that the external cause does not create a manifest effect. Instead it activates the internal cause, which together with the latent effect produces the manifest effect. The difference is extremely important.

Manifest effect, being in the physical or phenomenal world, contains the elements of time and space, and there is an apparent time lapse between the moment of the cause and the appearance of the effect. In fact, however, the manifest effect actually comes into existence at the same moment as the cause, even though this may not be immediately evident. Phenomenal changes seem to be discontinuous in time, but in fact in the macrocosmic world they are continuous. The development of the manifest effect may be likened to a child's growth. Children grow continuously by the second, day, month, and year, but we notice the growth only after a fairly long interval of time. In similar fashion, the manifest effect begins to make its appearance at the moment when the cause comes into existence, but some passage of time may be required before we perceive it.

To sum up, the law of causality inherent in a human being's inner life can be understood only within the categories of the spiritual world, and the manifest effect exists only in the physical world. Inherent cause and latent effect are present simultaneously, but cannot be observed with the tools of physics or chemistry. From the psychosomatic viewpoint, inherent cause, latent effect, and manifest effect are inseparable, because of the principle that mind and matter are united in perfect harmony.

In order to understand the vital operation of continuously changing human life, we must not only examine the nature of life itself, but weigh external influences and how the inner self reacts to them. Since life is complete in each single instant, it is in one respect like a geometrical point, and our analysis of the direction in which it is moving is rather like a differential calculus problem in which we determine the slope of a curve at a given point by an increasingly minute examination of the factors immediately around the point. The direction of life at a given point in time can similarly be determined only by a detailed and increasingly minute examination of power, influence, inherent causes, external causes, latent effects, and manifest effects in operation in the vicinity of the point.

These first nine of the Ten Factors are the analytical tools we use to examine the workings of life and the laws governing these workings from moment to moment. It remains to synthesize the elements into a meaningful whole, and this is where the last of the Ten Factors, consistency from beginning to end, comes in. Of this, the *Threefold Secret Teachings* says, "Appearance is the beginning and manifest effect is the end. Consistency from beginning to end is the totality of factors."

THE PRINCIPLE OF INDIVIDUALITY

Since each of the Ten Worlds includes all the others, Buddhist writings speak of the One Hundred Worlds, that is, each world as it exists in each of the other worlds. Furthermore, since each of the Ten Factors exists in each of the Hundred Worlds, we have the concept of the Thousand Factors in the Hundred Worlds (*hyakkai sennyo*, *sennyo* being an abbreviation of *sen-nyoze*).

I will take as an illustration a widely publicized photograph of a young Vietnamese mother clutching her dead baby to her chest. The expression on her face was sheer horror and despair. Anyone familiar with the theory of the Ten Worlds would assume the woman is in the state of Hell. With respect to the Ten Factors, we can say that her appearance, her internal nature, and her entity are all suffering the agonies of Hell. There is no way of knowing from the picture exactly how the baby died, but the death has clearly moved the mother to sob and groan as she holds the child to herself in a belated effort to protect it. The baby's death, the external cause, has evoked the inherent cause of grief lying deep within the woman's life. Power has moved her to a futile action, the nature of which is determined by latent effect, and the manifest effect of which is visible. The consistency from beginning to end, caused by the fusion and interaction of the first nine factors, is a life in the ultimate throes of sorrow.

If true peace were to come to Vietnam, this mother might possibly enter the state of Humanity, or that of the Bodhisattva Nature, or that of Buddhahood, for all these states are latent within the state of Hell. Her conduct would then accord with another set of factors. If she entered the state of the Bodhisattva Nature, for example, the memory of the baby's death might be the external factor that moves the inner cause of compassion, leading her perhaps to take a war orphan into her house.

Not only in this mother, but in all life, the Ten States are always present in all their permutations, together with the Ten Factors. All truth and all life can be analyzed with reference to these concepts. The idea of the Thousand Factors in the Hundred Worlds is a universal and objective principle, applicable to any single instant in the life process.

And yet this is not all of reality, because in each of the states of being we find people behaving differently, and the personalities and characteristics they display are distinctly their own. No two persons are exactly alike, and this remains true whether the people we are comparing are in the state of Hell or in some other state. Consider, for example, the condition of a man doubled up because of an excruciating pain in his stomach. He is in Hell too, and the Ten Factors of this state all apply to him as to the grieving Vietnamese mother. Both are overcome with agony, which activates their potential for suffering and saps much of their vital energy. There are differences between the sick man and the Vietnamese woman, and his suffering is of a different character from hers. It remains for us to explain the difference.

To put it in a more general way, all forms of life are alike in that they are inherently understandable in terms of the Thousand Factors in the Hundred Worlds. And yet all things are different, because it is possible to discriminate between any life in the universe and all the others. The basis for discriminating each individual entity from all the rest is what I call the principle of individuality.

Just what is the difference between the man in agony and the grief-stricken woman? On the face of it, they are of opposite sexes, and their bodies are different. Strictly speaking, all human bodies are different one from the other, and since the physical element and the spiritual element are inseparable, it follows that all human spirits are different one from the other.

In her grief, the mother thinks of her child all the more vividly. She remembers its innocent smiling face, its tiny hands, and its once sparkling eyes. Her mind goes back to a happier day when she and her family were together. Perhaps a smile crosses her face, until she remembers that her husband is also dead now, and she must face the world alone. The prospects of hardship and destitution are frightening, but despite the hopelessness of her situation, she has the will to go on. In love and defiance, she holds on tightly to her dead child.

What goes on in the sick man's mind is very different. He tries to find the exact location of the pain. Is it in the top of his stomach or over to the right? He senses that the pain is not going away soon, and he wonders when the doctor will arrive. Is it an ulcer? Could it be cancer? With these thoughts whirling around in his brain, he twists his body in any way that seems to bring momentary relief.

The mother and the sick man have much in common. Both of them are displaying distinctly human reactions; both of them are speculating about the meaning and probable effects of the situation confronting them. More important, perhaps, both are trying to assimilate their experience into their selves. At the same time, their specific thoughts are very different, and their physical expression of these thoughts is different. A key provided by Buddhism to the diversity we see here and in all aspects of human life is the theory of the Five Aggregates. This theory explains how our idea of reality is formed.

THE FIVE AGGREGATES

The Five Aggregates (*go-on*) are form (*shiki*), perception (*ju*), conception (*sō*), volition (*gyō*), and consciousness (*shiki*). If we apply the principle of the identity of the physical law of life and the spiritual law of life (*shikishin funi*), we can say that form signifies the physical law of life—matter and the entire physical composition of life. The other four belong to the spiritual law of life. But since the physical and the spiritual are one and inseparable, form is the prerequisite for the other four aggregates, and they for it. Consciousness, which includes discrimination and wisdom, is the starting point for perception, conception, and judgement, and at the same time it is the integrating force tying them together. To put it simply, all the mental activities center on consciousness.

Consciousness supports human life from within and functions to endow it with meaning. It is consequently usually mentioned last in the list of five, but it is a mistake to think of the Five Aggregates in sequential arrangements, for in fact they are inseparably entwined.

In discussing the Three Thousand Possible Worlds in Every Life-moment, Nichiren Daishonin wrote: "*On* means 'aggregate,' and the first aggregate is form, which is everything perceivable to the senses. The second is perception, which means receiving or taking something in. The third is conception, which according to the *Kusha-ron* is 'the forming of a mental image.' The fourth is volition, which means 'to act upon.' The fifth is consciousness, which means 'discernment.' The fifth volume of *Great Concentration and Insight* (*Maka Shikan*), quoting from Nagarjuna's *Jūjūbibasha-ron* says, 'First there is consciousness, which is discernment; next, perception is the act of taking in; conception is to form an image; volition is to decide whether to accept it or not; form is sensed through the workings of volition.' "

This profound statement calls for further elucidation, particularly with respect to Nagarjuna's definitions. In saying that consciousness means "discernment," I believe Nagarjuna meant that consciousness is the ability to consider something, define it, and grasp its meaning. Consciousness includes unconscious or subconscious impressions and is in fact the totality of mental and spiritual activity, reaching back to the essence of cosmic life. The ability of the mind to perceive an object begins with consciousness.

Perception means taking something in, receiving it into the mind. The mode of perception can be either subliminal or supraliminal. Conception is, as the *Kusha-ron* says, to form a mental image. This image may be an exact reflection of something external, or it may involve the use of imaginative powers reaching beyond time and space into the universe itself. It may be influenced by recollections from the past or ideals for the future. At times it may be little more than empty fancy, but in any case, it leads to volition, which involves not only accepting or rejecting what has been perceived, but deciding how to act on it. The question is whether we take an active or a passive approach to what has been perceived. You might regard the Vietnamese mother as having reacted positively by embracing her child tightly, whereas the sick man reacted passively.

The statement that "form is sensed through the workings of volition" can be interpreted in several ways. In one sense it is an illustration of the inseparability of the physical law of life and the spiritual law of life, for the form cannot exist without the idea. Our perception of physical objects is due to the reflection of our mental impulse in the objects themselves. In another sense, our mental volition becomes manifest in our bodily reactions. If the mind did not function to motivate action, we could perceive neither our physical movements nor existence itself. In the case of the mother clutching her dead baby, the action of the mind was simultaneously expressed by her arms. She may well have been unconscious of the strength in her arms, but power flowed into them as a result of the idea in her head. The energy of the body and the workings of the mind are inseparably interrelated. Our life-energy, which is the manifestation of our life itself, becomes volition within the mind, and the result is a surge of physical energy, which is the aggregate of form.

We can conclude that consciousness, perception, conception, and volition are manifestations of spiritual energy. They are perfectly fused with the actions of our body, and the fact that we sense objects to be real only through the action of our volition is a further demonstration of the inseparability of the physical and spiritual laws of life.

Having examined the relationships linking the Five Aggregates, we may go on to the important point that these aggregates differ with the individual. Together, the Five Aggregates make up what is called the "World of the Aggregates" (*go-on seken*). The word *seken* means "world," but the *Threefold Secret Teachings* states with regard to *go-on seken*, "*Seken* connotes division." The idea here is that the world is made up of many different people, each of whom has his own individual World of Aggregates. Each person's personality is differentiated from other personalities by the action of these aggregates, for they determine how he will respond to reality, and hence what reality actually is for him.

Through the function of the Five Aggregates, an infinite variety of mental and physical activities becomes possible. The workings of the aggregates can fill life with sorrow and sadness, or they can cause compassion and wisdom to become manifest. There are countless possibilities. The configuration of aggregates of a person in torment may work only to deprive him of vitality, so that he goes from one Hell to another. He is then among the sentient beings of Hell.

In discussing the meaning of the Five Aggregates, the *Threefold Secret Teachings* says: "The Five Aggregates of life are form, perception, conception, volition, and consciousness. If these are all present in people who base their lives on any of the nine worlds other than Buddhahood, they will obscure the merciful True Law of Life. Their actions form causes which eventually become an accumulation of many kinds of suffering. However, should one's life be based on Buddhahood, it will accumulate lasting happiness because it is filled with compassion."

If a sentient being is in any of the first nine states, the aggregates work to conceal the true Law of the Buddha and to cause the multiplication of sorrows, but if a sentient being is in the state of Buddhahood, the aggregates lead to an understanding of the Law of the Buddha and an accumulation of happiness.

In reality, our life activities take place within the bounds of the nine states, and the effect of consciousness and the other aggregates is to weaken our potential energy for creation, which originates in the cosmic life-force. The more active we are in mind or spirit, the further we obscure Buddhahood from ourselves. We hinder the functioning of our life-force. The effect of this is to increase our suffering. This is the meaning of the statement that "the aggregates lead to repetitive cycles of life and death," for "cycles of life and death" is synonymous with suffering.

When we realize the presence of Buddhahood within us and establish the state of Buddhahood as the basis of our lives, the aggregates function to accumulate happiness for us. Instead of stemming the flow of our life-force, they release the energy of compassion, with the result that our actions, instead of locking us within the lower states of being, further reveal Buddhahood and strengthen the foundations of our life in the state of Buddhahood.

SENTIENT BEINGS AND THE ENVIRONMENT

The World of the Five Aggregates is intimately connected with what is known in Buddhism as the World of Sentient Beings (*shūjō-seken*). This may sound more difficult than it really is, for what is intended is simply a world in which each living being is considered to be different from all other living beings. This, after all, is the way the world is, for as I pointed out earlier, no two individual beings are exactly alike physically, and it follows that no two are exactly alike mentally.

The *Threefold Secret Teachings* says: "The World of Sentient Beings is the name for all the sentient beings in the Ten States. The temporary fusion of the Five Aggregates is called a sentient being. The most exalted sentient being is in the state of Buddhahood, and for that reason *The Treatise on the Wisdom Sutras* (*Daichido-ron*) says, 'The sentient being than whom there is none higher is the Buddha.' "

A living being, according to this, is a "temporary fusion of the Five Aggregates." In other words, an individual human being is at any moment a temporary configuration of form, perception, conception, volition, and consciousness. This is another way of saying, first, that a human being is a fusion of physical and spiritual elements, and, second, that his personality at any moment represents a coming together of the five constantly changing aggregates.

It is a question of emphasis. If we are considering the instantaneous forces in operation within us, we consider the Five Aggregates: how we conceive of something, how we form an opinion of it, how our volition works upon it. If, on the other hand, we are considering the life entity as such, we are concerned with sentient beings, which as the previous quotation tells us, exist in all of the Ten States. In each of the Ten States, it will be observed, the sentient beings are different one from the other. Consequently, in the examples we took up some time ago, the Vietnamese woman and the sick man are both in the state of Hell, but they are different from each other both in particular circumstances and in individual personality.

Everyone is in one of the Ten States, and everyone has the potentiality of going instantly into any of the other nine states. In everyone, the Ten Factors are always in operation. That everyone is, nevertheless, different from everyone else is owing to the activities of the Five Aggregates, the fusion of which is the individual living being. We need only one more element to complete the Buddhist view of a human entity, and that is the World of Environment.

The *Threefold Secret Teachings* says, "The World of Environment signifies the place where people in the Ten Worlds live." We can understand more fully what this means if we recall the principle of the inseparability of life and its environment (*esho funi*). Each life is individual, and as it manifests itself in this world, the unique existence it forms simultaneously shapes an environment which it can find compatible. To see the truth of this, we have only to look at the environment of a particular person, for in his surroundings, we can see clearly all the inclinations and characteristics of his life. If we try to imagine a human being without an environment, we can be talking about nothing but a mythical being.

As life extends its influence into its surroundings, the environment automatically changes in accordance with the life condition. An environment, then, which is a reflection of the inner life of its inhabitants, always takes on the characteristics of those living within it. Moreover, since the earth is a form of life, the Ten Factors and the theory of the Mutual Possession of the Ten Worlds are applicable to each and every environment.

In chapter six, I discussed at length the Ten Worlds, or States of Being, and the characteristics of each. Here, I would like to add a few words about the states of life in relationship to their environment.

A passage in the *Threefold Secret Teachings* tells us that "Hell is a dwelling of red-hot iron, and Hunger is a place five hundred *yujin* beneath the human world." On the one hand, this expresses very graphically the agony of the environment of Hell, a state in which living beings are deprived of both their desire and their right to live. At the same time, it reminds us that the abode of a person in the state of Hunger, that is, one whose instinctive desires cannot be satisfied, lies at a great distance from the world appropriate to human beings. It is as if that person were confined in a deep underground pit, and could obtain neither food nor water.

The passage continues, "Beings in the State of Animality live in the water, on the land, and in the air." This signifies more than it seems to at first, because it causes us to think of the role played by water in the life of fish, of land in the life of animals, and of air in the life of birds. Thinking of this, we realize that each environment functions in an indispensable way to fulfill the instinctive needs of its inhabitants. In the case of human beings, however, those in the state of Animality use their environment in a limited way. They are at the mercy of selfish desire, so the only use they have for their environment, whether it be home or office or the great outdoors, is to obtain satisfaction for these instinctive urgings.

What the passage has to say about Anger is seemingly obscure: "Anger is on the seashore or the seabed." We have to think first of the life condition of a person in the state of Anger. His mind is warped by desire, and in any situation there will be something that arouses the desire for competition.

The sea itself is important in this image, too, for Anger was traditionally the Realm of Ashura, and it seems likely that in ancient Indian myth Ashura were related to the sea. In the state of Anger, one is buffeted and mauled by raging waves. Even a sea where the waves are quiet contains a great reserve of energy capable of overcoming any form of life in a moment. In sum, Anger is a world of conflict, and being in this state is like perpetually treading water.

"Humanity," according to the *Threefold Secret Teachings*, "is life on earth, and Rapture is life in a palace." Here again, "earth" means not our planet, but surroundings that are conducive to comfort, stability, and a life replete with human value. Anger spoils the feelings of people in its grip. Even if they are calm on the surface, there is inner rancor, and suspicion, jealousy, or hatred. In contrast, the feelings of those in the state of Humanity are calm and peaceful.

"Palace," too, is metaphorical. As we noted earlier, desire is a source of energy in life. "Palace," then, is an environment wherein all the desires associated with the Six Lower States can be gratified.

An important point distinguishing the Six Lower States from the Four Noble States is this: human beings in the lower paths have as their objective the satisfaction of their desires and impulses. Their happiness depends totally on environmental conditions. It is only when people can attain one of the noble states that they can manifest the power necessary to control their life-force in a positive way.

The passage I have been quoting goes on to say, "Those in the state of Learning or Realization live in a transitory land, Bodhisattvas live in a land of actual rewards, and the Buddhas, in the eternal, enlightened land."

The reason the states of Learning and Realization are referred to as a "transitory land" is that human beings, wherever they may actually live, can change their environment into that of these two states. This is because the self in these states, as we noted earlier, is a reflective self; it can penetrate the law inherent in all phenomena and perceive their impermanence. Particularly in the state of Realization, the individual can discover the truth, beauty, and good hidden in the ever-changing world.

Where the Bodhisattvas live is not an otherworldly place. They dwell among people in society as it is, but by the exercise of benevolence and the practice of altruism, they forthrightly challenge conceit, selfishness, and evil, thereby transforming any environment into one that will allow their compassion to find expression. Thus, their environment is "a land of actual rewards."

The world of the Buddhas is even more brilliant, for the wisdom it brings forth radiates through the veil of illusion and uncovers the Buddhahood in all living things. Those in the state of Buddhahood are not only in perfect harmony with the Mystic Law, but have the true power of compassion, which is to say, a power that is invincible and never rests and is great enough to alleviate suffering. In contrast to Hell, which deprives us of the very right to live, the eternal, enlightened land of Buddhahood guarantees this right. And it does more. It recharges everything with creative vitality and, indeed, provides the power to create new life.

THREE THOUSAND POSSIBLE WORLDS

Previously, I mentioned the principle of Three Thousand Possible Worlds in Every Life-moment (*ichinen sanzen*). Now we must form a more exact concept of the meaning of this principle, for it is at the core of Buddhist philosophy, and by understanding it, the view we gain of the true entity of life becomes both complete and impartial.

In the *Threefold Secret Teachings*, the question is posed: How can the life-moment, which is infinitesimally short, contain three thousand worlds? The answer given is this: " 'Three Thousand Possible Worlds in Every Life-moment' has two meanings according to the Lotus Sutra: 'to contain' and 'to permeate.' The entire universe is contained in each life at every moment of its existence. Conversely, each life-moment continually permeates the entire universe. The life-moment is a particle of dust holding the elements of all worlds in the universe. It is a drop of water whose essence differs in no way from the vast ocean itself."

Human beings in the states other than Buddhahood are apt to see only the moment-to-moment phenomena of human life. In doing so, they fail to grasp its essence and end up mistaking the evanescence of the life-moment for its true nature, which it is not. The life-moment is directly conjoined with the cosmic life-force, and it is boundless in terms of time and space. We only become aware of this as we extend our search for the truth ever deeper into the spheres of life.

Another way to understand the life-moment is to conceive of it as an entity, while at the same time recognizing that all entities interrelate harmoniously with the totality of cosmic life without losing their uniqueness.

The significance of uniqueness can be seen if we ask why "three thousand worlds"? When we discussed the concept of the Ten Worlds, we saw that the number ten was not chosen at random, but was both the maximum and the minimum number necessary to encompass all the states of being. Nor is the number three thousand arrived at arbitrarily. It comes from multiplying the Thousand Factors in the Hundred Worlds (*hyakkai sennyo*) by three, three being the three principles of individuality. Individuality exists, of course, in the unique configuration of the Five Aggregates, but there are two other sources of individuality. Individuality exists and is manifested among sentient beings (*shūjō*), and it exists and is manifested in the World of Environment. What this means is that Three Thousand Possible Worlds, by evoking the myriad forms life can take, is an expression of the totality of all phenomena.

Numbers, however, should not divert our attention from the profound meaning of the principle itself. Buddhism provides us with a deep and exhaustive analysis of life's totality, and brings to light its depth, breadth, expansion, motion and motivating force, as well as the law of cause and effect. It remains, then, to delve into how a life-moment can penetrate the entire universe.

The necessary condition for this is a life in the state of Buddhahood. The law of causality, in this case, operates both inwardly and outwardly. As Buddhahood becomes manifest, it grows into an ever-stronger, integral part of the life-force. A person in this state fully realizes the potential of the Five Aggregates in his own life, and he can build lasting happiness, never subject to changes in the environment.

Outwardly, the power of compassion and wisdom emerges and becomes active. Buddhahood reaches out and influences all other people. Those as low as the state of Hell, those confined to Transmigration in the Six Lower States, those in whom the expression of the life-force is curtailed by conceit or self-satisfaction—all who are touched by the influence of Buddhahood experience the opportunity to create their own human revolution and improve their karma, until their own innate Buddhahood comes to the fore.

I think an analogy in the realm of physics is appropriate. When nuclear fission takes place, the splitting of the first atom is all but undetectable. But then two more atoms split, then four, and so on. In other words, a reaction starting with a single atom increases in intensity until a great number of particles bombard the main mass of fissionable material. And when criticality is reached, a tremendous amount of energy is released. I have spoken out repeatedly against the evils of nuclear weapons, but we must remember that nuclear energy can have peaceful applications too. Nor should we forget that atomic reactions are natural, as well as man-made, phenomena.

A person who attains the state of Buddhahood is similar to the atom triggering a fission reaction. His life-flow is pure and profuse, and it causes remarkable changes in the depths of other lives. Just as grass which has begun to wither can be restored by a good rain, or a caravan stopping at an oasis is revitalized by the fresh water, individuals and their environment will be infused with the power and joy of living when they find themselves in the life-flow of Buddhahood. This chain reaction can spread in any kind of environment: from the individual to the family, and to neighbors and the community. Or from doctors or nurses to patients and a whole hospital. As it spreads, it imparts to the environment a new, vibrant quality, changes take place on an ever-larger scale, and the whole world is transformed. And this, I believe, offers the only hope of saving mankind and our planet from destruction.

In practice, the principle revealed in Three Thousand Possible Worlds in Every Life-moment requires the highest ideals, the utmost determination, and constant effort. Then, and only then, can those who understand this principle profoundly and positively influence all types of people and change their environments. Men of faith whose lives are one with the Mystic Law strive to live by it and are entrusted with the mission of beginning the chain reaction leading to the creation of the eternal, enlightened land, a world where all people can develop their own Buddhahood.

III

LIFE AND DEATH

THE NATURE OF DEATH

DEATH THE INEVITABLE

One of life's basic questions is "What is death?" Is death a final termination, beyond which nothing exists? Or is it the portal to a new kind of life, a transformation rather than a final ending? Conversely, are we to consider life to be merely a brief phase of activity that eventually ceases? Or does it go on forever in some form or another?

Throughout the ages of man these have been among the most fundamental questions in philosophy and religion. Nichiren Daishonin said, "Learn first about death and then about other things." Similarly, from an existentialist viewpoint, Martin Heidegger wrote that human life is "an existence directed toward death," and that the death-potential is inherent in human life from the time of conception. These are statements by thinkers who have sought, by facing the unavoidable fate of death, to enrich human life and make it more vital.

Any study of life that fails to take death into account cannot yield significant results. Deep down, we all know this, but still we have a tendency to avoid the subject. Even when we are in the very presence of death—as when someone close to us passes on—we cling unconsciously to an illusion: we ourselves are somehow exceptions, immune to death and under no compunction to consider it in connection with ourselves, at least for the time being.

The truth is that the consciousness of death is a peculiar privilege of mankind. Other mortal beings, it would seem, have only the briefest awareness of death as an approaching reality, if indeed they have this. Apprehension of death, therefore, is one of the qualities distinguishing man from the lower animals; it is to be considered a mark of man's higher intelligence. Still, because of this blessing, man often becomes obsessed with the fear of death and even goes to absurd extremes to avoid it.

The meaning of Nichiren Daishonin's words is that instead of averting our eyes from the inevitable, we must face death calmly and dispassionately, thereby developing in ourselves the courage and determination to make our lives more abundant and fruitful. If everyone avoided thinking of death, there would be no philosophy and no religion, and our lives would be correspondingly impoverished, not to say bestialized.

The confrontation of death has been described as the mother of philosophy. It might also be called the mother of science, for a large proportion of all scientific investigation is directed toward lengthening life expectancy. Modern medicine is a result of man's effort to control his own destiny, and all the blessings brought by medical research are traceable ultimately to our fear of death.

Medical scientists would be the first to agree that death has not been conquered and probably will not be in the future. So long as we remain living organisms, it is impossible to free ourselves from death. The cells of our bodies are constantly being renewed, but this does not apply to our brain cells, whose longevity places a biological limit on our life span. Some say brain cells have a maximum life of 125 years. If this is true, 125 years may be the greatest age to which life can be extended by medical means. Actually, the certifiable cases of people having reached this age can be counted on the fingers of one hand.

Although science and medicine can protect us from numerous illnesses and to some extent prolong our existence, they provide no fundamental solution to the problem of death itself. It is to philosophy and religion that we must look for the ultimate answers.

That human beings have grasped this point since the dawn of human existence is evident from our studies of the past. In a report on the remains of Neanderthal man in Iraq, the American anthropologist R. S. Solecki stated that he had found traces of flower pollen scattered around a tomb. This indicates that even the Neanderthals honored their dead by placing flowers on their graves, and we may infer that these early people believed in the continued existence of life after death. Solecki hypothesizes Neanderthal society had already conceived of a "heaven" of some sort, transcending the normal limits of reality. I myself suspect that, like men of later times, they intuitively sensed the fundamental life-force that pulses within nature and the universe.

Primitive men in Oceania, who were biologically identical with *Homo sapiens*, believed in a supernatural force called *mana*, which they thought inhabited all things in the universe. They seem to have believed life was the state in which *mana* is active and increasing, whereas death is the opposite.

People, no matter how primitive, observe the rhythms of the seasons and the movements of the celestial bodies, and sense that human life is also subject to continuous change in accordance with the pulsations of the universe. Life, they see, returns to the Earth Mother with death and reappears with birth. Belief in recurring cycles of birth and death is very common among primitive peoples. The *mana* of Oceania is conceived of as an inherent vitality which makes possible death and rebirth in all living things. The idea is fundamentally the same as the more sophisticated Greek concept of *pneuma*. Even among the most primitive ancestors of man, then, human wisdom perceived an omnipresent force acting throughout the universe.

At a later stage, men developed various types of animism, according to which all living things in the universe, people included, possess souls of their own. In religions of this sort, life is usually believed to be the state in which the soul inhabits a particular body, and death the state in which the soul is released from its physical confines. This idea leads directly to the doctrine of the immortality of the soul, a common tenet of many of the higher religions.

In the Judaic-Christian religions, the immortality of the soul is linked with the concept of creation by an almighty deity. In general, they hold that the soul is created by God at the time of conception, and that it continues to exist after death. The souls of believers who have faith in God can ascend to heaven and live eternally; those of the unfaithful are forever condemned to purgatory or Hell.

Christianity also maintains that there is to be a final judgement—the trumpet shall sound, the dead shall be raised, and everyone living or dead will appear before God to receive the ultimate dispensation of his soul. It is to be noted, however, that although Christianity believes in rebirth after death, it holds that there is only one resurrection, after which the soul continues to exist eternally.

Belief in personal immortality is also a tenet of Islam. According to Islamic belief, at the final judgement the dead will be divided into three groups: those summoned to remain near the throne of Allah, those sent to a paradisical heaven, and those condemned to a fiery Hell. In Zoroastrianism, the belief is in two kinds of judgement: one to which each individual soul is subjected immediately after death and another to which all persons living or dead are ultimately subjected simultaneously.

These religions, together with Judaism, from which both Christianity and Islam are descended, show a number of similarities. In the first place, all hold that individual life is created by the deity at the time of conception. Secondly, every soul continues to exist after corporal death. Finally, the dead will all be brought back to life on the final judgement day, when the deity will decide the everlasting fate of all.

It is to be observed that none of these faiths, which for practical purposes may be classed as Occidental, has acquired a dominating influence in the Orient. The Oriental attitude toward life and death, as seen in India and East Asia, is fundamentally different from the Occidental. In contrasting the two, I am reminded of an analogy employed by the late Count Coudenhove-Kalergi, who said that Orientals consider life to be one page in a book, whereas Occidentals consider it to be the whole book. In the Eastern view, to die means to arrive at the end of the page and turn to a new one; in the Western concept, to live is to read through the book one time and come to the end. Christianity and the other major religions of the Occident (including Western Asia) teach that the manner in which one lives out a limited life-span—the manner in which one reads one's book—determines one's destiny once and for all. The Oriental religions, on the other hand, regard a human lifetime as being only one act in a never-ending drama.

Materialism, we might note in passing, is widespread in most lands today and is like the Occidental religions. Life is the whole book, the principal difference being that for the materialists, when the book ends, it really ends—there is no soul that continues to exist after the body has died. This is roughly the difference between those who believe in religion and those who do not.

The Oriental attitude toward life and death can be seen in both Hinduism and Buddhism, for despite their dissimilarities, these two great religions both embody the doctrine of transmigration, the idea that life, being eternal, passes through an endless chain of deaths and rebirths. Physical death is not a final ending, but merely a transformation of the factors and functions that collectively make and sustain an individual life. Life is unbroken and extends from the infinite past to the infinite future. Though a given life is, as in Count Coudenhove-Kalergi's simile, a page in a book, the book itself is without beginning or end. No matter how many pages are turned, the story continues on indefinitely.

Transmigration is closely associated with the Oriental belief in karma, the sum total of the causes accumulated in a particular life, which determine the future of that life. The Western religions in general consider a man's destiny in life to be determined by God's will, and the fate of a man's soul in the afterlife to be subject to God's judgement. The Oriental faiths, on the other hand, believe that a man's destiny is determined by his karma, and thus it is the natural result of the laws of cause and effect.

Buddhism in particular sees the joys and sorrows of the present life as being determined by causes accumulated in previous lives. Furthermore, it sees the causes being accumulated in the present life as determining factors in future lives throughout eternity. As we have already noted, the great Chinese master Chih-i wrote in his *Profound Meaning of the Lotus Sutra* (*Hokke Gengi*), "My present sufferings all result from the past; the fruition of my present practice of the faith will come in the future."

It seems to me that in Christian belief, if one leads a life of agony from the day one is born to the day one dies, all one can do is reproach God for his lack of mercy. Logically speaking, it must be God who creates evil as well as good. If we accept Buddhism, however, we become aware that the essential causes of our troubles lie within our own lives. It is thus possible, by accepting responsibility for our own sufferings, to allay them and arrive at an indestructible state of peace and happiness. When people discover they themselves are the masters of their destiny, they also find a bright star of hope enabling them to see through the veil of illusion. In my opinion, the Buddhist concept of life makes far more sense to modern man than the idea that everything is up to God.

In 1972 and 1973, I had a series of discussions with the late Prof. Arnold Toynbee. I think he was one of the greatest intellects of our age, and was gratified to find we agreed on many points. One of them was that the Buddhist-Hindu concept of karma represents a more reasonable and plausible explanation of man's fate than is found in the Judaic-Christian tradition. Prof. Toynbee spoke frequently of Christianity, Islam, and Buddhism as "higher religions," by which he meant those religions seeking to put human beings into direct contact with "the ultimate spiritual reality." Since these religions have similar views of the ultimate principle of life and the cosmos, they agree on the eternity of life.

THE NATURE OF DEATH

Some of the world's numerous religions can be described as little more than superstition; others concern themselves primarily with the casting of spells. Even among the higher religions, one finds reference to fanciful worlds and irrational beliefs—heavens peopled by angels with wings and harps, paradises with Buddhas seated on lotus flowers, and so on. Through all of this, however, there does run a fundamental belief in the eternity of human life that has been in the back of man's mind for millions of years.

Prof. Toynbee saw in the higher religions the accumulated wisdom of past thinkers who sought communion with the ultimate spiritual reality. If we equate "ultimate spiritual reality" with "cosmic life," it becomes evident that the higher religions are constantly searching for this original and essential life element. In short, human wisdom, by grappling with the problem of death, has reached toward the inner meaning of cosmic life in order to explain the eternity of life.

Prof. Toynbee thought that all the higher religions eventually arrive at some equivalent of the Buddhist concept of *kū*. *Kū*, then, is the locus of the ultimate spiritual reality. Though all religions attempt to explain the eternal presence pulsating in the state of *kū* and thereby to understand the eternity of life, the search has yielded a wide variety of conflicting doctrines. If we are to find the true aspect of life in relation to death, we must sweep aside partial, incomplete concepts of *kū* and go to the truly Buddhist view.

LIFE AFTER DEATH

In writing of transmigration, Prof. Michitarō Tanaka, an authority on Greek philosophy and professor emeritus of Kyoto University, cited the case of Pythagoras, who upon seeing a dog being badly treated, told its tormentors to leave it alone because he recognized it as the reincarnation of a dead friend. Prof. Tanaka also mentions a Greek comedy in which a debtor, brought before a judge, argued that there was no reason to pay his debts because he was now a different person from the one who had borrowed the money.

There is an element of truth in the debtor's plea: have you never seen a picture of a smiling baby whom you know to have grown up to be a perfect reprobate? Have you never had difficulty spotting a friend's face in a class photograph taken many years earlier? Part of a person's character remains the same as he grows older, but a greater part changes, often to the extent that the person's disposition is completely transformed. If his appearance has changed beyond recognition and his disposition is greatly altered, does he remain the same person, or does he become somebody else, as the debtor in the story fancied himself to be?

Needless to say, he remains the same person, for in real life there is no one who believes himself to be a totally different being after a certain passage of time. We have something in us that guarantees our self-identity. Prof. Tanaka reached the conclusion that unless we postulate something on the order of a "soul," we cannot explain this continuing identity. In my opinion, what Prof. Tanaka has called a soul is identical with what I have spoken of as entity (*nyoze-tai*), one of the Ten Factors of Life. It manifests itself in appearance (*nyoze-sō*) and nature (*nyoze-shō*). Entity is free from phenomenal change, but manifests itself in all change.

Prof. Tanaka wrote: "In the doctrine of transmigration, it is a basic premise that the soul retains its identity and its continuity. If a dog is reborn as a man, he must in the process drink the waters of Lethe, which blot out the memory of the earlier existence. Actually, in this present lifetime, there is no continuity of memory between my infancy and the present. What, therefore, makes me the same person now as I was when I was a baby? People today often object to talking about the immortality of the soul, but is there really much difference between believing in an identity linking us with our infancy and the belief of our ancestors in the immortality of the soul?" If for "soul" we read what I have called the essential self, Prof. Tanaka's view is identical with my own.

Since man has no memory concerning his life before birth, he is apt to believe he first came into being in his mother's womb. By the same logic, it would seem that because a person cannot remember his childhood perfectly, a grown-up's identity has changed since his childhood. However, if you believe you are the same entity now as at the time of your birth, you cannot simply dismiss the idea that you might have been something else in a previous life.

Materialists laugh at this idea, and the fashion among intellectuals seems to be to ignore it, or try to ignore it. In a book entitled *The Way We Die* (*Ningen no Shinikata*), Yoshio Nakano expressed himself as follows: "My own wish is that my soul will be destroyed together with my body. This would be the happiest solution, and it is the one for which I pray."

Though there are those who long for extinction, there are others who, on the very brink of death, force themselves to live on in an effort to satisfy some ambition or grudge. In either case, no one can be certain that existence actually ends with death. Nakano himself went on to say: "Still I have no proof that life after death is impossible. I can only assume that when the cells of my body cease to function, my soul will also be extinguished. I feel such a death would be a beautiful release, but my wishing this does not make it so."

The idea of death as the total extinction of life is usually supported by one of three types of arguments. One of these is the citing of "empiric evidence," by which is usually meant the accounts of people who by their own testimony have come close to death and believe death must be an extension of what they experienced. More scientific than this approach is the view that life cannot continue after the body has been reduced to simple chemical compounds or elements. More serious materialists carry this argument somewhat further and insist that spiritual activity cannot exist without physical activity; in this view the spirit is the function of our brain cells and cannot continue to exist after the brain cells have died.

Typical of the first type of argument—the brush-with-death story—is a passage from Michio Takeyama's *Ningen ni tsuite* (*On Man*). At the age of six, the author lost consciousness after being severely injured in a fall. He came to for a time just as he was about to be given a general anesthetic, and later it seemed to him that the effect of the anesthetic must have been nearly the same thing as dying. "A mask was put over my mouth and nose," he records. "Chloroform fell on the mask drop by drop, and the smell seemed to smother me. . . . As instructed, I counted 'one, two, three, . . .' I felt waves beating in my head, and as they became louder I heard a creaking, rushing noise. Just as I thought my head would split, the noise subsided and I felt I was going to sleep. I was drawn into a whirlpool of confusion, from which I passed into complete oblivion." To the objective mind, this is a far cry from actually dying, but Takeyama is not alone in believing that "complete oblivion" of the kind people occasionally experience is what we must expect after death.

Fundamentally this is no more than a guess, possibly based on the superficial similarity of death to sleep. A deep loss of consciousness does not, after all, even mean a temporary loss of being. As in sleep, life continues in the vast areas of the subconscious mind.

In any case, for every account in which those who have "nearly died" have reported the extinguishing of their mental activity, one can find another suggesting that consciousness may continue in some form after death. I am reminded of a striking personal experience described by the late physician and professor Lord Patrick Geddes (1854–1932), whose words are quoted by Rosalind Heywood in *Man's Concern with Death* (edited by Arnold Toynbee and containing a thought-provoking essay by him). Lord Geddes wrote: "On Saturday, November 9th, a few minutes after midnight, I began to feel very ill and by 2 o'clock was definitely suffering from acute gastroenteritis. . . . By 10 o'clock I had developed all the symptoms of acute poisoning . . . pulse and respirations being quite impossible to count. . . . I realized I was very ill and very quickly reviewed my financial position: thereafter at no time did my consciousness appear to me to be in any way dimmed, but I suddenly realized that *my* consciousness was separating from another consciousness which was also me."

Reminiscent, is it not, of those dreams we have in which part of us is aware that we are dreaming? In this case, doctors speak of a splitting or separation of the self. Lord Geddes, in describing his condition, used the terms body-consciousness and ego-consciousness. The ego-consciousness witnessed the gradual collapse of the body-consciousness as it felt the heart, liver, and brain weakening. Simultaneously, it seemed to Lord Geddes as though the ego-consciousness was in the process of splitting off and merging with a larger flow of life. This is what is known as an "out-of-the-body" experience. Rosalind Heywood wonders if death itself is not something like that—the disintegration of the body-consciousness accompanied by the joining of the ego-consciousness with a larger flow of life. My own feeling is that though consciousness may seem to vanish at the time of death, just as it does when we are in a deep sleep, it is not actually annihilated. Rather it submerges in the depths of life and becomes one with the universal life-force of the cosmos. In any case, such experiences as that of Lord Geddes render the second type of argument against life after death—the idea that life must cease completely with the breaking up of the body into basic chemicals—inconclusive at best.

As for the materialistic idea that spiritual activity cannot exist without physical activity, there is a certain element of truth that must be recognized. Spiritual activity is known to be related to the brain cells; without the working of the cerebral cortex there could be no intricate thought processes or religious speculations. It does not follow, however, that consciousness itself springs from the brain. Instead, I see the brain as the physical manifestation of root consciousness. It is the tangible location where mental activity takes place.

Henri Bergson's comprehensive and logically impeccable refutation of materialistic theories on life and death is well known. In a lecture called "Mind and Body," delivered in 1912, he explained the relationship between the brain and consciousness by likening them to a clothes peg with clothes hanging from it. The clothes represent consciousness and the peg represents the brain. Though the clothes depend for support on the brain, they are a separate entity from it. You cannot learn about them by examining the peg, any more than you can learn about the peg by examining the clothes. If the peg falls, so do the clothes, but the peg is only the support, not the originator, of the clothes.

Nevertheless if the brain cells are injured, the mind is apt to suffer spiritual damage. When the brain cells die, consciousness loses its physical manifestation, but this is not to say that the entirety of life, including the conscious and the subconscious, has been annihilated. Various functions of the mind may continue to exist and to move in harmony with the cosmic life of which all individual lives are a part.

Having discussed the brain and consciousness, Bergson concluded that the workings of the mind extend far beyond the scope of the physical brain. It was his contention that the mind continues to exist after death. Indeed, so confident of his argument was he that at the close of his lecture he asserted that the burden of proof now lay with those trying to deny the possibility of life after death.

Bergson's views have been enjoying a new vogue of late. I find this gratifying, for it tends to confirm my belief that he who speaks the truth will always be heard, even though his views may go through periods of eclipse.

In attempting to explain life after death, all higher religions (not to mention many philosophies) arrive ultimately at the concept of *kū*, or latency. What I have tried to make clear here is that the key to the riddle is in the long run to be found only in religion, for there is no completely satisfactory scientific explanation and perhaps there never will be one. By the same token, there is no scientific proof that life after death does not exist. Those who believe in the religious approach certainly need not quake before the arguments of materialists. Close examination reveals that much of the scientific logic they parade is superficial, if indeed it is even factual.

A LAW OF CONSERVATION

An interesting approach to the subject of life beyond death is seen in a book entitled *Ningen wa Shindara dō Naru Ka* (*What Happens to Man after Death*?) by Dr. Kinjirō Okabe, professor emeritus of Osaka University. Being a physicist, Dr. Okabe employs a method he describes as "scientific sleuthing," which means in effect drawing inferences from known scientific fact as to the nature of the unknown and the unknowable. For a man basing himself on the laws of physics, Dr. Okabe comes remarkably close to Buddhism in his conclusions concerning life and death.

The key element in Dr. Okabe's argument is the principle of conservation of energy. This fundamental principle of modern science states that energy is never lost, although it may be converted into other forms of energy, either dynamic or potential. For example, the electric energy supplied to a light bulb is not dissipated; it is transformed into an equivalent amount of optical and thermal energy. Dynamic energy can result only from the transformation of an equivalent amount of potential energy and vice versa. Energy, in short, cannot be either created or destroyed. Since matter can be expressed in terms of energy, there also exists a law of the conservation of matter.

Dr. Okabe reasons that a similar principle must apply to life, which is a form of existence and ought logically to be subject to the universal laws of physics. This seems to me an understandable position; if living beings are seen as energy complexes, then this energy must be composed of physical energy and spiritual energy. I see no reason why either kind should not be subject to the principle of energy conservation.

Dr. Okabe introduces a concept he calls the "core of the soul," similar, if not identical, to the soul postulated by Michitarō Tanaka. Our life, says Dr. Okabe, is the active state of the core of the soul, while death is its passive state. The meaning of active state and passive state, which seem to be terms borrowed from physics, is clear enough. Active state refers to the visible manifestations of life: movements of the limbs, the functioning of the brain, the expression of emotions. With death, these life functions enter a latent or dormant phase. Superficially, they appear to have ceased to exist, but in reality they retain their life potential. This condition is Dr. Okabe's passive state, or death. Dr. Okabe believes the nucleus of existence, in response to surrounding circumstances, travels back and forth between the active and the passive states, that is, between life and death.

Though Dr. Okabe arrived at his theory by extrapolation from the laws of physics, his conclusions are very close to the age-old concept of transmigration. The idea of life and death alternating in cycles can perhaps most easily be explained by an analogy, though I might note in passing that to more than half of the world's populace—that part living in India and East Asia—the concept of transmigration needs no explanation, it being more logical to most people than any analogy that comes readily to mind.

We may liken life to the rain falling outside the window. Having fallen, the rain either seeps into the ground or flows into rivulets, then larger streams, which empty into rivers, and eventually the rainwater finds its way to the ocean. From the ocean's surface, water rises in the form of vapor and is incorporated into clouds, from which it once again falls to earth as rain. The water from the rainfall is liquid part of the time and vapor part of the time, but its chemical structure remains unaltered throughout the hydrological cycle.

Life and death are like the physical form of the rain. Water is a liquid and visible; vapor is a gas that is often invisible. But both consist of molecules containing two hydrogen atoms and one oxygen atom. In the same way, life and death are but two aspects of the same fundamental existence, which moves from one state to the other and back again in endless cycles.

By combining physics with an original line of reasoning, Dr. Okabe peered deeply into the nature of life in its incessant transformations through past, present, and future. The Buddha, by means of religious insight rather than scientific induction, discovered not only the true nature of life and death, but also all the laws governing the working of life and the cosmos. Let us turn now from science to religion, from energy conservation to the flow of life and death as the Buddha saw them.

DEATH THE EXPEDIENT

Shakyamuni said that life is composed of four basic sufferings: birth, sickness, old age, and death. To find a way to free men from suffering, he retired from the world and entered upon his search for enlightenment. I suspect that his principal aim was to find the kind of knowledge that would enable people to overcome the suffering caused by death. Not to evade death, but to overcome the sorrows it entails.

For death is the basic problem. Old age brings its annoyances and its griefs: we lose our freshness and our beauty and become wrinkled; we watch our family and our friends depart; we find ourselves alone and failing in strength. No doubt the greatest terror of old age is that it is a process leading inevitably to death. Sickness may bring physical and mental anguish, but the awareness that illness is often the precursor of death causes far greater distress. Birth is regarded as the beginning of all suffering primarily because a person once born cannot avoid dying.

The four sufferings all derive ultimately from man's vulnerability to and abhorrence of death. All living things instinctively fear death, but man's fear is special because he is the only animal with the mental ability to apprehend death and wonder what lies beyond it. This awareness gives birth to terrors unknown to other animals and causes men to yearn for immortality. In the past, kings and potentates sought above all else to find an elixir of life; common people dreamed of living forever in paradise. Recently, I have read of Americans with incurable diseases wanting to have themselves deep-frozen and placed in cold storage in the hope that doctors will one day be able to thaw them out and heal them. Though attachment to life is not often carried to such morbid extremes, it is strong enough to cause a large number of people to try to hold death in mental abeyance, as though it were a debt that can be left unpaid indefinitely. When people finally face the fact that a final accounting must be made, they seek solace in the concept of an indestructible soul or of another world into which they will be reborn and immune to death. As we have already seen, such ideas are expressed or reflected in many, if not all, religions.

Even in Buddhism there exists the idea that the faithful will upon dying be reborn in a Pure Land in the west, where they will live in bliss and glory and perfect enlightenment forevermore. Though this idea has a large following, it was first put forth not as a definitive theory of life after death, but as a means of attracting people to Buddhism. Shakyamuni's original purpose was to wipe away man's futile attachment to this world so as to be able to face the problem of death directly. He took great care to clarify the real nature of death. Whereas most men do not want to die or even to think about death, he bravely rose above this instinctive human aversion and accepted the four sufferings as the normal condition of life. With full awareness of human suffering he contemplated the essence of life and death.

Buddhism has been criticized as negative because it places strong emphasis on the suffering that life brings. But what could be more positive than confronting the reality of death, along with its concomitant sufferings, and finding a way to cope with them?

Although Buddhism preaches the eternity of life, the Buddhist theory on the subject is certainly not simply an easy palliative for those who find death horrifying. On the contrary, the impermanence of all things and the prevailing misery of human life, which are among Buddhism's most fundamental teachings, are doctrines the average human being is likely to find sobering, if not as frightening as death itself. Far from glossing over the truth, Buddhism bids us accept it calmly and fearlessly. It squarely faces the fact that everything alive will die. We ask, why must we die? Are life and death fundamentally separate, or are they intimately related? What sort of current or flow is life? With courage, forbearance, and open eyes, Shakyamuni sought to find the true answers to these questions with respect to his own life. And the enlightenment he found is eternal life.

In describing his enlightenment, Shakyamuni said: "Thus I remembered my various past lives—the first life, the second life, the third life, the fourth life, the tenth life, the twentieth life, the thirtieth life, the fortieth life, the fiftieth life, the hundredth life, the thousandth life, the hundred thousandth life, the countless formations of the universe, the countless destructions of the universe, the formations and destructions of the universe. I remembered what my given names had been, what my surnames were, what my tribal names were, what I ate, what pleasures and sorrows I experienced."

It is mistaken thinking to take either life or death as absolute and ignore the other. Both are intrinsic phases of human existence. Human life flows on eternally in great waves, life and death alternating back and forth throughout time. Shakyamuni perceived this by recalling the flow of his own lives. His was no romantic doctrine of immortality born of a yearning for life. Instead, he perceived that life must be eternal because of the law of cause and effect running through his own series of existences. In his concept, death occurs so that there can be new life. Its function is like that of sleep; it is a period of rest before a new awakening.

This idea is expressed in the chapter of the Lotus Sutra on the Eternal Life of the Buddha, where death is seen to be an expedient, not to be ignored, but subordinate to life. This view is in many ways a hymn to life, but not one that urges us to avoid death or forget about it. The aim of the Lotus Sutra, like that of Shakyamuni, is to enable us to taste the joys of life without remaining ignorant of the nature and essence of death.

Let me emphasize that Buddhism is not, as some critics argue, a pessimistic or otherworldly religion. At the same time, it does not preach unbounded optimism. Its message is that the joy of living is to be found not by evading life's sufferings, but by grappling with them to the finish. True happiness is not born of escape; ecstasy based on delusion does not continue. Enlightenment comes from seeing the truth, no matter how unpleasant it may be.

The idea of death as an expedient is a revelation, but it is not a complete explanation of the relationship between life and death. Perhaps life, too, should be regarded as an expedient, devised to lead people toward a healthier view of death. Nichiren Daishonin's explanation of life and death as the two aspects of the same entity is more profound. In the *Orally Transferred Teachings* (*Ongi Kuden*), he is quoted as follows: "To hate life and death and try to separate oneself from them is delusion or partial enlightenment. To perceive life and death as essential is enlightenment or total realization. Now, when Nichiren and his disciples chant *Nam-myōhō-renge-kyō*, they know that life and death are intrinsic workings of the fundamental essence. Being and non-being, birth and death, appearance and disappearance, worldly existence and future extinction—all are essential and everlasting processes."

Death, in the final analysis, is neither an impermanent phenomenon nor an expedient. Together with life, it is inherent in fundamental existence and coexistent with cosmic life. Shakyamuni's enlightenment demonstrated that death was neither to be avoided nor to be taken as an object of dread. Nichiren Daishonin gave us a clearer and more comprehensive view of life and death as belonging to the eternal flux of universal being.

Enlightenment revealed to Shakyamuni the vast panorama of human life as it spreads out over time and space. He must have seen people whose lives are snuffed out soon after birth, as well as people who lived to a ripe old age. From the opposite viewpoint, there must be, among those who die, some who are reborn almost immediately and others for whom death drags on for eons. Though death can be a peaceful continuum, it can also be a seemingly interminable nightmare. In either case, it will eventually be transformed into life again. For the individual existence at least, death is a means of storing up energy for life, a period of rest preceding a return to action.

The life-death cycle is often likened to the alternate periods of sleep and wakefulness in ordinary life. The analogy is apt, for a few hours of sleep do restore us and make us ready for a new day, as death prepares us for a new life. A second point of similarity, I might note, is that neither sleep nor death destroys our identity. Just as a person who goes to sleep remains the same person when he wakes up, a life entity that dies is the same life entity when it is born again. In this sense, death may indeed be considered an expedient.

We should note in passing that psychologists consider sleep to play a more active role than has traditionally been assigned to it. When we sleep, we dream, and psychoanalysts from Freud on have maintained that dreams are expressions of our hopes and frustrations. They relieve pressures we have been unable to respond to while awake. An example often cited is that of a man who is angry at another person, but is prevented in real life from venting his anger. If this man has a dream in which he takes out his wrath on the other person, he is likely to awake refreshed and relieved of his ill feelings. In this way, dreams often function as cathartics for the mind.

Not infrequently, good ideas or inspirations come to us when we are asleep or half asleep. "It came to me in a dream" is an expression we have all used at one time or another. About this phenomenon, Prof. Teruo Ōkuma of Tottori University has written, "Dreams are expressions of the real self. They release desires and worries usually suppressed during the waking hours." In certain situations, the mind can arrive at a more efficient or creative idea when asleep than when awake.

That sleep is a subordinate state is no longer a tenable idea. Sleep is as much a part of our life action as what we do when we are awake. In the words of Prof. Junji Matsumoto of Tokushima University, "Being awake and being asleep can be regarded as alternate states in a continued flow of consciousness. These changing states combine with the various other functions of the brain to produce spiritual and vital activities." It should be observed that "consciousness" as used here includes the subconscious and the unconscious.

But, to return to the subject of life and death, we are now in a better position to examine the profound explanations offered by the philosophy of Nichiren Daishonin.

Shakyamuni, in his wisdom, described the phases of life and death, but did not see fit to define the indestructible essence of the universal flow of existence. Though he preached that Buddhism's ultimate teaching was the perception of this essential reality, he never described it clearly in words.

The ceaseless flow of life as fundamental existence wells forth like ocean waves from the innermost depths of all being. While playing out the unceasing rhythm of life and death, it develops continuously from infinite past to infinite future. Our self, which is the fundamental essence of our life, manifests the unceasing momentary changes, but remains anchored in the great flow of nature as it proceeds on its eternal journey. At times the self experiences the joy of living; at times it basks in the tranquillity of death. For some, both life and death may be filled with suffering and sorrow. In any case, life and death are both functions or expressions of the eternal flow of life. And all individual life currents are fused with the elemental reality of the universe. This total flow is a cosmic tide, one and indivisible. The universal life current that underlies and is immanent in all actions and all things is the Mystic Law propounded by Nichiren Daishonin. The merciful power of the Mystic Law resides in the inner depths of everything in the universe. Our lives exist, have always existed, and will always exist simultaneously with the universe. They neither came into being before the universe, occurred accidentally, nor were created by a supernatural being. Nichiren Daishonin taught that life and death are the alternating aspects in which our real self manifests itself, and both are part of the cosmic essence.

In *On the Ultimate Teaching Confirmed by All Buddhas* (*Sanze Shobutsu Sōkammon Kyōsō Hairyū*), Nichiren Daishonin wrote: "The idea that life and death are two is the reasoning of dreams, deluded and inverted. If when wide awake we examine our true nature, we will find no beginning that requires our being born and no end that requires our dying. What we will find is the essence of life, which can neither be burned by apocalyptic flames, nor worn away by flood, nor cut down by sword, nor pierced by arrow. It is not too large to enter the seed of a flower without the seed's expanding. It is not too small to fill the universe without the universe's contracting." The "essence of life" is the Mystic Law, which is the totality of universal existence, immanent in all beings. Nichiren Daishonin is reaffirming here that our natures do not begin and end, but are coeval with the universe.

The first forms of life on earth are thought to have come into existence 3 billion years ago. Human beings are thought to have appeared a million, or perhaps as much as 2.5 million, years ago. But to say that life itself began at either of these times, or that the self of human existence came into being when human beings first appeared, would be superficial. Life and the self existed long before either took on a manifest form on this earth. Similarly, they will continue to exist throughout eternity, through endless reenactions of the drama of life and death.

Recently I was asked whether a person weary of life might escape it all by committing suicide or by paying someone else to kill him. The answer, which is no, is implicit in the above quotation: "The essence of life . . . can neither be burned by apocalyptic flames, nor worn away by flood, nor cut down by sword, nor pierced by arrow." Since all forms of life exist originally and concurrently with the universe, they are undestroyable. To borrow Dr. Okabe's terminology, cosmic energy—the inexhaustible source of all activity, physical or spiritual—operates in accordance with the law of conservation of energy. It is neither created nor annihilated, no matter how often or in what varied ways it might transform itself. The self is imperishable, and suffering does not cease with death.

The passage stating that the essence of life can be contained in a flower seed or can fill the entire universe cannot be explained without reference to the concept of *kū* (latency), for it is by being in the state of *kū* that the mystic entity transcends the confines of space and time. We tend to regard the state of *kū* as inactive, like the water at the bottom of the ocean, but in fact it is eternally charged with the vibrant energy of life.

Nor is death static. Just as we speak of life's activities, we can properly speak of death's activities, though these are not visible to us. Many life entities must enjoy a period of peace and tranquillity after death, but for others death brings terror, worry, misery, torment. Death's activities can be likened to the countless radio waves being transmitted through the air. Some are happy waves, carrying music or laughter or good news; others contain violent, hateful propaganda. Whatever they convey, none of them interrupts or hinders the others so long as it is not on the same wave length. Without a receiver we cannot detect the presence of these waves, but with one we can see or hear whatever we are tuned in to. Broadly speaking, the self that dies remains "tuned in to" the state of existence as before. Just as there may be a "self" that undergoes anxiety and suffering, there may be a "self" that moves along on waves of joy. The functions or operations or activities of death, though different in texture from those of life, are nevertheless sustained by the essence of life. Death, being one with life, is also original and eternal.

While manifesting either death or life, our self is an integral part of cosmic life. Even within a person in the state of Hell, the supreme state of Buddhahood remains alive, for the energy of the Mystic Law permeates the deeper undercurrents of death. Filled with deep compassion, the Buddha illuminates the realities of life and death just as they are. This is the reflection of the Buddha's insight into a constant and ultimate reality for all forms of life, as well as the expression of the possibility of salvation, provided to calm the suffering of the dead.

LIFE IN OUTER SPACE

PROBABILITY

We have discussed life and death as alternating phases of eternal existence, but so long as we limit our discussion to ourselves and the planet we live on, we cannot really speak of eternity. Earth is only one of a number of satellites circling the comparatively small star we call the sun. There are countless similar stars in the Milky Way galaxy, and the galaxy itself is but one of innumerable galactic islands in the known universe.

The earth is thought to be more than 4 billion years old. The sun must be older, but how much older is uncertain. What does appear definite is that both will eventually die, whether in a gigantic explosion of the sun or by internal disintegration or through some other process. At all events, neither the earth nor the sun is eternal in the strictest sense; even the life of the Milky Way is presumably limited in comparison with that of the universe. The observable fact that all celestial bodies are constantly undergoing change may be seen as a spectacular physical manifestation of the Buddhist doctrine that all phenomena are impermanent.

From the astronomer's viewpoint, the Milky Way resembles other galaxies and the sun resembles other stars. Is it not possible that there exist, in the enormous vastness of the universe, solar systems like our own in which there are life-sustaining planets like the earth? Today, when simple organic matter can be created in the laboratory, the existence of life in other parts of the universe seems more likely by far than in the days when it was thought organic matter could not be synthesized from inorganic ingredients.

Some years ago Dr. Cyril A. Ponnamperuma, noted biochemist and professor at the University of Maryland, reported the discovery of a pyrimidine-type compound in a meteor fragment. Previously, Dr. Ponnamperuma and his group had found amino acids in another meteorite. In both cases, the substances isolated were so different from counterparts found in living things on earth that they must have come from outer space together with the meteorites. Since pyrimidine is a component of the nucleic acids found in living matter and amino acids are constituents of protein, Dr. Ponnamperuma's discovery suggests that the basic building blocks of life exist outside our planet. And since the meteor fragments studied are but a tiny sampling of those that have fallen to earth and an infinitely tinier sampling of those that must be flying about in space, the temptation is to believe that nucleic and amino acids must be widely distributed throughout the universe.

The mere presence of the materials, however, does not mean that life has come or will come into being. Certain environmental conditions must be fulfilled: it is difficult to suppose that life in any form we could recognize could exist in circumstances very different from those prevailing on our own planet. In the first place, since all stars so far observed are, like our sun, too hot to sustain living beings, the site would have to be a planet. It would also have to move in a stable orbit neither too near nor too far away from its star, or else temperature variations would be too great for life to exist. A third condition would be that the planet would have to be large enough for its gravitational field to trap oxygen, steam, or other gases needed to support living beings.

Because planets do not give off light of their own, those outside our own solar system cannot be seen. Theoretically, it should be possible to detect the presence of planets by measuring irregularities in the motions of the stars, but such irregularities are slight and the measurements difficult to make. It is nevertheless thought that Barnard's star, discovered in 1916 by the American astronomer Edward E. Barnard and located about six light years from the earth, has a planet about the size of Jupiter. A number of other stars in the general neighborhood of our solar system are also believed to possess planets.

The enormous number of stars makes it improbable that our solar system is the only one of its kind in existence. And if there are two, then why not three or four or fifty or a hundred or a thousand more? Most astronomers today believe the universe contains hundreds of millions of planets with more or less the same environmental conditions as the earth.

There remains a question of probability. In the best circumstances, it may take a long time for the potentialities for life to bear fruit. Note, for instance, that in the only case we even begin to know about, that of the earth, it is generally thought the first organic life came into being no fewer than 2 billion years after the planet itself was formed.

If we look at one of a pair of dice, we see it has six faces, and there is consequently one chance in six that a particular side will face upward when you toss it. But this does not mean the faces will appear in succession once every six times, nor is there any way to predict how many times you will have to throw to get the number you want. The conditions for the generation of life are like a face on a die, except that scientists still have no idea how many faces there are in all: there may be dozens; there may be billions.

With religious rather than scientific insight, Buddhist philosophers long ago developed the idea of the universe containing an infinite number of Buddha-lands extending out in all directions in the universe and encompassing all time, from the infinite past to the eternal future. They spoke of *sanze*, which means three temporal realms (past, present, and future), and of *jippō*, meaning ten (or all) directions, all of which are part of universal life. In his "Reply to Tayu-no-sakan," Nichiren Daishonin wrote, "A world (*shitenge*) is composed of Mt. Sumeru and the four continents surrounding it and other planets. Ten billion worlds compose one Minor World System, a thousand Minor World Systems form one Intermediate World System, and a thousand Intermediate World Systems compose one Major World System." In more simple language, this means there is an infinite number of life-sustaining worlds, each having its own Buddha. Buddhism is thus neither closed nor anchored to our small world. It expands indefinitely and encompasses all phenomena and all laws, both microcosmic and macrocosmic.

It does not seem likely we earth people will be able to make contact with extraterrestrial beings in the foreseeable future because of the extreme distances separating us from other stars and planets. Our science fiction writers are therefore free to go on inventing little green men from Mars and amorphous monsters invading earth from foreign planets. It is quite possible that living beings on other celestial bodies are too different in form from us even to be imagined by our writers. Considering the almost incredible variety of living things found on our own planet, there is little reason to suppose creatures in other worlds necessarily bear a physical resemblance to earthmen. All we can say in this respect is that the human form has proved itself suitable for the development of mental faculties, and it possesses the sensory organs needed to perceive sound, light, and smell. It is consequently reasonable to assume that at least some forms of life on other planets would resemble us in general structure.

On the other hand, even if there is a similarity, there might be some rather radical variations, owing for example to such differences as a lower or higher force of gravity. On Mars, where the surface gravity is only 0.38 that of gravity on earth, living beings otherwise similar to humans might be expected to be much taller and thinner; on Jupiter, whose gravity is 2.65 times as great as ours, men would presumably evolve into a more squat and sturdy form. Extraterrestrial people would most likely differ in color, and their sensory organs might have greater or less capacity.

We must also take into consideration the possibility of chemical differences. Animal life on earth, including humans, is based on the fact that protein molecules are active in water. Our bodies are composed of proteins and sustained by water and its constituents. It is said, however, that fats and fatty materials, known in general as lipides, could serve as the principal material for living cells under the proper circumstances. Lipides have sufficient growth capacity, which is to say sufficient instability, to sustain life, and they are distributed widely throughout the universe. Being capable of forming macromolecular groupings, they have the potentiality of becoming highly organized life entities. Isaac Asimov, a noted American biochemist, believes fluorocarbon and silicon fluoride could also form macromolecules and serve as the substance for living bodies.

Proteins are active not only in water, but also in liquid ammonia. Since ammonia liquefies at between minus 50° and minus 70°C., protein-based life would be possible at these low temperatures. Lipides could live in methane with hydrogen as their "water." Both fluorocarbons and silicon fluorides could form macromolecules in a medium of liquid sulfur. Asimov has listed six combinations that could result in the generation of life: (1) lipides in hydrogen, (2) lipides in methane, (3) protein in ammonia, (4) protein in water, (5) fluorocarbon in sulfur, and (6) silicon fluoride in sulfur.

Since hydrogen liquefies at about minus 240°C. and sulfur melts at more than 100°C., life based on these chemicals is possible at temperatures that would destroy life on earth. This raises the possibility that life of some kind might yet be found in other parts of our own solar system. In any case, the potentiality for life in other parts of the universe is vastly increased by including substances other than protein.

Silicon, one component of silicon fluoride, is very different from carbon, which is an essential component of proteins. We associate silicon with rocks, but if a type of organic substance developed from silicon, it would probably have a consistency like that of rubber. Presumably, a living body made of such a substance could resemble rock while functioning like an organism.

Whether it would be possible for us to communicate or share ideas with living beings not made of proteins is another matter. Certainly the sensory perception and ways of thinking of such beings would be very different from our own. From the physical and chemical standpoint, the air we breathe might be a virulent poison to beings formed of non-protein "flesh." Even supposing these beings had the same mental capacity as we do, would there be any subject on which they could converse with us?

It seems possible that beings of higher intelligence would have arrived at similar concepts of mathematics, physics, and chemistry. An American space program called Project Ozma has attempted to establish contact with beings in outer space by broadcasting mathematical formulas. On the other hand, unless such beings are similar to us, there seems little possibility of their being able to communicate with us in the fields of literature, social sciences, or the arts.

LIFE ON EARTH

No hard and fast conclusions being possible with respect to extraterrestrial life, let us turn our attention again to life as it has developed on earth, where mutual communication and understanding are possible. The fact remains that "Spaceship Earth" contains the only life of which we have any definite knowledge. In developing a philosophy of life, we must ask ourselves how it came about that living beings, including animals, plants, and innumerable microorganisms, happened to be born on this planet.

In general, there are two theories. One is that life arrived on earth from outer space; the other is that it was generated here. The first theory leaves us with the problem of explaining how life originated elsewhere.

Partly for this reason, and partly because the idea that the earth is not the center of creation is comparatively new, man's thinking on this subject has been dominated by the second theory. The Old Testament describes how God made the universe and all therein within a period of six days and rested on the seventh. Christian theologians long ago calculated that this took place about 4 thousand years before the birth of Christ. The idea of a world created by a deity is found among the mythologies of nearly all peoples, and was the generally accepted explanation until the age of science. As human knowledge expands, however, there are more and more people who doubt the very existence of gods, let alone the idea that one of them created the world.

If the world was not created by a deity, there is little choice but to regard life as a spontaneous development occurring in the course of the earth's evolution. This idea itself is not new. Aristotle believed eels were born of heated mud and bees from dew. The notion that living creatures came into being from the air persisted until Pasteur disproved it by showing that the organisms causing fermentation were produced from similar organisms suspended in the air. Scientists now believe primitive life came into being as a result of certain chemical and physical reactions that took place 2.5 or 3 billion years ago.

Because of the discovery of organic matter in meteorites, we cannot totally rule out the possibility that some form of life came to our planet from outer space. But since we have even less knowledge of conditions there than of those on earth, we might as well suppose life to have begun on our planet. To ascertain how, we must consider what the earth was like in the early stages of its development.

So far as scientists can tell, 3 billion years ago or so the planet was covered by cloud masses. Volcanic eruptions occurred incessantly, and molten rock spread over much of the earth's surface. Smoke and flames spat forth from fissure after fissure; vapor streamed upward even as rain poured down. Gradually the surface cooled and a crust was formed. Water gathered to form oceans. The atmosphere consisted of volcanic fumes, containing steam, methane, nitrogen, ammonia, hydrogen sulfide, and carbonic acid. There was little or no free oxygen and consequently no protective layer of ozone such as exists today. The sun's ultraviolet radiation beat mercilessly on the planet's surface.

Paradoxically, this hellish environment, which would presumably have destroyed any life coming in from without, was a prerequisite for the life that actually came into being. Only in such heat could the amino and nucleic acids making up proteins take form.

The most popular explanation of what happened next was offered in 1922 by the Russian biochemist Aleksandr I. Oparin, who argued that life came about in two stages. First, with the aid of ultraviolet rays or lightning, atmospheric constituents such as methane and ammonia were synthesized into the amino acids and adenine (a basic component of nucleic acid). The resulting organic compounds were carried by rain to the ocean, which gradually became a sort of nutrient "soup." In this milieu, repeated chemical reactions eventually led to a new stage, which was the creation of what Oparin called coacervates, the first primitive living cells.

There are important variations on this theme. John D. Bernal (1901–71) of the University of London, for example, theorized that life was generated on the surface of moistened clay on seashores, rather than in the sea itself.

Theories of this type have two points in common. One is that the primitive earth's surface presented conditions suitable for the generation of life. The other is that the life thus formed made its first appearance spontaneously on earth. It was neither created by some external being nor imported from some outside source.

Some scientists and philosophers have, while accepting these basic premises, hypothesized that the appearance of life on earth was a purely chance occurrence—a one-time event which might never happen anywhere else at any other time. The implication is that life as we know it is unique to earth. Among the facts supporting this idea, the most important relates to the chemistry of living bodies.

Protein molecules are composed of hundreds of amino acids. These exist in two known forms: L-amino acids and D-amino acids, which are in the geometric sense mirror images of one another. When amino acids are made in the laboratory, the L-amino forms and the D-amino forms are produced in equal proportions. Curiously, all living things on earth are made solely of L-amino acids. According to one view, only a completely accidental set of reactions could have led to this result.

In reply, it has been suggested that D-amino life forms which may have once existed became extinct during the course of the earth's subsequent evolution. This and perhaps several other theories are possible, but assuming that only L-amino acids existed at the beginning are we left with no other explanation than that of pure chance? I don't think so.

A chance origin flies in the face of probability. Among the many arguments cited, I am particularly attracted to one set forth by Prof. Haruhiko Noda of Tokyo University in his *Seimei no Kigen* (*Origins of Life*), which strikes me as being both graphic and easily understandable.

The number of different kinds of amino acids found in the structure of proteins is only twenty, and we must assume that they were all present on our planet at a very early stage. (To assume that any was lacking would be illogical, because all are essential to life.) These acids are strung together in chains to produce protein molecules.

Prof. Noda starts by considering a protein molecule composed of amino-acid chains of one hundred links. By his calculation, the probability that the given molecule would be produced by chance alone is only one in 10^{130}. Even if maximum yields were obtained, at least 10^{100} occurrences would be required to produce a single molecule of the designated type. Hypothetically, to carry out an experiment leading to the production of this one molecule would require 10^{75} tons of matter, whereas in fact all the matter in the known universe is thought to weigh no more than 10^{49} tons. Thus, even if the entire universe were composed of amino acids, which it is not, it would not contain enough material to fulfill the probability requirements for the yielding of one particular protein molecule. It is said, in fact, that if the entire universe consisted of the primary ingredients of nucleic acids, it is still not certain that the simplest nucleic acid would be generated in a billion years of consecutive reactions.

Probability is only probability. We cannot absolutely rule out the possibility of life's appearance on earth being a once-in-eternity event. Yet there is much more reason to suppose that the universe itself is endowed with an intrinsic tendency to develop toward life. Or, to put it figuratively, that the universe is a great womb, pregnant throughout with the miracle of life. As Prof. Noda said, "Should the 'impossible' have occurred, once and for all, without any reason, there is no room for further argument. But it is uncomfortable to have no answer at all. There remains the possibility that all matter in the natural world contains an inner urge to produce life."

If we accept the alternative—that nature is always prepared to create life; that the inclination toward life is immanent in the universe itself—it follows that macrocosmic life must possess some integral force enabling it to bring forth and nourish all the existing forms of life and induce them to perform their own acts of procreation. Prof. Noda is saying that even inorganic matter is oriented toward life.

Teilhard de Chardin seems to have thought in much the same way. He likens life to some sort of compressed gas always ready to burst forth from any tiny fissure in the universe. The earth itself, having taken form some 5 billion years ago, was in existence for some 2 billion years before life actually appeared. Chardin saw these 2 billion years as a time of preparation, during which the stage was set for the transformation of inorganic matter into organic matter.

In a sense, the difference between life and non-life is not as distinct as we are accustomed to thinking. On the face of it, organic compounds such as methane and ammonia are as devoid of life as inorganic substances. Yet when the organic chemicals are synthesized into complex amino acids, nucleic acids, and proteins, they undergo a transition that leads to primal life. Both Noda and de Chardin, different though their theories are, seem to point to a single conclusion: even prior to the genesis of life the earth was a gigantic mass of life-potential capable of giving birth to all the myriad beings which ultimately emerged.

Many scientists believe all the substances and environmental conditions required for life must have been present in the earliest stages of earth's development. I would go a step further and say there was also present an essential life-force, which must be inherent in the universe as a whole. For in the final analysis it is as difficult to explain why one planet or one solar system alone should contain this potentiality as it is to suppose that life came about on earth by sheer chance.

At the very least, we can say that the probability of life is determined by a life-directed force in the universe, which causes certain planets to possess the basic materials and conditions for the emergence of life in some form. A seemingly perfect environment will not necessarily produce life. We must suppose that in some cases the evolution of life is impeded by certain external forces. We do not know—perhaps cannot know—the formula or formulas governing the formation of life. Many chance factors, such as accidents of time or place, may be in operation—indeed almost certainly are in operation. It must be possible, as I see it, that in any place where the stage is set by cosmic-life's potential, new manifestations of life will appear, bearing characteristics suited to the specific conditions. The universe is a limitless expanse of space, and there is a limitless flow of activity. There is every reason to suppose that the raw materials of life are present in many parts of it, as well as manifold types of living beings or potentially living beings.

With the expected decline of the solar system and the earth, life as we know it will presumably be destroyed. But if it can be proved that other realms in the universe offer life-potential and life-supporting conditions, we will have scientific verification of the possibility that birth and death flow on throughout the cosmos, eternally repeating the cycle of transmigration. Even without that scientific verification, there is nothing to prevent our accepting this idea on faith.

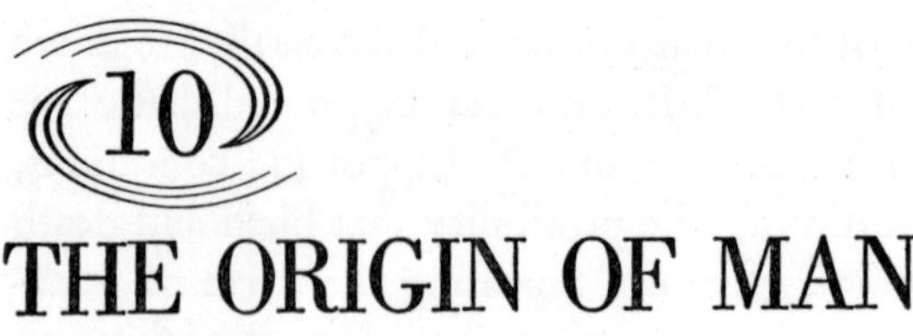

THE ORIGIN OF MAN

HUMAN EVOLUTION

The time generally thought to have elapsed between the formation of organic life on our planet and the appearance of human beings is about 3 billion years. During this time countless forms of life came into being and later died out. No fewer than one million animal species and a quarter of a million types of plants survive today. To describe evolution in its entirety would involve going into all the extinct organisms as well as those now alive. Since this is a practical impossibility, the subject is usually reduced to terms of specific types, of which the most important to us is man himself.

The American geneticist Theodosius Dobzhansky posited three basic stages in the development of the human race. The first, discussed in the previous chapter, is the period when primal life took form from inorganic matter. The second is the age in which what we normally regard as living creatures evolved. The third is the comparatively short period in which the ancestors of man became distinct from the rest.

Most current evolutionary theories are concerned with the second and third stages. The basic text is, of course, Charles Darwin's *Origin of Species*, in which the author modestly stated, "Light will be thrown on the origin of man and his history." Although there remain many mysterious points concerning the evolution of living creatures in general, and man in particular, Darwin's book set the basic guidelines for all later scholarship in this field. The principles it states are so widely accepted today that it is difficult to imagine the furor it aroused when first published in 1859.

At that time nearly everyone in the Christian world believed the story of creation as presented in the Bible. The Book of Genesis, having told how God created heaven and earth, recounts that on the fifth day he caused the waters to "bring forth abundantly the moving creature that hath life," and on the sixth day said, "Let us make man in our image, after our likeness." Learned theologians had long since calculated that this took place in 4004 B.C.; only agnostics were prepared to deny that the Old Testament should be taken literally. Even Thomas H. Huxley, the great biologist, was skeptical of Darwin's theory until he wrote a review of the *Origin of Species* for the London *Times*, though when he finished he exclaimed, "How stupid not to have thought of that!"

Controversy over Darwinism reached a height of sorts at the meeting in Oxford of the British Association for the Advancement of Science in June, 1860, when a celebrated confrontation took place between the now convinced Huxley and Bishop Samuel Wilberforce. When Huxley appeared to have won the day for Darwin, the bishop arose and said sarcastically, "I'm told you claim to have descended from apes. Well, is this on your grandfather's side or your grandmother's?" Amid the laughter, Huxley replied gravely, and tellingly, "If I were forced to choose my ancestors from between the pitiful ape to which you refer or a man who, though blessed with brilliant talent and great influence, devotes his energies to humiliating a sincere seeker for truth—without the slightest hesitation I would prefer the ape."

Neither Bishop Wilberforce nor many others were capable of understanding what Darwin really meant. Aside from the question of Biblical truth, Christian Europe was disturbed by the idea that man was not unique but rather a distant relative of lower forms of life. As the bishop's remark shows, most people knew Darwin's theories only in a vastly oversimplified version, and thought they meant that man was descended from the same sort of simians that inhabit the earth today.

In fact, modern scholars generally regard the forebear of both human beings and apes to have been a creature called *Dryopithecus fontani*, which first appeared about 40 million years ago and inhabited the earth for approximately 30 million years. During that interval, man's remotest ancestors must have begun an independent path of evolution separate from that of the apes. Yet since Darwin's time it has become impossible to regard man's existence as being set completely apart from the animal kingdom. Man and beast belong to a living continuum, there being animal characteristics in humans and human characteristics in animals. Instinct and primitive impulses, which govern the lives of lower creatures, are also important factors in man's psychology; conversely something resembling parental affection is found in many birds and beasts. As scientists have discovered, quite a few animals possess means of communication similar to the elementary speech processes of human beings. No doubt the overlapping explains why many people accept the idea that humans can transmigrate as animals and vice versa.

Still, human beings are undoubtably very different from animals, and the most crucial theme in the theory of evolution is the question of when and how they became so. In discussing this subject, we must of necessity try to define the essence of humanity—to pinpoint the quality or qualities only human beings have.

Among the creatures which may be direct ancestors of modern man is *Australopithecus*, who lived perhaps as early as 2,000,000 years ago and is sometimes described as "man ape" or "near man." This creature is thought to be related to *Pithecanthropus*, who dates from between 400,000 and 500,000 years ago; to *Homo erectus*, who does not go farther back than 100,000 years ago; and to *Homo sapiens*, who first appeared about 50,000 years ago. Today, all hominoids other than *Homo sapiens* are extinct. That the earlier types were progenitors of *Homo sapiens* is inferred from remains —including skulls, teeth, and pelvic bones—which indicate that they were erect bipeds who made use of tools, fire, and language.

It is thought that some apelike type of creature began to stand and walk on its hind legs not long after the time of *Dryopithecus*. Traces of roughhewn stone implements have been found in conjunction with *Australopithecus*, and the later *Sinanthropus pekinensis* left remnants of man-made fires. Neanderthal man, who belonged to the *Homo erectus* group, created the stone-age culture known as Mousterian, while Cro-Magnon man—considered an early specimen of *Homo sapiens*—left behind an impressive body of cave art. Verbal communication probably dates back millions of years.

Our only sources of information about hominoids or early men are fossils, stone implements, and a few other remains. New discoveries in this line will doubtless expand our knowledge and possibly reveal many other extinct hominoid types. For all their importance, the result of our diggings can at best disclose only a small fragment of prehistoric life. Of greater importance is the fact that some essential quality of man's early ancestors inspired him to make tools, weapons, and (later) art objects. This quality has been described by philosophers as intelligence, reasoning power, consciousness, or spirit. Bergson called it the "intellectual consciousness" and said it was implicit in man's tools.

What enabled man to survive in a hostile environment was not, after all, stone tools or weapons, but the intelligence that led him to produce these implements. The same mental power impelled him toward language and toward various technical skills. More important: it gave him a consciousness of self and a knowledge of an inner world within the self.

Immanuel Kant argued most eloquently that moral laws derived from practical reasoning are an indispensable element in the human state. In the *Critique of Practical Reason*, he wrote, "Two things fill the mind with ever new and increasing admiration and awe, the oftener and the more steadily we reflect on them: the starry heavens above and the moral law within." He continues, "The second (the moral law), on the contrary, infinitely elevates my worth as an *intelligence* by my personality, in which the moral law reveals to me a life independent of animality and even of the whole sensible world. . . ." I think we may say that an ability to reason and an innate moral law nurtured in primitive man the spiritual qualities that made it possible for him to sense oneness with his fellows. Without this, the development of the human race would have been impossible.

The latent potentiality for the development of intelligence and self-consciousness must have existed in all living things at the earliest stage of their evolution, but until the appearance of man its highest expression was instinct. The light of reason, as it were, was concealed within the limitations of an animal brain. Only when man came into being did this light become visible and effective. Once it did, however, it permitted man to take leave of the apes and proceed along an evolutionary path of his own.

Did *Dryopithecus* possess what we call intelligence and reason? It is difficult to say. Even the much later *Australopithecus* and Neanderthal man do not appear very intelligent in the various reconstructions we see. But this is perhaps misleading. One American anthropologist, Earnest A. Hooton (1887–1954), stated as he gazed at a Neanderthal skull that from it he could draw either the face of a chimpanzee or that of a philosopher. Intelligence, it seems, does not always appear on the surface.

In this connection, it may be observed that the brain of *Australopithecus* is considerably larger than that of a chimpanzee—500 cc. as compared with 300–400 cc. Brain size increased to about 1,000 cc. in *Homo erectus* and perhaps to as much as 1,500 cc.—the same as for modern human beings—in some Neanderthal men.

Even if our ancestors of 10 million years ago had far less mental capacity than modern man, he had what we may call the "fire of human intelligence." Even in the use of rough-hewn stones or pebbles as tools he was far beyond the ancestors of the apes in mental development. Though the subsequent growth of the intellect required millions of years, it was vastly more rapid than the progress of evolution prior to the first appearance of hominoids. Intelligence bred intelligence: the possession of certain mental faculties led to the rapid growth of the frontal brain lobe, where all higher mental activity takes place.

If we compare a human baby's intellect with that of a chimpanzee, we find them not very different. The baby can neither walk nor talk, and he appears to live entirely by instinct. In contrast to the chimpanzee, the baby's brain contains all the potential mental powers needed for his future as a human being. Though undeveloped, it has the essential qualities that make growth as a human being possible. This is not true of a baby chimpanzee.

To put it in different terms, no matter how immature or barbarous a human being may seem, he is endowed with the full range of human qualities, at least in a potential form. The light of intelligence and morality had already appeared in *Australopithecus*. It may be that his brain structure inhibited the flowering of the intellect, but his potential was perhaps as great as our own. The realization of this potential was the growth of brain capacity, which made possible the development of human culture.

THE NATURE OF HUMAN DEVELOPMENT

Since Darwin's time, scientists concerned with evolution have spoken in terms of mutation, natural selection, and adaptation. Mutation is the appearance of random variations in the hereditary process, caused in general by unusual combinations of genes. Suppose that among a group of like living creatures, a type is born that has certain special features. If these features are unsuited to the environment, the type will die out; but if they are better suited to the environment than the hitherto "normal" characteristics of the species, the type will tend to survive and pass its "idiosyncrasies" on to its progeny, which will gradually replace the earlier norm. By a process of natural selection and adaptation, those types best fitted to the circumstances survive and the others perish.

In traditional Darwinism, this process is regarded as more or less accidental. Prime importance is attached to environment, and the fittest individuals are thought to survive because of their chance relationship to it. Darwinism does not really concern itself with what goes on inside the living creatures themselves.

Lamarck, the French naturalist (1744–1829), placed emphasis on the independent, spontaneous activities of living things. His idea was that evolution takes place when living creatures try to adapt to their surroundings and deliberately pass on their acquired characteristics to the next generation. When a new environment requires new qualities, living beings seek to develop them in whatever way possible. Change in the species is thus brought about by an inner will to adapt. Stated somewhat dramatically, this means living creatures have control over their own destinies. Mutation is not entirely random, but at least to some extent directed.

A noted Japanese biologist, Dr. Kinji Imanishi, believes Lamarck was in some respects closer to the truth than Darwin. In discussing his own theory of the "mutation of frequent occurrence," Imanishi wrote: "In response to environmental change, a species of living beings increases the frequency of mutations. Then they encourage the mutations to develop in the most suitable direction. Since there is a great number of individuals within the species, random variations are bound to occur, and some mutations do not proceed in the proper direction. But little by little the number of mutations proceeding in the right fashion increases to the point that the well-adapted types become the mainstream. The pace of change, no doubt, varies with the particular species." I believe this idea is applicable to evolution as a whole. Just as other species produced frequent mutations moving in a particular direction, so man produced more and more mutations tending toward the development of brain power and other human characteristics.

I am reminded of Dr. Yuichi Okamura's very interesting book *Homo Sapiens?* (the question mark expresses the author's doubts as to whether *sapiens*—wise or knowing—is really applicable), in which he discusses the evolutionary divergence of men from apes. According to Okamura, human beings first came into being when the temperature of the earth was lowered to the extent that the size of the forests inhabited by the common ancestors of man and ape was being drastically reduced. Loss of forests meant loss of sustenance, but at least some of the man-apes had the drive to come down out of the trees and settle on the ground. These became the ancestors of man.

Though other scientists differ with Okamura on specifics, most are agreed that man's forebears were brought out of the trees by climatic change and resulting famine. This can be regarded as an adjustment to environmental change on a global scale. The accommodation was a dangerous step, because the ground to which the proto-humans descended was inhabited by all sorts of fierce animals.

If the hominoids had remained in the forests, they would either have starved to death or been vastly reduced in number. Their departure made it somewhat easier for those that remained to evolve into the apes and orangutans and chimpanzees of today, but it remains a fact that man's ancestors are the only creatures who attempted to solve the environmental problem by an exercise of will. From the biological viewpoint, their "moment of decision" was a mutation leading toward the development of man. This successful mutation continued to develop more and more human characteristics and eventually to display what we think of as the light of human intelligence. Though we may think of the first step as resulting from frequent consecutive mutations, we cannot avoid the conclusion that the life-activity leading toward human evolution was different from the life-activity in countless other species that have appeared and disappeared in the course of evolution as a whole. Physical impulse or instinct led other creatures to produce one new species after another, but the transition from beast to man was not an unconscious development. It involved the workings of some sort of inner intelligence—a light that did not shine in other species.

Teilhard de Chardin spoke of a *noösphere*, or spiritual sphere, which humanized the ancestors of man and set them apart from other creatures. I like to think of this as a primitive "frontier spirit," which is one of the terms Okamura uses to describe the "mind" latent in primordial human life. Interestingly enough, Okamura also speaks of this as the "insanity of genius," since, as he comments, "our ancestors' choice of migration [from trees] to an earth overrun with killers would have seemed like madness to an objective observer."

According to Okamura, the progenitors of the human race threw their energies and their exceptional ability into the invention and manufacture of weapons—the only means with which they could overcome the sharp fangs and claws of beasts. These fighting implements were in one sense the tools primitive man needed to enable him to win the struggle for existence. Speculation and insight—genius of a sort—led him to make use of sticks and stones to protect himself, and the use of such implements in turn opened the door to greater intellectual growth. In order to employ his weapons more effectively, he tried and eventually mastered the extremely difficult feat of standing and walking on his two legs. Okamura classes this as a "world-shaking concept—sheer genius."

Climatic changes and environmental threats, then, were among the stimuli necessary for the development of man's remote ancestors. If the primitive forests had continued to be livable, presumably the will to reach beyond would never have been asserted. Yet there always remains the question of what it was that made man seek different conditions when apes and other similar creatures did not. Granted that it was a "frontier spirit" of sorts, how did it happen that man alone came to possess it?

We have almost no clues as to the inner life of such early forms of humanoid life as *Dryopithecus* and *Australopithecus*. The best we can do is try to draw a few assumptions from the information we have about much later primitive types, Neanderthal and Cro-Magnon man. Even here, our knowledge is largely conjectural.

As I noted in an earlier chapter, Dr. Solecki, while excavating a Neanderthal site in Iraq, discovered pollen from flowers around a burial site, suggesting that Neanderthal people honored their dead and had certain definite ideas about death. It is only man, among the earth's many creatures, who has the intellectual power to form such concepts. Animals, living by instinct alone, do not seem even to be consciously aware of their own death.

Once primitive man developed the ability to think about death, it must have troubled him deeply. For him, the hostility of his surroundings meant that one careless move could mean sudden destruction. He was almost completely at the mercy of natural calamities, which presumably often wiped out whole groups. Even for Neanderthal man, the average life span seems to have been less than thirty years. Death was consequently a more immediate reality than it is for modern man. Fear of obliteration was probably an important part of everyday life, for the danger of death was ever-present.

As his intellectual powers developed, primitive man must have begun to wonder whether the dead simply ceased to exist or went to another world beyond the perception of the living. Neanderthal man seems to have believed in life after death, though he may have regarded it as a sort of eternal sleep. Near Le Moustier, in southern France, where the remains of the Neanderthal Mousterian culture were found, excavators discovered the grave of an eighteen-year-old boy who had been laid on his side with knees bent, his head pillowed on a pile of flint chips. In other graves, the remains of two adults and four children were found placed in the same way, with their heads facing east. Stone implements and animal bones were buried with the dead, presumably for their use should they once again awaken.

Among Dr. Solecki's more interesting discoveries was the skeleton of a man of about forty whose forearm had been amputated. This suggests not only that Neanderthal men may have had some primitive form of surgery, but, what is more important, that they at least on some occasions cared for the aged—in those times, a man of forty must have been too old to live on his own. Although a sort of parental affection is observed in animals, cooperative behavior directed toward the protection of the old and weak would not have been possible if early man had not possessed something on the order of Kant's "inner moral law."

I believe primitive man speculated on the mystery of life and death. His speculations led him to a belief in an existence beyond death, and also to a search of the innermost recesses of his own life. Dr. Solecki used the word "heaven" to describe what Neanderthal man sensed about the reality of human life and death. "Heaven," in this context, signifies a superior existence supporting and underlying all things in the universe and controlling all natural phenomena. It is, in short, cosmic life. Even in the distant past, man's ancestors held this fundamental reality in awe, for it gave them the power to overcome the difficulties they faced, including violent natural upheavals. Contemplation of death must have developed in Neanderthal man an intuitive knowledge of the essence of his own life and of the constant changes going on in nature. His eagerness to know, despite his lack of science and logic, was in no way inferior to our own.

The flowers at the grave sites may have been expressions of affection and respect, but they may also have come from the concept of a universal presence sustaining all phases of life and death. Perhaps these early men were confident that death was a return to the eternal flow of life—a rejoining of the fundamental reality beneath all phenomena. They may have sensed that this fundamental reality exists in all living beings, making them a part of the four cosmic stages of birth, maturation, destruction, and latency.

The idea that there can be communion with some greater reality, more lasting than individual life, is essentially religious, and I think it likely Neanderthal man experienced strong religious impulses, as a number of scholars have suggested. When we come to Cro-Magnon man, who is regarded as a direct ancestor of modern man, we find many beautiful works of art that are regarded as expressions of religious sentiment or of prayers. Such works as the famous wall paintings in a cave at Altamira testify not only to artistic ability, but also to a complex spiritual life.

In general, this cave art seems to have had ritual significance. The Cro-Magnons may, for example, have created the paintings as part of ceremonies designed to bring success to their hunts—expeditions on which the survival of the community depended. We may envision rites carried out by chanting magicians to secure the good fortune and fertility of the tribe. Though we regard these as primitive, they indicate the wish of the paleolithic hunter to express reverence for the immense power of nature. Cro-Magnon man was probably seeking some connection or identification with the universal forces of life.

What was true of Neanderthal and Cro-Magnon man may not have been true of *Australopithecus*, 2 million years earlier, but I believe that even the earlier pre-men must at least unconsciously have perceived something of cosmic life. So long as there is a spark of human intelligence, there will inevitably be an awareness of death. When even the most primitive laws of morality and practical reason come into being, then human wisdom begins to search for their source.

Religious feelings are a necessary element in humanity. They emerge simultaneously with intelligence and seek to fuse with the ultimate truth within. Intelligence and morality are communicated by such concrete means as language and the production of tools, which leave traces; but religious impulses are difficult for later observers to fathom, because they are completely inner processes.

Religious sentiment developed simultaneously with intelligence and other inner energies. But since the flow of cosmic life is an eternal reality, the religious sentiment of the individual man—along with his desire to unite with the ultimate—must be the origin of intelligence and morality. Religion is, in effect, a more essential aspect of human life than intelligence, morality, or conscience. Neither intelligence nor conscience can unlock the great door of life; the key to human existence is the inborn religious impulse that springs from and aspires to return to essential universal life. This is true today, and it has been true throughout human history. Hominoids could not have become human without intelligence, but only the religious feeling could have enabled them to develop intelligence and the other spiritual or mental capacities associated with our species.

The life-force is omnipresent, its functions underlying the cyclic birth and death of all living phenomena. Universal life was operating throughout the three-billion-year process required for the evolution of living creatures, and where there is universal life, there must also be religious sentiment and a continuing evolution.

The dynamic functions of cosmic life reached their zenith with the appearance of man. Adapting and responding to an enormous variety of external conditions, this essential force channeled evolution toward the human form. This means that each human being has a deep and intense communion with the infinite, eternal entity that constitutes the essence of universal life. The basic evolutionary plan of life as a whole and of man in particular must hold true throughout the macrocosm, even on planets beyond our power of observation. Although religious sentiment functions inseparably from many other human qualities, it is the principal impulse causing the development of intelligence and morality. It is the impulse that caused man to make his appearance in the world.

THE ETERNITY OF LIFE

FROM SENTIENT TO NON-SENTIENT

The first successful heart transplant, performed by Dr. Christiaan Barnard in late 1967, focused attention on the question of just when a human being may be said to have died. The idea of replacing a faulty heart with a healthy one is no more than a logical extension of the principle whereby corneas or kidneys are transferred from one person to another, but there is a vital difference: a heart transplant can be carried out only at the cost of the donor's life. The purpose of the operation, in a sense, is to convert one person's death into life for another.

Since the heart must be alive, it must be removed from the donor at the earliest possible moment. But if it is removed before the donor dies, the physician is guilty of murder. It is important then to know at just what point the donor may be said to be dead.

Curiously enough, medical authorities are not completely agreed on what constitutes death, or what phenomena represent the cessation of life. Usually a patient is said to have died when his heartbeat stops, his pupils no longer respond to light, and his breathing ceases. At this point, however, the patient is "too dead" for his heart to be transplanted. Dr. Barnard consequently used as his final criterion the absence of brain waves, thereby accepting the principle of "brain death," as opposed to "heart death."

While understanding the attitude of the physician who feels that it is better to transplant the heart of a patient he considers helpless to the body of another patient than it is to allow both of them to die, I nevertheless look askance at the application of the principle of "brain death." The fact is that the cessation of brain waves in the cerebral cortex does not mean the patient has absolutely no hope of recovery. Encephalographic specialists in particular deny the validity of "brain death," because they know of cases in which people whose electroencephalograms (EEG) have been totally flat for hours have eventually recovered. A report from the Toranomon Hospital in Tokyo states that out of fifteen patients registering no EEG activity, ten died, but five showed a resumption of brain activity. Two of the five later returned to their jobs.

Even if the probability of survival is as small as one in a hundred, it is not right to decide that the patient is completely hopeless. Obviously, the idea of "brain death" is based on an incomplete understanding of death itself.

"Brain death" means the death of cells in the brain. But in fact our body cells are constantly dying and being replaced by new cells. Skin cells, for example, are renewed daily, and the cells in our gastroenteric and respiratory systems are constantly undergoing metabolism. Tens of millions of cells in our body die every day, and tens of millions of new cells are born to replace them. As we noted earlier, the human body contains something like 60 trillion cells, all of them engaged in the continuous cycle of birth and death. Without this constant breakdown and renewal, human life cannot sustain itself. We might say, then, that the death of untold numbers of cells is one of the factors making life possible.

The life and death of a human being are matters of a higher order than the life and death of cells. Life is the process of harmonizing, integrating, and systematizing the life and death of various cells and organs. It is a state in which vital energy flowing in abundance unifies all the intrinsic functions of the body at every moment. And a living organism, which is an integrated unity comprising physical and spiritual phases, is able to exert an influence outside itself.

Human life expresses itself through both the body and the mind. Working in harmony and balance, our spiritual and physical elements integrate our being while at the same time acting upon our external surroundings. In Buddhism, life is considered to be formed of Three Bodies: the manifest body, or *ōjin*; the body of reward, *hōshin*; and the body of the Law, *hosshin*.

The functions that harmonize the buildup and breakdown of cells and govern metabolism correspond to the *ōjin*. But the *ōjin* is not merely the body; it is the total mechanism forming and controlling the physical aspect of life. As cells and organs, while possessing a separate life cycle of their own, go together to form the human body, so the various parts of our physical life integrate to form the *ōjin*.

Similarly, the *hōshin* consists not merely of knowledge, philosophy, and memory, but of all the mental activities that work to collect knowledge, retain it, and control emotions or impulses.

The *hosshin* is life's essential motivating force, perceptible only in the activities of the *ōjin* and *hosshin*. *Hosshin* is the core of life, or the self.

In *Great Concentration and Insight* (*Maka Shikan*), Chih-i states, "Life as the truth is *hosshin*, life as wisdom is *hōshin*, and life as it functions is *ōjin*." *Hosshin* is what would be seen if we could view life with complete objectivity and grasp its fundamental nature. It is the nucleus or generating force and it brings about the workings of the body and the spirit. *Hōshin* is the wisdom and other elements inherent in the spirit, while *ōjin* is the bodily activity that forms the physical aspect of life. Within our lives, the three are one and inseparable; each necessarily includes the other two.

Leaving this question aside for the moment, let us return to the case of people whose brains have become inactive, but whose other vital organs are still functioning. Such people are often said to have become "vegetables." Are they to be considered alive or dead?

In situations like this, the cerebrum is presumably dead, but the body is still alive. One might say that the transition from life to death has been interrupted midway. Yet so long as it has not been completed, there is still life. It is important to remember that death is not instantaneous. Though it sometimes seems very rapid, there is always a gradual change, a process whereby the inhibiting force of death shuts off life's functions one by one. One can find innumerable analogies in nature.

An oasis in the desert, for example. Its spring provides life-giving water, and life in the surrounding area takes the form of green trees, flowering plants, and tiny animals. But if the spring runs dry, the plants gradually wither, the animals die, and the oasis itself returns to the desert, no longer distinguishable from the vast stretches of sand around it.

The oasis is a form of life. While clean water wells forth from the earth, plants change with the seasons and the inhabitants live on from generation to generation. The individual plants and animals and human beings are all parts of the oasis's total life. They correspond to the cells and organs in a human body. The spring is the core of life—the *hosshin*. The water is the essence that makes physical and spiritual functions possible. If the water dries up, death ensues.

Human vegetables have a flat EEG reading, indicating the absence of life in the brain. The cerebral cortex, the seat of reason and emotion, has stopped functioning. This does not mean, however, that all the brain cells are dead. Huge numbers of them may be quite alive, though the energy or capacity to coordinate their functioning is missing. The strength of the *ōjin* insofar as it is connected to the cerebral cortex has disappeared. In normal life, the integrating force of the *ōjin* pervades not only the frontal lobe, but the whole of the cortex; in human vegetables the integrating and motivating energy of the *ōjin* is too weak to affect the cortex. The life of a person in this state is like an oasis running dry. As the flow from the wellspring diminishes, it reaches fewer and fewer places. The area dries up, beginning at the outer edges.

The still-living self is trying desperately to maintain enough energy to keep the physical and spiritual elements going, but its force reaches only to the brain stem, where it can control breathing and blood circulation, but not integrate the whole system. Even in this state, something inside the human being is doing everything it can to regain vital power. I do not believe it is right to terminate that effort from without. That "something inside" is, from the Buddhist viewpoint, the combined force of the *ōjin* and *hōshin*, both of which are struggling to stave off death.

In the vegetable state, a human being is unable to express emotions, but the *hōshin* is still there. Desire, impulse, sentiment, intelligence, and other mental faculties withdraw from the conscious mind, but continue to remain alive within the unconscious mind. They are among a vast number of mental currents continuing to flow in the depths of life. No matter how serious a patient's condition, the impulse to remain alive continues to exist. This remains true even after all the workings of the *hōshin* have merged with the universal life. The desire to continue living manifests itself as the fundamental energy that is life itself.

Some individuals experience a stronger desire for existence than they had ever imagined they would, while others are remorseful as they approach death and are faced with the reality of their lives. Sometimes the living self feels an intense hunger to survive and fights to hold on even to a bitterly painful existence rather than succumb to the unknown.

By way of contrast, some people enjoy a sense of tranquillity and fulfillment after the surging waves of emotion and impulse have died out; some retain a conviction that overcomes the fear of death. Such sensations belong to a different dimension than physical pain, spiritual distress, or the conscious feelings of sorrow or hate. They come into play after the transition of all conscious activity to the realm of the unconscious. As life is transformed into death, the deeper self within life regulates the workings of *ōjin* and *hōshin*. It has a sense of life that is completely unaffected by outside influences. Perhaps we could call it the sense of life of the *hosshin* itself.

In a collection of essays on death compiled by Dr. Michio Matsuda, I was particularly interested in one called "Phantom of Death" (*Shi no gen'ei*), by Masaru Kobayashi. Kobayashi being a professional writer, his account of his own brush with death is exceptionally articulate and realistic. "I was lying on an operating table," he relates. "As soon as the pain became absolutely unbearable, I felt myself coming apart and beginning to fly away. I was being transported at tremendous speed through the vast reaches of space." He felt himself leaving the warm earth and entering a cooler atmosphere. The space around him gradually changed from light to deep blue and then to a more and more impenetrable black. He somehow sensed that death was at the end of the absolute blackness.

Kobayashi's experience may have been influenced by his knowledge of astronomy. To others, the experience of coming close to death may be very different. In the ancient Oriental tradition, the souls of the dead must cross a mythical river leading to three evil worlds. This may be based on feelings people have had as they seemed to be approaching death. Kobayashi's account, it seems to me, being that of a modern individual, is more acceptable than ancient lore. It has much in common with the description Lord Geddes gave of his feelings at the time when an attack of gastroenteritis nearly carried him away. As noted earlier, Geddes perceived that the consciousness attached to his brain was beginning to break up, and that the consciousness related to his heart, kidneys, and other organs had already almost disintegrated. In this case, the self of life was witnessing the loss of the *ōjin*'s integrating power. Kobayashi, it will be observed, said that he felt himself to be "coming apart."

As the functions of the *ōjin* decline, the consciousness that goes together with the cells and organs is gradually separated from them and merged into the flow of the earth and the universe. It is as though the spring in our oasis had lost touch with the exterior and retreated into the desert's subterranean currents. Like the *ōjin*, the *hōshin* also subsides and, together with the *hosshin*, fuses back into the great flow of cosmic life.

Kobayashi's sensation of flying through space may have represented the beginning of the unification of the individual self with the cosmic entity. For death is not the extinguishing of life, but the merging of individual life with the greater, permanent life of the universe.

We might recall again our comparison of the life of a human being to an iceberg. The consciousness and the physical activities of the human being are like the portion of the iceberg visible above the water. Beneath these lies the vast unconscious. Death is like the melting of the iceberg into the boundless sea. As death comes, both the visible tip and the massive base of the iceberg of human life melt into the sea of universal life. But the human life is not destroyed: as the iceberg becomes an integral, potential part of the ocean, so the human life becomes an integral, potential part of cosmic life.

As for Kobayashi's feeling that everything was getting colder and colder, the sensation may well come from leaving the world of the sentient and entering that of the non-sentient. Sentient beings, as we know, possess emotions, sentiments, feelings, and conscious thoughts—man is the archetype. Non-sentient beings, on the other hand, are life entities in which emotional and conscious forces are inactive or dormant. Trees, rocks, stones, and the like are examples. I would assume that as Kobayashi's life hung between the sentient and the non-sentient, his deeper self sensed the approach to the latter state as increasing coldness.

When our life undergoes the transition from manifest to latent—from the sentient to the non-sentient—both its physical and its mental aspects are conjoined with the physical universe, which is itself non-sentient. Kobayashi's deepening cold, then, must represent the vastness of physical space. Interestingly enough, Kobayashi reports no sense of emotion—no loneliness, no pain, no grief. The only inextinguishable sensation seemed to be an indescribable feeling of annoyance. This I interpret to be the life-feeling of the *hosshin*, which becomes clearer as every other feeling disappears. Kobayashi wrote that to die with this sense of annoyance must be the greatest despair of all. That he experienced no sorrow or grief may well mean that he had lived a full and proper life. As it happens, Kobayashi had previously viewed death as a complete obliteration, the absolute end of a human being's life. Even a person who has lived a worthwhile life must be seized at the end with annoyance or regret if he thinks his life is coming to a complete halt. Had Kobayashi believed in eternal life, he might well have experienced hope instead of annoyance.

If people would only realize that life is a perpetual repetition of birth and death—if this belief were allowed to become not only a philosophy but an integral part of life—then it could provide the strength to overcome the fear of death, as well as the accompanying spirit of despair. But even then, unless one's philosophy is a great deal more than skin-deep, it will disintegrate in the passage from sentient to non-sentient being. Kobayashi himself admitted that if the philosophy he regarded as his spiritual foundation was only a borrowed idea, it could not help him confront the appalling reality of his own physical destruction.

If we succeed in establishing the concept of eternal life as more than an intellectual idea, if over the years we make it an integral part of our lives, then it will serve us as a powerful weapon when it comes our time to face death. I only hope that what I have written will help my readers build a stronger, more positive attitude toward the eternity of life.

THE PERMANENT SELF

In his work entitled *On the Ultimate Teaching Confirmed by All Buddhas* (*Sanze Shobutsu Sōkammon Kyōsō Hairyū*), Nichiren Daishonin said, "The Buddha, perfectly enlightened in the Three Bodies, takes the entire universe as his true body, takes the entire universe as his spiritual nature, takes the entire universe as his physical existence." It is clear from these teachings that the "Buddha, perfectly enlightened in the Three Bodies" refers to ourselves in an enlightened state. Since Nichiren Daishonin taught that life and death are but two aspects of eternal life, it follows that the Three Bodies can be found in death as well as life, for they are inherent in cosmic life itself, whether they are in the sentient state or the non-sentient state. The *ōjin* is united with the physical universe; the *hōshin*, with the spiritual universe; and the *hosshin*, with cosmic life itself. It must never be forgotten that in cosmic life, the spiritual and the physical are one.

At the time of death, the Three Bodies become one with the eternal flow of the universe. For this reason, death is said to be inherent in life. After death, the individual workings of the *ōjin* and *hōshin* become indistinguishable from the whole, because they are in the potential state of *kū*. The *hosshin*, the self, is also absorbed within the cosmic whole. Unlike certain other religions, genuine Buddhism does not hold that the self of the individual dwells in heaven or wanders from place to place within the unseen world. In the Buddhist belief it is united with the universal life.

In *Man's Concern with Death*, Prof. Toynbee speaks of an "immortal sea," which is mentioned in a poem by Wordsworth. Of it, he writes: "We might think of a human person—which is the only kind of person that we know—as being a wave that rises and falls, or a bubble that forms and bursts, on the 'immortal sea's' surface. Like a wave or a bubble, a human person is ephemeral in himself. . . . The person who lives and dies in a psychosomatic organism on this planet may be a manifestation of Eternal Spiritual Reality."

Elsewhere, Prof. Toynbee says: ". . . it would seem to follow that, at death, the aspect of a human being that we call his spirit or his soul ceases to be the ephemeral separate personality that it has been during the now dead human being's lifetime, but continues to exist as the ultimate spiritual reality with which, even in bodily life on Earth, it has never ceased to be identical in the spiritual vision of observers who have the inward eye to see."

Toynbee's "ultimate spiritual reality," which he describes as pervading the universe, is at least akin to the Buddhist cosmic life, and his analogy of a wave rising and falling on the " 'immortal sea's' surface" is similar to the iceberg I spoke of. Yet Toynbee seems to suggest that the communion between the individual and universal life that takes place at death means the total extinction of human individuality, whereas we believe that individuality continues to exist in a dormant state. If asked whether a human life is existent or non-existent in the state of death, we would have to reply neither, for it is in the state of *kū*, transcending existence and non-existence. At the time of death, the individual life changes from perceptible existence to latency, but since *kū* itself cannot be fully defined, we can offer no complete description of exactly how the self continues in this state.

In the *Orally Transferred Teachings* (*Ongi Kuden*), Nichiren Daishonin says, "*Kū* means nothingness, but not absolute nothingness. This nothingness transcends what appears to be existence." I interpret this to mean that *kū* is the potential-void combining Provisional Perception, Perception of the Latent, and Perception of the Middle Way. After death, our *ōjin* merges with Provisional Perception (*ketai*); our *hōshin*, with Perception of the Latent (*kūtai*); and our *hosshin*, with Perception of the Middle Way (*chūtai*). All are one, and all are identical with the life of the cosmos, but the life composed of the Three Bodies continues even in this state to possess its individuality.

One is tempted to think that if the self retains its individuality it must of necessity occupy some definite space, as it does in normal life. It is impossible, however, to consider *kū* as being limited to a spatial dimension. The best clue as to how an individual exists after death is probably the last sensation of the *hosshin* that emerges as death draws near. This sensation, I believe, is governed by the basic state of the individual's life.

We come back, in the long run, to the Ten States of Being, which were discussed in part two in considerable detail. In life, we are constantly moving from one state to another, but over the years each person manifests a basic tendency toward a particular state. Unless he experiences the human revolution and it causes him to become a Bodhisattva or Buddha, he is constantly reverting to one of the lower states of being. There are, for example, human beings whose basic tendency is toward the state of Hell. Even though they experience other states from time to time, they are constantly returning to this condition of extreme agony. Other people are similarly inclined toward the states of Hunger or Animality or Anger or Humanity or Rapture.

So long as one is a sentient being, it is possible to change one's basic tendency. The path is open toward self-reformation and the creation of a new life-tendency. But with the transition from sentient being to non-sentient being, the individual loses the capacity to enter any other realm than the one that has become basic for him. In becoming non-sentient, he loses the power to respond to external stimuli.

In life, desires and emotions are as a rule conditioned by outside factors. A person suffering from an illness can obtain relief by taking an appropriate medicine—he can, in other words, leave the state of Hell and enter that of Humanity through the influence of an external factor. A person thirsty for love can find fulfillment, and one hungering for knowledge can come across the information that takes him into the state of Learning.

As death approaches, external means of altering one's state of being gradually drop away. Money, power, social standing, even love can no longer bring about a basic change. As the three phases of life undergo the change from sentient to non-sentient, the power to influence the environment or be influenced by it is lost. The basic condition experienced in life thus becomes fixed. One whose life is directed toward Hell falls further into the abyss of agony after he dies. One who was constantly succumbing to desire becomes even more tortured by a sense of frustration. One basically inclined toward Animality experiences a permanent state of dismal terror.

On the other hand, a person whose fundamental tendency is toward Humanity or Rapture surmounts the physical pain of death and becomes filled with a sense of satisfaction or elation. The person directed toward the state of Realization will experience spiritual contentment even after death. More important, a life based on the compassion and altruism of the Bodhisattva will retain these feelings throughout the experience of death and its aftermath. Such a person, when about to die, might literally offer his life to guide the living. The self consumed by compassion sees death as the same sort of challenge as life. To him, it may be a rare opportunity to do good for mankind. The higher understanding he has achieved may cause him to regard his own death as an expression of the compassion of cosmic life.

Buddhahood is the wellspring of compassion, courage, and wisdom. Only those who succeed in establishing the supreme state of Buddhahood as the central tendency of their lives can subdue the fear of death to the point of causing it to lead directly to the salvation of others. But the state of the Bodhisattva Nature and of Buddhahood cannot be feigned. If a person's apparent compassion in this life is nothing more than a pretense, death will reveal it.

Death is the great unmasker. The pain and fear it brings put an end to false philosophy and religion. Before them, false emotions are revealed and base desires uncovered. Death invariably reveals an evil nature, even one successfully concealed throughout a long life. Only by living a genuinely good life can one be sure one's death will be a source of strength and truth to those who survive.

Once dead, we lose all power to change ourselves. Self-motivated change is impossible because the forces that move the Three Bodies—*ōjin*, *hōshin*, and *hosshin*—have all become dormant. If, of course, a person is in the state of the Bodhisattva Nature or Buddhahood, there is no need for reform. But if he is in one of the evil states, his suffering becomes more intense than in life. Instead of going from one state to another, he is locked in the one toward which his life was directed. If it was Hell, he experiences not personal but universal Hell; if it was Hunger, he experiences not occasional but continuous Hunger. In the cosmos, as in our individual lives, the Ten Worlds exist within each other, but the dead, who are non-sentient, can experience only the one to which their lives led them.

In his "Reply to Soya," Nichiren Daishonin wrote, "People in the state of Hunger see the Ganges River as fire; people in the state of Humanity regard it as water; people in the state of Rapture find it to be nectar." The dead self experiences that which it has been prepared in this life to experience.

People in the six lower realms of existence are more acted upon than acting. It consequently follows that when death has deprived them of all means of positive action, they are entirely subject to the conditions of the realm their self inhabits. The situation is different for those who dwell in the four higher states, for they have achieved this status not through outside influences but through their own effort. When they die, they too become non-sentient, but the worlds they inhabit are by their nature endowed with cosmic life-force.

The self in the state of Learning or Realization no longer retains the power which it had before death to seek and practice the Law, but it can still experience joy because of the causes it made during its lifetime. In the case of the life that is in the state of the Bodhisattva Nature, any realm it inhabits becomes a place for the exercise of compassion. The life of the Bodhisattva fuses with the cosmic Bodhisattva-world—it becomes an integral part of the infinite compassion that works to relieve men of suffering and grant them peace. In the same way, the self that is in the state of Buddhahood becomes one with the very source of cosmic life, merging into the ultimate reality of the universe, seeing all phenomena as the actions of the Buddha, becoming identical with the eternal land of enlightenment.

Even in death, the life in the state of Buddhahood possesses the boundless wisdom of cosmic life and the power to exercise infinite compassion, whether deep inside the earth's scorching depths, or in the coldest iceberg, or amid raging seas, or in the continual changing of the seasons, or in the complex interaction of egos and desires we call human society. Buddhahood is infinite and eternal, whether in life or in death.

CONDITIONS FOR REBIRTH

Sophocles wrote, "Best of all is never to have been born, and second best, second by far, if one has made his appearance in this world, is to go back again, as quickly as may be, thither whence he has come, that is, to die young." This is a view that may appeal to many pessimists today, and one that is not far from the Hinayana Buddhist belief that one can enter nirvana only by escaping from the cycle of transmigration.

But the Lotus Sutra, which is the essence of truth, tells us that the perpetual repetition of birth and death is an essential principle of life. The achievement of perfect peace lies not in dying but in the attainment of Buddhahood in this life. Nor does death offer a relief from suffering, for he who has not achieved the higher state of being may be fated to suffer far greater anguish in death than in life. Had Sophocles been a Mahayana Buddhist, his wish would have been the opposite: he would have wanted not to die at all, or, failing that, to remain in the state of death as short a time as possible.

In the writing called *On Revealing Slanders* (*Kenhōbō Shō*), Nichiren Daishonin said a person dying in a state of extreme agony is doomed to suffer the flames of the lowest Hell for one thousand kalpas or more. One kalpa usually being regarded as either 8 or 16 million years, this is a long time indeed, though, as I have pointed out earlier, we are talking in this case about subjective time rather than conventional time. If death confines the self in one of the evil states, the agony suffered therein is all the greater for being inescapable. Even if the time spent there is short in the absolute sense, to the self that senses it subjectively it might endure for countless eons.

Since the state in death of those in the upper realms of existence is a happy one, it might be supposed that the self in the state of the Bodhisattva Nature or the self in the state of Buddhahood would be content to remain dead for an indefinite length of time. But the contrary is true: the sense of responsibility for others—the feeling of infinite compassion for others—causes the Bodhisattva or Buddha to reappear in the world of the living immediately. A life whose main tendency is toward Buddhahood never for a moment ceases to shift from life to death and back to life.

In *On the Ultimate Teaching Confirmed by All Buddhas* (*Sanze Shobutsu Sōkammon Kyōsō Hairyū*), Nichiren Daishonin says, "The believer of Nichiren will be reborn in the land of eternal enlightenment, yet, in an instant, return to this dreamlike world of birth and death in the Nine Worlds, his body becoming one with all lands in the infinite cosmos and his mind reaching all sentient beings. Thus he will inspire them from within and guide them from without. With internal and external causes fusing in harmony, the all-powerful, mystic strength of compassion spreads itself throughout, bringing benefit to all sentient beings." Here we may take the phrase "reborn in the land of eternal enlightenment" to mean the death of the person who has established Buddhahood as the basic direction of his life. Nichiren Daishonin is telling us that this person in the state of Buddhahood no sooner dies than he returns to the world of the phenomenal with its cycles of life and death.

Such a person must sense his reappearance in the world as occurring instantly after death. To him the subjective time interval approaches zero, and even in this momentary passing he experiences infinite kalpas of perfect bliss.

I have been asked why there is such a huge difference between the death interval for the self suffering in Hell and that for the self rejoicing in Buddhahood. To answer this question, we must consider the connection between life-death and the transition we call rebirth. How and why does this transition take place?

A valuable clue appears in a passage of the *Orally Transferred Teachings* (*Ongi Kuden*) in which Nichiren Daishonin says, "Becoming and departing are equal to birth and death. . . . Becoming is the condensation of the cosmos into one heart; leaving means opening out into the universe." In other words, birth means the gathering together of universal life into one self, while death is the dispersal or redispersal of that self into the universal continuum.

In describing *kū*, I have previously used the analogy of radio waves in the space around us, which contain potential pictures, sounds, and data that can be translated into reality only through a proper receiver. At the time of death, the self enters the state of *kū*, in which it is fused with all sorts of potential forces, just as radio waves are mingled together in space. When the proper "receiving apparatus" is available, the self can reappear as a perceptible entity in the ordinary world.

Josei Toda, the second president of Soka Gakkai, compared the relationship between life and death to a game of *go* between two experts. Often it becomes necessary for the players to stop for the night and resume the game in the morning. When they do this they remove the black and white stones from the board and replace them in their boxes. The following morning, the stones are set out on the board just as they were the night before. In the case of experts, the game is so fixed in their minds that there is no chance of a mistake in putting the stones back on the board.

Toda said that death is like the breaking up of the formation on the board at bedtime, while life is the ongoing game. During the night, the stones retire from the scene of action, but the game itself remains alive in the minds of the players. This is another way of expressing Nichiren Daishonin's statement about becoming and departing. Just as the *go* stones leave at night and return in the morning, so the dying self disperses into the universe, to return again in a pattern that accords with its previous life-tendency. The entity of life thus continues throughout the phases of dispersion and condensation.

When a life in the state of Hell reappears in the world, its activities retain the same tendency. The same is true of lives in the state of Hunger or Animality or any of the other states of being. There is no guarantee, of course, that a person in one of the lower states will not be reborn as an animal or an amoeba or a curious being on another planet.

Assuming the self is reborn as a human being, let us give some thought to just how this comes about, for in a way the phenomenon of birth illustrates the principle of becoming and departing, as stated by Nichiren Daishonin.

A human life is conceived when a sperm cell (spermatozoon) unites with an egg cell (ovum). The sperm cell resembles a tadpole; it consists of a head and a long tail that enables it to swim. When the sperm cell collides with the egg cell, the tail breaks off and the head alone makes its way to the nucleus of the egg. As the two unite, in the process of fertilization, they produce a zygote, which is the smallest form of human life. The zygote then begins the process of cellular division by which it grows into an embryo.

The two principles, sperm and ovum, are both independent, highly specialized life cells. The zygote, too, is a single cell, not materially different in appearance from the unfertilized ovum, which is much larger than the sperm. Yet the zygote resulting from their combination functions quite differently from either of its components, for the zygote is a human life, containing all the basic information needed to determine the character of the human being into which it will grow. Having incorporated the potential elements in the sperm and ovum, it begins new activity as a separate sentient being.

Until the ovum and sperm unite, the entity of human life is still in a potential or "dead" state, waiting for the opportunity to manifest itself. Fertilization is the process whereby the individual life entity is transformed from *kū* into a living organism. The zygote is endowed with the Three Bodies, *ōjin*, *hōshin*, and *hosshin*. The zygote has *become*, in the sense in which Nichiren Daishonin used this word: it may be regarded as the "condensation of the cosmos into one heart."

Like all other living entities, the zygote is composed of universal matter and has an indissoluble relationship with its surroundings. Its atoms and molecules come from the ovum and sperm cells, which are physical parts of the parents. Conception takes place within the mother's womb. The mother herself is connected by infinite ties with her environment. From the beginning, then, the zygote is related to the natural and social surroundings in which its mother lives.

Fertilization might be regarded as the external cause of rebirth. The internal cause is the potential inherent in the self that has been in the state of *kū*. The strength of this internal cause—which is to say the strength of its potential for rebirth—depends on the state of being in which the self resides. If it is in one of the Six Lower States, its energy is relatively weak; but if it is in the state of Buddhahood, its energy is equal to that of the universe. Hence the enormous difference between the length of time a person in Hell remains dead and the almost non-existent interval during which a Bodhisattva or a Buddha is dead. The self in Hell is almost too weak to reappear at all, but in the case of Buddhahood, "the all-powerful, mystic strength of compassion" comes into play.

In a work entitled "On Compassion" (*Jihi-ron*), Josei Toda said, "To begin with, the entire universe is the true body of the Buddha, and the phenomena taking place in the universe are all the work of compassion . . . Since the universe itself is compassion, what we do every day is naturally the work of compassion. But as human beings, we must not content ourselves with being like ordinary animals or plants. We must try instead to perform acts of a higher order so as better to serve the Buddha." Compassion is essential for faith; it is also the fundamental source of energy. While we are alive, it brings us together with the cosmos and guards our actions. While we are dead, it becomes the energy that will eventually bring about our rebirth. The energy of compassion within a dormant self leads it to acquire the form of life in which it can best express compassion. As Josei Toda implied, the human being is a better suited instrument of compassion than plants or animals.

Many people ask me whether there is nothing a dead person can do to influence his next life. The answer, I fear, is no. The self in the state of death (of *kū*) is totally incapable of self-motivation. The dead person must await the power of such compassion as he has within him.

Yet Buddhism does recognize one, and only one, way in which the condition of a person in the state of death can be improved. That is through the actions of the living. While we cannot communicate with the dead or summon them back to life through magic, it is possible, through our own Buddhist practice, to draw on the cosmic life-force and transfer this energy to our dead loved ones. This possibility was mentioned earlier in connection with our discussion of the Ten States of Being.

A scripture called the *Ubasokukai* Sutra states, "Even though a father dies and descends into the world of Hunger, if his child sends him good fortune, he will receive it." The meaning is that the son's gift of energy tapped from the ultimate cosmic compassion will be bestowed upon the dead father, thus improving the lot of his dormant self. The more energy a dormant life receives in this fashion, the greater its potential for remanifestation as a living being, possibly even one in a higher state of existence than before. We can say that Buddhist memorial services offer a means of salvation which the Buddha has provided even for those so unfortunate as to enter death in one of the lower states of being. The energy in question, however, can be evoked only by the living.

IMPLICATIONS FOR OUR PRESENT LIFE

I have written at some length about the Buddhist view of eternal life as compared with the idea that death is final, and with other doctrines of immortality. It remains for me to suggest the import of these theories for the living. Unless our ideas concerning death have some bearing on the way we conduct ourselves in this life, they can amount to little more than idle speculation on a subject that cannot in the nature of things be fully known.

Among those who believe life is a one-time proposition, we have both hedonists and pessimists. In general, the hedonist believes that since death is final, we had best try to find as much pleasure as possible before it occurs. The pessimist often argues that even life's pleasures are too fleeting to be satisfactory and, consequently, death is ultimately preferable to life. These two trains of thought seem to me to be particularly common in the modern world. A special form of pessimism encountered today is the idea of opposing the *system* or the *establishment*, to which are attributed all of life's miseries. More often than not this results from a feeling of emptiness, which then seizes upon a flaw in the social system as the cause or symbol of life's meaninglessness. It may well be a sign not so much of a rebellious spirit as of a lack of spiritual roots.

There are, to be sure, those who, though rejecting the idea of an afterlife, attempt to make their present lives as worthwhile and noble as possible. Such people often devote themselves to work which they believe will contribute to the benefit of mankind. Others consciously overcome the normal fear of death by creating works that will survive their own passing. We find this type of attitude among a number of philosophers who dedicate their lives to searching for the truth and doctors who devote themselves to relieving the world's suffering. I am reminded, in this connection, of a statement made by Dr. Hideo Kishimoto, a professor of religion, as he described his own bout with terminal cancer: "In this state when one feels totally oblivious of the world, humans, and time, one feels rich and specific experiences open in the depths of his mind. This must be the sensation of eternity, transcendence, and absoluteness. When this brilliant experience pervades the entire psyche, he can feel eternity in each and every moment. The reality of eternity is now, in the present moment."

In a somewhat different context, I think of the Meiji-period writer Chogyū Takayama, who believed he himself would live on in his literary works and staked his life on completing them. One cannot help admiring people who, despite their disbelief in a hereafter, nevertheless lead brave and beautiful lives. Still, as Josei Toda pointed out, it is difficult for the great majority of people to behave in this way. A handful of people may realize specific spiritual goals without faith in eternity, but this is too much to expect of ordinary mortals, who are inclined either to try to put the fear of death out of their minds or turn to any expedient that seems to offer a chance of forestalling it. In this sense, those few people are in the state of Learning or Realization, unable to offer any help to others. Any philosophy promising a person a full and meaningful life in the present, even though he believes there is no life to come, is to be valued, but it cannot usually do much for people dominated by the dread of dying.

There are those whose belief in the finality of death leads them to feel a strange attraction to it. The inclination to suicide, it would appear, is particularly strong in literary figures. Not a few people, it seems, fear the prospect of becoming old and ugly to the extent that they do away with themselves before they reach that stage. In fact, the egoism of suicide does more to impair the value of their existence than the ravages of age could possibly do.

As for the relatively common belief that immortality means being reborn in some heavenly realm, it seems doubtful to me that any creed of this sort can really enrich a person's life on earth. Indeed, I suspect the opposite is more frequently the case, because the hope for a future paradise seems to encourage a feeling of resignation in the face of life's difficulties.

A good example is the doctrine of the Pure Land faith, according to which believers are reborn in a western paradise after they die. In Japan, what this belief actually produced was not hope, but an abandonment of expectations of happiness in this trouble-ridden, "impure" world. Believers ended up becoming escapists of a sort, seeking utopia only in the afterlife. It is significant, I think, that the suicide rate in Japan was extremely high in the periods when the Pure Land sects flourished.

A view of life particularly objectionable to Buddhism is the idea that all living things undergo an eternal fixed cycle of transmigration. In other words, a man is always reborn as a man, a dog as a dog, and an ear of wheat as an ear of wheat. No matter what a person does, he can never change his fundamental destiny. The Buddhist theory of cause and effect, which is basic to the Buddhist faith, is a denial of this type of thought.

To Nietzsche, we might note, eternity was in a sense circular; he used the term *ewige Wiederkunft* to refer to the eternal recurrence of the same events at gigantic intervals. But even Nietzsche claimed that one could attempt to perfect oneself in this life—a view which is in many ways inconsistent.

It is a mistake to describe transmigration as a closed circuit on a plane. We must think of it as a three-dimensional, open cycle—a spiral that may lead upward or downward. As life undergoes the eternal repetitions of birth and death, it expands in a free and dynamic fashion, always charged with limitless potential for self-improvement. This view of eternal life accords with the Buddhist philosophy of causality.

Living organisms eternally go back and forth between life and death, which are themselves but two phases of existence. The causes formed by a person in the present become manifest as effects in the future. If people apply this simple law to their lives, it is possible for them to develop a constructive, hopeful attitude toward their daily activities and to recognize the true value of life in this present world. The future does not exist apart from the present, nor will it remain fixed in a single plane. What and how we will be in lives to come depends on what we do now. Every single act and thought plays a role in shaping our future existence, both in life and in death. The law of causality is valid for every life, because it permeates and molds the great, eternal flow of cosmic life.

What, then, are the practical implications of this philosophy? How should it affect our conduct and our attitudes?

In the first place, it provides us with the courage to challenge both life and death. It enables us to see death not as some terrifying unknown, but as a normal phase of existence that alternates with life in an eternal cycle.

Second, it teaches us to treasure the life we are now living and to try to make it as worthwhile as possible. If we believe in our hearts our present behavior creates and determines our future existences, we will strive to cultivate ourselves and to make the most of what each day offers.

Third, it teaches us that the only way to fulfill the potential of the human race is to live just, kind, benevolent, and compassionate lives. We are helped by being aware that each activity in which we engage can be the source of growth and self-reformation. It is comforting to know that the good fortune we amass by means of our conduct is undiminished by death, that it is integral with life itself and enhances our eternal self.

Finally, this way of thinking enables us to control and subdue our instinctive desires, redirecting them in such a way as to elevate our state of being. We learn to avoid the pitfalls of hedonism and pessimism, to find joy and truth in compassion rather than in an ephemeral hope for rebirth in paradise.

Some people familiar only with Hinayana or with Pure Land ideas see Buddhism as pessimistic or nihilistic—something designed only to prepare people for death. In fact, Mahayana Buddhism aims at teaching all human beings how to enjoy their lives in the truest sense of the word. A phrase in the Lotus Sutra says plainly: *this world itself is where people can live in happiness and peace.* Far from being negative, true Buddhism affirms and exalts life. For the Buddhist philosophy of eternal life is not an expedient designed to persuade people to accept their mortality; it is a realistic and unfailing view of life established through myriad struggles against the sufferings of birth, old age, sickness, and death. It teaches us to face up to the harsh realities of life with conviction and hope; it enjoins us to devote all our actions and our thoughts to the welfare of others, because compassion is the ultimate source of cosmic life.

By cherishing this philosophy we can turn each difficulty into a source of power bringing joy to our lives. The trials we face become ingredients for the building of our characters. Hardship becomes the fertile soil in which tiny new shoots spring up and flourish. Each bead of sweat expended in the struggle for self-protection and the betterment of our society becomes the seed of greater energy.

The only sure remedy for the ills besetting modern civilization is to establish Buddhist teachings in the hearts of each and every individual alive. This is the key to the twenty-first century—the means whereby we may achieve the ultimate victory for humanity.

BIBLIOGRAPHY

Chapter 1, The Body and the Spirit

page

13. Scientific American Magazine Editors. *The Physics and Chemistry of Life.* New York: Simon & Schuster, 1956.
16. Carrel, Alexis. *Man, the Unknown.* New York: Harper & Brothers, 1935. pp. 4, 23.
20. Nichiren Daishonin. *Orally Transferred Teachings* (*Ongi Kuden*). In *Gosho Zenshū.* Tokyo, Soka Gakkai, 1952. p. 708.
23. Nichiren Daishonin. *The Ten Factors* (*Jūnyoze-ji*). In *Gosho Zenshū.* p. 410.
25. Nichiren Daishonin. *Orally Transferred Teachings* (*Ongi Kuden*). In *Gosho Zenshū.* p. 742.

Chapter 2, Man and Nature

28. Whitman, Walt. *Leaves of Grass and Selected Prose.* New York: Random House, 1950. p. 306.
33. Makiguchi, Tsunesaburo. *Geography of Human Life.* In *Makiguchi Tsunesaburo Zenshū.* Tokyo: 1965. Vol. III, pp. 151–2; vol. IV, p. 131; vol. IV, p. 243; vol. IV, p. 247.
34. Nichiren Daishonin. *On Good Omens* (*Zuisō-gosho*). In *Gosho Zenshū.* p. 1140.
39. Ibid.
41. Nichiren Daishonin. *The True Entity of Life* (*Shohō Jissō-shō*). In *The Major Writings of Nichiren Daishonin.* Vol. I, p. 89.

Chapter 3, Eyes That Can See Life

46. Natsume, Sōseki. *Ten Nights of Dreams.* Tr. Aiko Ito and Graeme Wilson. Tokyo: Tuttle, 1974.
48. Nichiren Daishonin. *The Ten Factors* (*Jūnyoze-ji*). In *Gosho Zenshū.* p. 410.
55. *Sutra of Infinite Meaning* (*Muryōgi-kyō*). In *Myōhō-renge-kyō.* Tokyo: Soka Gakkai, 1961. pp. 72–3.
56. Doi, Takeo. *Seishin Bunseki.* Tokyo: Kyōritsu Shuppan, 1956. p. 23.

Chapter 4, The Riddle of Time

67. Goethe, Johann W. von. *Johann Wolfgang von Goethe Gedlichte.* Leipzig: Reclan. p. 202.
70. Hatano, Seiichi. *Toki to Eien.* Tokyo: Iwanami Shoten, 1943. p. 3.
72. Frankl, Viktor E. *Nacht und Nebel: Ein Psycholog das K. Z.* Vienna: Verlag

für Jugend und Volk, 1947.

72. Nichiren Daishonin. *Orally Transferred Teachings* (*Ongi Kuden*). In *Gosho Zenshū*. p. 753.

Chapter 5, The Essence of the Cosmos

79. Sutra of the Benevolent King (*Ninnō-kyō*). In *Gosho Zenshū*. p. 79.
80. Nichiren Daishonin. *The True Object of Worship* (*Kanjin no Honzon-shō*). In *The Major Writings of Nichiren Daishonin*. Tokyo: Nichiren Shoshu International Center, 1979. Vol. I, p. 66.
81. Pascal, Blaise. *Pensées*. Paris: Librairie Hachette, 1950. p. 126.
85. Nichiren Daishonin. *On Attaining Buddhahood* (*Issho Jobutsu-shō*). In *The Major Writings of Nichiren Daishonin*. Vol. I, p. 3.

Chapter 6, The Ten States of Being

92. Nichiren Daishonin. *New Year's Writing* (*Mushimochi Gosho*). In *The Major Writings of Nichiren Daishonin*. Vol. I, p. 271.
93. Nichiren Daishonin. *The True Object of Worship* (*Kanjin no Honzon-shō*). In *The Major Writings of Nichiren Daishonin*. Vol. I, p. 52.
96. Ōta, Yōko. *Shikabane no Machi*. Tokyo: Ushio Shuppansha, 1972. p. 6.
97. Solzhenitsyn, Alexander. *The Cancer Ward*. New York: Dell, 1974. p. 155.
99. Nichiren Daishonin. *On the Bon Observance* (*Urabon Gosho*). In *Gosho Zenshū*. p. 1427.
99. *Risse Abidon-ron*. In *Kokuyaku Issaikyō*. Tokyo: Daito Shuppansha, 1933. Ronshūbu Vol. I, p. 114.
101. Nichiren Daishonin. "Letter to Niike" (*Niike Gosho*). In *The Major Writings of Nichiren Daishonin*. Vol. I, p. 254.
101. "Letter from Sado" (*Sado Gosho*). In *The Major Writings of Nichiren Daishonin*. Vol. I, p. 34.
102. Ibid.
103. Nichiren Daishonin. *Gosho Zenshū*. p. 430.
105. Nichikan Shonin. *Threefold Secret Teachings* (*Sanjū Hiden-shō*). In *Fuji Shūgaku Yōshū*. Tokyo: Sankibō Ltd., 1958. Vol. III, p. 16.
105. "Letter from Sado" (*Sado Gosho*). In *The Major Writings of Nichiren Daishonin*. Vol. I, p. 35.
106. *Risse Abidon-ron*. In *Kokuyaku Issaikyō*. Ronshūbu Vol. I, p. 115.
108. Nichikan Shonin. *Threefold Secret Teachings* (*Sanjū Hiden-shō*). In *Fuji Shūgaku Yōshū*. Vol. III, p. 17.
109. Ibid., p. 16.
111. Ibid., p. 17.
115. Nichiren Daishonin. *On the Curing of Disease* (*Jibyō-shō*). In *Gosho Zenshū*. p. 997.

117. Nichiren Daishonin. *The True Object of Worship* (*Kanjin no Honzon-shō*). In *The Major Writings of Nichiren Daishonin*. Vol. I, p. 52.
121. Nichiren Daishonin. *The Opening of the Eyes* (*Kaimoku-shō*). In *The Major Writings of Nichiren Daishonin*. Vol. II, p. 71.
124. Yukawa, Hideki; Ichikawa, Kikuya; and Umehara, Takeshi. *Ningen no Saihakken*. Tokyo: Kadokawa Shoten, 1971. pp. 91–92.
124. Nichiren Daishonin. *Orally Transferred Teachings* (*Ongi Kuden*). In *Gosho Zenshū*. p. 721.
125. Nichiren Daishonin. *The True Object of Worship* (*Kanjin no Honzon-shō*). In *The Major Writings of Nichiren Daishonin*. Vol. I, p. 53.
126. Nichiren Daishonin. *Causality within the Ten States of Life* (*Jippōkai Myōin-ga-shō*). In *Gosho Zenshū*. p. 433.
127. Nichiren Daishonin. *Orally Transferred Teachings* (*Ongi Kuden*). In *Gosho Zenshū*. p. 751.
128. Nichiren Daishonin. *The True Object of Worship* (*Kanjin no Honzon-shō*). In *The Major Writings of Nichiren Daishonin*. Vol. I, p. 65.
128. Ibid., p. 53.

Chapter 7, Mutual Possession

137. Nichiren Daishonin. *The True Entity of Life* (*Shohō Jissō-shō*). In *The Major Writings of Nichiren Daishonin*. Vol. I, p. 89.
137. Nichiren Daishonin. *The True Object of Worship* (*Kanjin no Honzon-shō*). In *The Major Writings of Nichiren Daishonin*. Vol. I, pp. 49–50.
145. Trumbo, Dalton. *Johnny Got His Gun*. New York: Bantam, 1970.
147. Lotus Sutra. *Myōhō-renge-kyō*. Tokyo: Soka Gakkai, 1961. pp. 154–5.
148. Nichiren Daishonin. *Ichinen Sanzen-riji*. In *Gosho Zenshū*. p. 407.
149. Nichiren Daishonin. *Jūnyoze-ji*. In *Gosho Zenshū*. p. 410.
149. Nichiren Daishonin. *Ichinen Sanzen-riji*. In *Gosho Zenshū*. p. 407.
150. Nichikan Shonin. *Threefold Secret Teachings* (*Sanjū Hiden-shō*). In *Fuji Shūgaku Yōshū*. Vol. III, p. 17.
151. Ibid.
151. Nichiren Daishonin. *Ichinen Sanzen-riji*. In *Gosho Zenshū*. p. 407.
152. Ibid.
152. Nichikan Shonin. *Threefold Secret Teachings* (*Sanjū Hiden-shō*). In *Fuji Shūgaku Yōshū*. Vol. III, p. 17.
152. *Shinjikan* Sutra. In *Gosho Zenshū*. p. 231.
155. Nichikan Shonin. *Threefold Secret Teachings* (*Sanjū Hiden-shō*). In *Fuji Shūgaku Yōshū*. Vol. III, p. 17.
156. Ibid.
159. Nichiren Daishonin. *Ichinen Sanzen-riji*. In *Gosho Zenshū*. p. 407.
160. Nichikan Shonin. *Threefold Secret Teachings* (*Sanjū Hiden-shō*). In *Fuji*

Shūgaku Yōshū. Vol. III, p. 17.
165. Ibid., p. 20.

Chapter 8, The Nature of Death
171. Nichiren Daishonin. *Gosho Zenshū*. p. 1404.
176. Tanaka, Michitarō. *Jinseiron-funi*. Tokyo: Shinchosha, 1968. pp. 53, 74–75.
177. Nakano, Yoshio. *Ningen no Shinikata*. Tokyo: Shinchosha, 1969. p. 107.
178. Takeyama, Michio. *Ningen ni tsuite*. Tokyo: Shinchosha, 1966. pp. 337–8.
179. Heywood, Rosalind, et al. *Man's Concern with Death*. London: Hodder and Stoughton, 1968. p. 195.
180. Bergson, Henri. "Mind and Body." In *L'Energie spirituelle*. Paris, 1919.
181. Okabe, Kinjirō. *Ningen wa Shindara dō Naru Ka*. Tokyo: Kyōritsu Shuppan, 1974.
185. Nichiren Daishonin. *Orally Transferred Teachings* (*Ongi Kuden*). In *Gosho Zenshū*. p. 754.
187. Nichiren Daishonin. *On the Ultimate Teaching Confirmed by All Buddhas* (*Sanze Shobutsu Sōkammon Kyōsō Hairyū*). In *Gosho Zenshū*. p. 563.

Chapter 9, Life in Outer Space
192. Nichiren Daishonin. "Reply to Tayū-no-sakan." In *Gosho Zenshū*. p. 1104.
197. Noda, Haruhiko. *Seimei no Kigen*. Tokyo: Nippon Hōsō Shuppan Kyōkai, 1966. pp. 337–8.

Chapter 10, The Origin of Man
200. Darwin, Charles. *On the Origin of Species*. Cambridge, Mass: Harvard University Press, 1966. p. 488.
203. Kant, Emmanuel. *Critique of Practical Reason*. In *Great Books of the Western World*. Chicago: Encyclopaedia Britannica, Inc., 1952. Vol. 42, pp. 360–1.
205. Imanishi, Kinji. *Watakushi no Shinkaron*. Tokyo: Shisakusha Publishing Co., 1970. p. 179.
205. Okamura, Yuichi. *Homo Sapiens*? Tokyo: Tamagawa University Press, 1972. pp. 50–53.

Chapter 11, The Eternity of Life
215. Kobayashi, Masaru. *Shi no gen'ei*. In Matsuda, Michio, ed. *Watakushi no Anthology* 7. Tokyo: Chikuma Shobō, 1972. pp. 39–42.
217. Nichiren Daishonin. *On the Ultimate Teaching Confirmed by All Buddhas* (*Sanze Shobutsu Sōkammon Kyōsō Hairyū*). In *Gosho Zenshū*. p. 562.
218. Heywood, Rosalind, et al. *Man's Concern with Death*. p. 184.

218. Toynbee, Arnold J. *Experiences*. London: Oxford University Press, 1969. p. 140.

218. Nichiren Daishonin. *Orally Transferred Teachings* (*Ongi Kuden*). In *Gosho Zenshū*. p. 783.

221. Nichiren Daishonin. "Reply to Soya." In *Gosho Zenshū*. p. 1025.

222. Nichiren Daishonin. *On the Ultimate Teaching Confirmed by All Buddhas* (*Sanze Shobutsu Sōkammon Kyōsō Hairyū*). In *Gosho Zenshū*. p. 574.

223. Nichiren Daishonin. *Orally Transferred Teachings* (*Ongi Kuden*). In *Gosho Zenshū*. p. 782.

225. Toda, Josei. *Jihi-ron*. In *Toda Josei Sensei Shidō Shū*. Tokyo: Seikyo Press, 1976. pp. 181–2.

227. Kishimoto, Hideo. *Shi o Mitsumeru Kokoro*. Tokyo: Kodansha, 1973. p. 113.

GLOSSARY

Anger: (Jap., *shura*) Fourth of the Ten States of Being. In this state, there is consciousness of self, and one is driven by the desire to dominate others.

Animality: (Jap., *chikushō*) Third of the Ten States of Being. In this state, one is subject to instinct and desire and does not think beyond self-preservation and immediate profit. The wisdom of self-control is lacking.

Anryūgyō: *See* Bodhisattvas of the Earth.

Ashura: (Jap., *shura*) Represents the state of Anger. In Indian mythology, they were devils who fought continually with the god Taishaku.

Bodhisattva: (Jap., *bosatsu*) One in the ninth of the Ten States of Being. Compassion (*jihi*) characterizes this state. Bodhisattvas seek enlightenment for themselves and for others.

Bodhisattvas of the Earth (Jap., *jiyu no bosatsu*) Bodhisattvas appearing in the *Yujutsu* (15th) chapter of the Lotus Sutra. They alone are charged with the mission of propagating the Mystic Law in the Latter Day of the Law. Four major ones are Jōgyō, Muhengyō, Jōgyō, and Anryūgyō.

Buddha: An Enlightened one.

Buddhahood: The highest of the Ten States of Being. In this state, one has achieved supreme wisdom and compassion and is in perfect harmony with the universe. In daily life, Buddhahood is manifested in the actions of a Bodhisattva.

Buddha-land: The world where a Buddha dwells. It also signifies absolute happiness and does not mean a paradise or a land removed from mortal suffering.

Buddhism: The teachings of Shakyamuni, transmitted by his disciples.

Chih-i (538–97): (T'ien-t'ai; Tendai Daishi) Chinese priest who founded the T'ien-t'ai (Tendai) sect. His three major works based on the Lotus Sutra are: *Hokke Gengi*, *Hokke Mongu*, and *Maka Shikan*. In *Maka Shikan* he revealed the principle of *ichinen sanzen*.

chūtai: *See* Three Perceptions

Daichido-ron: A hundred-volume commentary on the *Mahaprajnaparamita* Sutra, attributed to Nagarjuna (Ryūju) and translated into Chinese by Kumarajiva (344–413).

Daishonin: Title given to the Buddha of the Latter Day of the Law who appeared to save all mankind.

Devil of the Sixth Heaven: (Jap., Dairokuten no Ma-ō) Most powerful of all devils. He dwells in the highest of the six realms of the World of Desire and takes pleasure in enervating the life-force of others.

ehō: Objective environment. *See also* eshō funi, shōhō.

engaku: Self-attained Realization. One who has perceived the Twelve Links of Dependent Causation and thus has experienced a type of enlightenment.

en'yū santai: Unified harmony of the Three Perceptions.

eshō funi: Inseparability of subjective existence (*shōhō*) and objective environment (*ehō*).

fifty-two stages of the Bodhisattva's practice: These are: ten stages of faith, ten stages of security, ten stages of practice, ten stages of devotion, ten stages of development, *tōgaku* (a stage almost equal to enlightenment), and enlightenment. The Bodhisattva progresses through them to attain Buddhahood.

Five Aggregates: (Jap., *go-on*) An analysis of the way life functions to influence and assimilate its environment. The five are: form (*shiki*), perception (*ju*), conception (*so*), volition (*gyō*), and consciousness (*shiki*). *See also* three principles of individuality.

Four Evil Paths: The lowest of the Ten States of Being. Hell, Hunger, Animality, and Anger. People undergo these worlds of suffering because of evil karma.

Four Noble States: The highest of the Ten States of Being: Learning, Realization, the Bodhisattva Nature, and Buddhahood. In these states, one reflects on the impermanence of all phenomena and transcends the fluctuations of the Six Lower States.

Fugen: A leader of the Bodhisattvas of the theoretical teaching. He represents reason and learning.

go-on: *See* Five Aggregates.

Gosho: The individual and collected writings of Nichiren Daishonin. Includes letters of personal encouragement, treatises on Buddhism, and recorded oral teachings. The complete works are called *Gosho Zenshū*.

Hell: (Jap., *jigoku*) First of the Ten States of Being. This state is characterized by suffering, despair, and the impulse to destroy oneself and others.

Hinayana: Literally, the "lesser vehicle." Also called the Theravada school, one of the two major streams of Buddhism. This conservative doctrine resulted from a schism in the community of monks about a century after Shakyamuni's death. Salvation is held to come from strict adherence to the practices as originally formulated by the Buddha. It spread mainly to Burma, Cambodia, Laos, Sri Lanka, and Thailand. *See also* Mahayana.

Hoben chapter: "Expedient Means." This second chapter of the Lotus Sutra is a key to the theoretical teaching. Shakyamuni revealed that the Ten Factors are common to all states of life from Hell to Buddhahood. Thus, Buddhahood is not separate from the nine worlds below it, and Buddhas appear in the world solely for the purpose of enabling all people to attain Buddhahood.

Hokke Gengi: "Profound Meaning of the Lotus Sutra." This commentary by Chih-i explains the profundity of the title of the Lotus Sutra, *Myōhō-renge-kyō.*

hōshin: *See* Three Bodies.

hosshin: *See* Three Bodies.

Humanity: (Jap., *nin*) Fifth of the Ten States of Being. Through reason, one in this state controls desire, exercises good judgement, and lives in harmony with his environment.

human revolution: An individual's total reformation in thought, word, and deed that leads to fulfillment of character and an improvement of karma.

Hunger: (Jap., *gaki*) Second of the Ten States of Being. A state of insatiability in which one is dominated by selfish desire for wealth, fame, or pleasure.

ichinen sanzen: Three Thousand Possible Worlds in Every Life-moment.

Ichinen Sanzen-riji: "On Three Thousand Possible Worlds in Every Life-moment." A *Gosho* written by Nichiren Daishonin in 1258. The three sections are: *Jūni-innen* (the Twelve Links of Dependent Causation), *Ichinen Sanzen-riji*, and *Sanjin Shaku* (Commentaries on the Three Bodies of Life).

jihi: Compassion. The supreme quality of Buddhahood, the capacity to relieve suffering and give happiness.

Jikkai: Ten Worlds. Ten States of Being.

Jikkai Gogu: Mutual Possession of the Ten Worlds.

Jōgyō: (Skt., Visiṣtacārita) Bodhisattva who represents self. In the *Yujutsu* (15th) chapter of the Lotus Sutra, it says that Jōgyō vowed to propagate *Myōhō-renge-kyō* in the Latter Day of the Law. In the *Jinriki* (21st) chapter Shakyamuni transferred all his teachings to the Bodhisattva Jōgyō. *See also* Bodhisattvas of the Earth.

Jōgyō: (Skt., Viśuddhacārita) Bodhisattva who represents purity. *See also* Bodhisattvas of the Earth.

Jūjūbibasha-ron: A fifteen-fascicle, thirty-five-chapter commentary on the first two of ten stages of a Bodhisattva's practice. Compiled by Nagarjuna and translated by Kumarajiva (344–413).

Jūnyoze: Ten Factors of Life.

Jūnyoze-ji: "On the Ten Factors." A *Gosho* written in 1258 by Nichiren Daishonin to his disciples. He teaches that people in the Latter Day of the Law can attain enlightenment only by chanting *Nam-myōhō-renge-kyō.*

Juryō chapter: "Life-span of Nyorai." This 16th, key chapter of the Lotus Sutra discusses Shakyamuni's Buddhahood in terms of its cause, effect, and land. Shakyamuni reveals that he attained Buddhahood in the remote past, and has remained in the mundane world ever since; thus, the Buddha is a common mortal endowed with the nine worlds.

kalpa: An extremely long period of time. Sutras and other treatises describe them as falling into two categories, of measurable and of immeasurable duration. There are three kinds of measurable kalpas: minor, medium, and major. A minor kalpa is approximately 16 million years long.

Kanjin no Honzon-shō: "The True Object of Worship." One of ten major writings of Nichiren Daishonin, written in 1273. It reveals the supreme object of worship in true Buddhism.

Kannon: According to the *Fumon* (25th) chapter of the Lotus Sutra, the Bodhisattva Kannon assumes thirty-three different forms to save the people.

ketai: *See* Three Perceptions.

kū: The state of latency. In life, it is a spiritual or qualitative realm and cannot be defined in terms of existence or non-existence.

Kusha-ron: The compendium of supreme truth written by Vasubandhu.

kūtai: *See* Three Perceptions.

Learning: (Jap., *shōmon*) Seventh of the Ten States of Being. Through self-reform and development, one in this state strives to attain a lasting world of contentment and stability.

Letter from Sado: This *Gosho* is named after the island of Sado, where Nichiren Daishonin was in exile when he wrote it in 1272.

Lotus Sutra: (Jap., *Hokekyō*) *Myōhō-renge-kyō*, Shakyamuni's ultimate teaching. Expounded in the last eight years of his life, it is generally divided into twenty-eight chapters.

Mahayana: Literally, the "greater vehicle." One of the two major streams of Buddhism, the Mahayana teachings place emphasis not simply on individual salvation, but on the importance of leading all mankind to enlightenment. It spread to Central Asia, China, Japan, and Korea. *See also* Hinayana.

Maka Shikan: "Great Concentration and Insight." This major work of Chih-i was compiled by his disciple, Chang-an, and reveals the principle of Three Thousand Possible Worlds in Every Life-moment.

Makiguchi, Tsunesaburo (1871–1944): He was converted to Nichiren Shoshu in 1928. He founded and became first president of Soka Kyōiku Gakkai, which later became Soka Gakkai, in 1930.

Maudgalyayana: (Jap., Mokuren) One of Shakyamuni's ten major disciples; said to have been particularly skilled in occult practices.

Miao-lo (711–82): (Jap., Myōraku) Ninth successor in the T'ien-t'ai sect in China. He is revered as the restorer of the sect and the author of profound commentaries on Chih-i's works, the three major ones being *Hokke Gengi Shakusen*, *Hokke Mongu Ki*, and *Maka Shikan Bugyōden Guketsu*.

middle way: (Jap., *chūdō*) The law of *Nam-myōhō-renge-kyō*. The ultimate reality underlying all phenomena.

Miroku: A Bodhisattva whose persistent questions induced Shakyamuni to expound the *Jūryo* chapter. He died before Shakyamuni. In the *Bosatsu Shotai* Sutra it says he will reappear in this world 5,670 million years after the Buddha to teach the Law.

Monju: A Bodhisattva who represents the virtue of wisdom. He is a leader of the Bodhisattvas of the theoretical teaching.

Mount Sumeru: The highest of all mountains. In ancient Indian cosmology, the world was divided into four continents with Mount Sumeru standing at the center of the world.

Muhengyō: A Bodhisattva who represents eternity. *See also* Bodhisattvas of the Earth.

Munetchi Lake: Literally, "lake without heat." This lake is inhabited by the dragon king Anavatapta, and its cool, clear water fertilizes Jambudvipa, the continent south of Mount Sumeru.

Muryōgi Sutra: "The Sutra of Infinite Meaning." In this introductory teaching to the Lotus Sutra, Shakyamuni explains that all principles and meanings (*muryōgi*) derive from the Law and implies that the Law will be revealed in the Lotus Sutra.

Mutual Possession of the Ten Worlds (Jap., *Jikkai Gogu*) The principle that each of the Ten Worlds has the potential of all ten within it. The main implications are that one can change his fundamental life condition and that ordinary mortals inherently possess the potential for Buddhahood.

Myōhō-renge-kyō: Title of the Lotus Sutra. True entity of life, the law of *Nam-myōhō-renge-kyō*.

Myōon: According to the *Myōon* chapter of the Lotus Sutra, this Bodhisattva propagates the Lotus Sutra by manifesting himself in thirty-four forms.

Mystic Law: (Jap., *myōhō*) The law of *Nam-myōhō-renge-kyō*, the ultimate law of life and of the universe.

Nagarjuna: (Jap., Ryūju) Major Indian philosopher of the third century. After studying the Hinayana tradition, he devoted himself to the study and propagation of Mahayana Buddhism. The *Daichido-ron* is one of many treatises he wrote which made a significant contribution to Buddhist philosophy.

Nam-myōhō-renge-kyō: Nichiren Daishonin defined it as the fundamental principle of the universe, and it is the invocation of Nichiren Daishonin's Buddhism.

Nichikan Shonin (1665–1726): The 26th high priest of Nichiren Shoshu. In *Rokkan-sho* (The Six-Volume Writings) and his exegeses of the *Gosho*, he clarified the correctness and orthodoxy of Nichiren Shoshu doctrine.

Nichiren Daishonin (1222–82): The Buddha of the Latter Day of the Law. The son of of a fisherman, he was called Zennichimaro. He began the study of Buddhism in 1233 and took the tonsure at the age of sixteen. After attaining enlightenment and mastering all the Buddhist sutras and literature, he took the name Nichiren (Sun-Lotus) in 1253 and declared the establishment of a new Buddhism. In 1279 he inscribed the Dai-Gohonzon, the principal object of worship, for the peace and happiness of all mankind.

Ninnō-kyō: "The Sutra of the Benevolent King." A pre-Lotus, Mahayana sutra. *Ninnō* means a benevolent king who protects his country and his people.

nirvana: In the Hinayana sutras, attaining enlightenment by extinguishing earthly desire and escaping the cycle of birth and death. In Nichiren Shoshu, nirvana means an enlightened life condition in the real world, based on faith in the Gohonzon.

Nirvana Sutra: (Jap., *Nehan-gyō*) In this teaching expounded on the last day of his life, Shakyamuni reconfirmed the major principles of the Lotus Sutra.

Nyorai: One who comprehends the true entity of life. Nyorai is one of the ten honorable titles of the Buddha.

ōjin: *See* Three Bodies.

Ongi Kuden: "Orally Transferred Teachings." Nichiren Daishonin's discourse on the Lotus Sutra, compiled by Nikko, his immediate successor.

Pure Land: Traditionally, the pure land, remote from the mundane world, where the Buddha dwells.

Rapture: (Jap., *ten*) Sixth of the Ten States of Being. In this state, one feels satisfaction and joy, as when a cause of suffering is removed, desire is fulfilled, or a goal is attained.

Realization: (Jap., *engaku*) Eighth of the Ten States of Being. One in this state learns the way to self-reform by consciously attempting to understand the ultimate truth of life.

sanjin: Three Bodies, *ōjin*, *hōshin*, *hosshin*.

Sanjū Hiden-shō: "Threefold Secret Teachings." The work of Nichikan Shonin, it includes comparisons of actual Mahayana (the Lotus Sutra) and provisional Mahayana (the other sutras), the first half of the Lotus Sutra and the second half, the Buddhism of Shakyamuni and that of Nichiren Daishonin.

santai: Three Perceptions, *chūtai*, *ketai*, and *kūtai*.

Sanze Shobutsu Sōkammon Kyōsō Hairyū: "On the Ultimate Teaching Confirmed by All Buddhas." A major work of Nichiren Daishonin (1279). The revelation of the life philosophy of Nichiren Daishonin, it also explains that the pre-Lotus teachings were provisional and that the Lotus Sutra is supreme among the doctrines of Shakyamuni.

Shakyamuni: The historical Buddha, he lived in India in the fifth and sixth centuries B.C. A prince of the Shakya tribe, he renounced the throne at nineteen (or twenty-nine) and set out to solve the question of the four sufferings: birth, old age, sickness, and death. After profound meditation, he attained enlightenment at the age of thirty (or thirty-five) and lived for another fifty years. He sought to pass on his enlightenment to all people, and his teachings are so numerous that they are called the "eighty thousand teachings."

shiki-shin funi: Inseparability of the physical law of life (*shikihō*) and the spiritual law of life (*shimpō*).

Shinjikan Sutra: Eight fascicles and thirteen chapters translated by Prajna and others between 785 and 810.

shōhō: Self; subjective existence.

Shohō Jissō-shō: "The True Entity of Life." A letter written by Nichiren Daishonin to his disciple, Sairen-bo Nichijo, in 1273.

shōmon: Men of Learning. Disciples of the Buddha who listened to his teachings.

shujō: Living beings. *See* three principles of individuality.

Six Lower States: Hell, Hunger, Animality, Anger, Humanity, and Rapture. These states are ones of delusion or suffering and contrast with the Four Noble States.

Taishaku: A main tutelary god of Buddhism. Originally the god of thunder, he was adopted as a protective deity.

Tendai sect: The name in Japan of the T'ien-t'ai sect, established by Chih-i in the early ninth century.

Ten Factors of Life: The Ten Factors common to all life in any of the Ten Worlds: appearance (*nyoze-sō*), nature (*nyoze-shō*), entity (*nyoze-tai*), power (*nyoze-riki*), influence (*nyoze-sa*), inherent cause (*nyoze-in*), external cause (*nyoze-en*), latent effect (*nyoze-ka*), manifest effect (*nyoze-hō*), and consistency from beginning to end (*nyoze-hommatsu-kukyōtō*). They clarify life's entity and functions.

Ten States of Being: (Jap., *Jikkai*) The states inherent in life and manifested in the physical and spiritual aspects of all human activities: Hell, Hunger, Animality, Anger, Humanity, Rapture, Learning, Realization, the Bodhisattva Nature, and Buddhahood. Also called the Ten Worlds. *See also* individual entries for each state.

Ten Worlds: The Ten States of Being.

Three Bodies: (Jap., *sanjin*) *Ōjin*, the manifest body, are the merciful actions of a Buddha to save people and the physical body of a Buddha in this world. *Hōshin*, the Body of Reward, is the wisdom to perceive the truth. *Hosshin*, the Body of the Law, is the truth of a Buddha's life.

Three Evil Paths: Hell, Hunger, and Animality, the lowest states of being.

Three Perceptions: (Jap., *santai*) *Ketai* is Provisional Perception and is concerned with the recognition of all phenomena of life. *Kūtai* is Perception of the Latent and means to observe the spiritual or qualitative aspects of life. *Chūtai* is the middle way and is the realization of the eternal and unchanging essence of the universe.

three principles of individuality: (Jap., *sanseken*) These are manifested in the Five Aggregates of Life (*go-on seken*), in the realm of living beings (*shujō-seken*), and in the World of Environment (*kokudo-seken*).

Three Thousand Possible Worlds in Every Life-moment: (Jap., *ichinen sanzen*) The principle that each of the Ten States of Being possesses the potential for all ten. *Ichinen* indicates the life-essence, *sanzen*, the phenomena it manifests. The theory was postulated by Chih-i, based on the Lotus Sutra.

Toda, Josei (1900–58): He became an adherent of Nichiren Shoshu in 1920 and assisted Tsunesaburo Makiguchi in founding the Soka Kyōiku Gakkai. Imprisoned with Makiguchi by the militaristic government during World War II, he began to rebuild the society in 1945 and was its second president. The society was renamed Soka Gakkai.

two vehicles: (Jap., *nijō*) Two kinds of teaching expounded for men of Learning and men of Realization. *See also* engaku and shōmon.

Vasubandhu: (Jap., Tenjin or Seshin) Buddhist scholar who lived in India in the fifth century and wrote the *Kusha-ron*. He originally studied Hinayana. Initially critical of Mahayana, he was converted by his elder brother Asanga and subsequently wrote many treatises clarifying Mahayana teachings.

Yakuō: A Bodhisattva who serves people by providing them with medicine to cure physical and spiritual diseases.

yujun: A measure of distance. There are various opinions, but it is thought to be the equivalent of about thirty kilometers.

INDEX

定価3300円
in Japan